MW00883647

Singing is My Life:
A Memoir of My Journey
from Homelessness to Fame

To: Megan.

Make Everyday
Victorious!

Sungbong Choi.

Singing is My Life: A Memoir of My Journey from Homelessness to Fame

Sungbong Choi

Singing is My Life: A Memoir of My Journey from Homelessness to Fame by Sungbong Choi.
Copyright 2012, Sungbong Choi.
English translation copyright Sungbong Choi, 2015.

All rights reserved.

This English edition is published by arrangement with Munhakdongne Publishing Corp.

All rights reserved. No part of this book may be reproduced, stored in a retrieval system, or transmitted in any form or by any means—including mechanical, electronic, photocopying, recording, scanning, or otherwise—without the prior written permission of the author and the publisher.

© 2015 FremantleMedia Ltd —*Korea's Got Talent* is a trademark of FremantleMedia Ltd & Simco Ltd.

Author: Sungbong Choi
E-mail: sungbongchoiofficial@gmail.com
Official website: www.sungbongchoi.co.kr
Facebook: www.facebook.com/sungbongchoiofficial
Instagram: www.instagram.com/sungbongchoiofficial
Twitter: www.twitter.com/sungbongchoi218

English translation by the Korean Translation Group
Website: www.koreantranslation.com

ISBN-13: 9781517229603
ISBN-10: 151722960X

Table of Contents

This book includes several Korean words that may be unfamiliar to readers.
To aid your comprehension, I have included a glossary at the end.

Preface to the English Edition

WHILE TRYING TO get my autobiography published in English, I encountered many obstacles and ran into some unexpected but realistic issues.

Three-and-a-half years had passed without any prospect of seeing my autobiography, originally in Korean, published in English. However, I have found and will continue to find hope in my lifelong journey.

All those problems that I had encountered in the past could not stop me from pursuing what I wanted. I had waited patiently for the right moment to come. Thanks to the generous support of the Julius Bär Foundation in Switzerland, I was finally able to get my book published in English via the self-publishing route.

What you are holding now in your hands—the English version of my autobiography—is the result of the three-and-a-half years' wait and of having overcome all the obstacles. I am glad that this whole process has turned out to be an opportunity for me to further mature.

I received a lot of help from many people this time, as always.

Once again I feel warmth in my heart with the support from all around the world.

On a spring day, 2015
Sungbong Choi

Preface to the Korean Edition
I Grew Up on the Streets

HELLO. MY NAME is Sungbong Choi.

I sometimes find myself reflecting on what might be the first thing that crosses people's minds when I introduce my name. *Korea's Got Talent*'s first-season first runner-up, "Nella Fantasia," Korea's Paul Potts, a gum-selling orphan...The numerous modifiers added before my name seem both to be and not to be who I really am.

Among the phrases that describe me, the one that is most familiar to you and also to me is probably "gum-selling orphan"—words that now evoke no special feelings in me, yet are still considered surprising by many.

Those words, after they were broadcast, brought to me many proposals from publishers to turn my story into a book, but I could not consent to them readily. It could be a story about all the moments I had lived through, but I did not know what I would really be able to talk about at the mere age of twenty-three. I also felt that it was not right to write a book at a point where I had just barely made a step into the world, and when there was still so much to learn. What I feared most of all was becoming the subject of a rumor that I was, as so often happens, trying to profit from selling the story of my past—especially in the delicate situation where my life had become more famous than my songs.

What made me decide to publish this book despite this was something that a fan with terminal cancer said to me. She said, "You made it through, whereas I just whiled away life grieving my misfortune." The fact that my existence was a source of consolation to her made me feel as though I was the one being comforted.

Among those who cheer me on are many people who continue on with hope through life's tribulations, like little children with leukemia and lonely elders who have nowhere to go. It was the consolation that they received from me and that I received from them that began the story contained in this book. If I had had no faith that writing this book was a consolation between them and me, I would not have overcome my reluctance to publish it.

Despite that faith, however, it was not easy for me to relive my past— stories that I had consciously or unconsciously forgotten, stories that I had buried deep and tramped down firmly inside my heart to keep from resurfacing as memories, stories that I had wished never to be dug up. While I was drawing out these stories, I realized how difficult it was to look at myself straight in the face. It was tremendously painful to uncover wounds that hadn't yet healed. This book is full of me that I did not want to believe was me, and which I obstinately dismissed.

My courage in confessing these stories was shadowed by the fear that I may lose your support once you had read all of them. What made me go on was your strength. If this book can be a small consolation to those who have been thrown down by life's storms, perhaps I, too, could be healed through it.

All those at Munhakdongne Publishing Corporation who toiled for this book, who wrote and edited the text, I thank you for not giving up on me despite all those difficulties I caused you knowingly and unknowingly. You who have opened this book—regardless of the situation you may be in now, whatever dream it is that you may hold—I hope you will brace up yet again today, and keep striving for your dreams tomorrow. I will be cheering you on with all of my strength.

Thank you.

On a spring day, 2012
Sungbong Choi

Acknowledgements

FROM THE BOTTOM of my heart, I would like to express my heartfelt thanks to the Julius Bär Foundation; Mr. Boris Collardi, vice chairman of the foundation and CEO of Bank Julius Bär; and Mr. Bernard Keller, the foundation's former chairman, for their belief in me, without which the English version of my book would not have been possible.

To PL, who does not want her name to be revealed, I am truly grateful to her for taking care of every aspect of the publication of this book into English, from securing the sponsorship for the book and finding translators to handling all the liaison work and reviewing the English manuscript, never expecting anything in return. A million thanks would not be enough. Without her help, this book would not have seen the light.

I would like to thank Jiyoung Park for reviewing the English manuscript, Liane Angerman for her literary support during the final stages of my book, Jinjoo Kim for lending her support in translation and interpretation, and all the volunteer translators for their help in translating and interpreting all the communications related to this book project.

To the team at Munhakdongne who helped with the publication of my original autobiography, I would like to send my thanks with a smile and love. They include Byungsung Kang, publisher; Younghee Seo, senior project manager and editor; Neosang Park and Jaeyoung Ha, who were responsible for the composition of the Korean manuscript; Sohjin Hyeong, Hyeonsook Yeom, and Donggyu Oh, editors; Heeyeon Lee, who was responsible for monitoring; Hyeri Um and Jooyoung Lee, designers; Younghee Woo and Hyejin Na, who were responsible for marketing; Sanghyeok Lee and Sunah Jang, who were responsible for online marketing; Jungsook Ahn, Dongkwan Seo, and Aejin Kim, producers; and Young-Shin-sa, the production company.

Last but certainly not least, to the readers of this book, I cannot thank you enough.

---✂---

Part 1:
An Unforgettable Childhood
That Is Best Forgotten
Ten Years on the Streets

I Was Only Five Then

A RED RUBBER tub. I was hiding inside a large rubber tub, the kind that is only used for making kimchi. I wasn't playing hide-and-seek or preparing to lark about. I was hunched up in the rubber tub because I was going to run away from the orphanage.

The orphanage was a place where people yelled at me. It was a place where people forced me to do this and not that. I waited inside the rubber tub until dark in order to escape from that place of yelling and oppression. I couldn't tell how many hours had passed, but as it neared sunset, my cramped feet began to ache.

They say that I was left at an orphanage at age three. I can't remember whether the orphanage I escaped from when I was five was the place where I had stayed for two years, or whether it was one of the many orphanages I had passed through. One thing I remember clearly even now, however, was that the orphanage was a terrible place. Was it because I had been beaten up and abused? I don't know. In any case, orphanages were the first memory and the last mark left in my mind about Seoul.

Only when I felt certain that no one was looking for me did I climb out of the rubber tub and hobble through the orphanage yard, with feet that had cramped up to total insensitivity. Even after the orphanage disappeared in the distance, I did not dare slow down for fear that someone might come up from behind and grab me by the neck.

How long must I have walked? A place where huge cars had been parked appeared before my eyes. Vehicles full of people were leaving or returning from somewhere. I got into one of them because I knew instinctively that sitting in that huge car would take me to a faraway place.

"Hey, kid, are you alone?"

The driver turned back and asked me with a dubious face.

"My mom and dad are...waiting."

He seemed to understand the words, that they meant my mom and dad were waiting at the destination. I sat like a real well-behaved child on his way to meet his mom and dad, staring through the window. When the huge car began to move, I could finally begin to feel that I had escaped from the orphanage. I wanted to whip the huge car to go faster—faster away, farther away. The fact that I was here and not at the orphanage anymore wasn't enough in itself; I wanted to go somewhere where nobody knew me and where nobody could find me. After some time, the bus stopped at an unfamiliar city. It was the East Terminal in the city of Daejeon.

The first street that appeared in front of me as I came out of the terminal was a red-light district with glaring neon signs and staggering, drunken people. I was swept along in the crowd to the center of the district. To a five-year-old boy whose view only reached grown-ups' waistlines, that world that I was encountering for the first time seemed to be of towering, gigantic scale. Looking up, I saw gaudy store signs shining their colorful lights against the pitch-dark night sky. It was an unfamiliar street, but I wasn't scared of the glaring signs and the staggering grown-ups. I actually felt comfortable there. I had been liberated. I was free. Now I would be roaming around streets where there would be nobody commanding me to stay still.

I walked through the night until dawn. The signs had been turned off and the drunkards had disappeared, but I was still roaming the streets.

Night fell and it was dawn again, and so a few days had passed. I had left the noisy red-light district behind and was walking alone down an empty back alley. Just as the day and night of the street were distinct, the front and back of the street were disparate. The front of the street was lined with restaurants and bars, whereas the back was sparsely marked with streetlights. I was famished to the point of being unable to walk any farther, yet not knowing how to find food, I had no choice but to lurch on. Then I blacked out and my feet gave out.

"Hey, get up."

Even through flickering consciousness, I could feel someone shaking my shoulders. When I opened my eyes, I found a grubby face blocking the sky, looking down on me. It wasn't a grown-up. It was a big brother who had on filthy clothes and an even filthier face.

"Your mom and dad?"

When I shook my head, he helped me to my feet. I'd thought I couldn't take another step, but when he supported me, I managed to follow him along, though just barely. The place he took me to was a Chinese restaurant. He ordered two bowls of jajangmyeon.*

I still like jajangmyeon. Even though I'm fed up with noodles because I've eaten too many noodle meals instead of proper meals with rice, I still eat jajangmyeon often. Glistening, dark, sweet, and salty jajangmyeon. Even when my throat was all sore from crying too much, I would have no trouble slurping down those oily strands.

And it was exactly this way on that day when I had my first bowl of jajangmyeon. That food that I was eating for the first time in my life seemed to somehow wrap around my hungry tongue, such that I almost couldn't tell whether it was the noodles or my tongue that was getting swallowed down. When I had made it through the entire bowl, with the brown sauce completely covering my face, the big brother began to tell his story.

---

* Noodles with black-bean sauce.

He'd run away from home, and since then he'd been selling gum in the town. The world, as it first revealed itself before my eyes in the red-light district of Yongjeon-dong, Daejeon, was crowded with taverns, karaoke bars, soju* houses, restaurants, and snack joints.

"All those stores are places where you can sell gum. First put the gum on the table. Then wait around with a pitiful face. Then people will come to buy the gum. I buy gum for two hundred won† but when I sell it, I get a thousand won. Then I'll make eight hundred won, right? See, a bundle of five like this is worth five thousand won."

A little kid who couldn't even understand words well obviously didn't have any concept of money; calculating numbers was out of the question. But the fact that I would be able to eat jajangmyeon by handing out gum and receiving money did vaguely make sense. Thus, I duly engraved in my mind the three steps: "hand out gum," "get money," "buy food." I had discovered the most important fact of life: that you could eat something if you had money.

I continued to follow the big brother along even after coming out of the Chinese restaurant. I learned by observing from the corner of my eye how he would buy gum and Bacchus‡ drinks to sell them in nightclubs and bars. But that only lasted for a while. After some time, he went on his way.

"Anyway, living on these streets, we'll be running into each other often enough."

He tapped my shoulder, talking like a grown-up. He didn't have any reason to continue to take care of me; he'd been more than generous in helping me back on my feet when I had collapsed on a street and in teaching

---

* Korean distilled liquor.

† One hundred Korean won is approximately 10 US cents. Although the exchange rate has fluctuated over the past couple of decades, it is usually between 900 won per US dollar at the least to 1,300 won at the most. In 1995, when Sungbong was five years old, 775 Korean won was equivalent to about one US dollar.

‡ A noncarbonated South Korean energy drink, manufactured since 1963.

me how to survive there. I wanted to follow him around, but it seemed that I should not bother him anymore.

I was afraid of being alone, but knowing how not to starve to death and having freedom were enough for me.

After parting ways with him, I became hungry again. I fiddled with the gum that he had given me. I decided to sell gum the way he had taught me. At the first store I entered, I got thrown out before I had a chance to start selling. The same happened at the second and the third.

I tried a few more times, but I couldn't even cross over the store threshold. There must be something that I was doing wrong. I stood outside a store and carefully watched the people entering. They said "Hello" when they entered. I learned how to say that: hello. The next time I entered a store, I began by first greeting the store owner.

"Hello. May I sell some gum here?"

Each store owner had a different attitude. Some of them ignored me, and though very seldom, there were some who gave me food and allowed me to rest in a corner in their store. Most of them, however, yelled at me to clear out, and quite a few even went right on to box me on my ears. After a while, I found myself a veteran gum seller who could sell gum and leave quietly without attracting the owners' attention. I had learned one survival method to live on the streets.

It's about having your wits about you.

Just as the big brother had predicted that we would run into each other again living on the streets, I sometimes saw him on the way to and fro.

"Did you sell some gum?"

After being knocked around by strangers, I was glad to meet someone who would ask with a friendly face how I was doing. Thinking how he must have also been slapped on the cheeks and assailed with swear words while selling gum, I was moved to tears as though he and I were the only ones on those desolate streets.

Selling gum started with the early-evening drinkers, and the morning crowd who were having their hangover soup rounded off my daily routine. Like the store owners, the customers also came in great variety. There would be some who would open their wallets with a sympathetic face as soon as I approached the table, while some would ignore me without any replies or gesture me to go away. Most of them ignored or gestured me away.

I, too, developed tact, and I came to figure out how to pit my situation advantageously over other gum sellers' situations and win over customers by arousing their pity. I was a beggar by all standards, but because I was a little kid with a pretty enough face, it was easier for me to gain sympathy than other gum sellers. There wasn't really any need to start acting pitiful— I was already a poor gum-selling orphan. It was easier when people were with their lovers or were drunk.

"Oh dear, what a poor kid."

When the lady looked at me with a commiserating face, the man would immediately open up his wallet. Even if they were not couples on a date, if one person from a group felt sorry for me, at least one of them would take out his or her money. But that was when I was lucky. There were more mean ones than nice ones, who would demand something in return.

"Still wet behind the ears and you dare go begging around? Can you drink this? I'll buy if you can!"

"Hey, squirt, you think there's anything free in this world? First let me give you a thick ear. Then I'll give you money."

I drank whatever they gave me, not knowing that it was alcohol. I got beaten up, not realizing that it hurt. Or I must have drunk even though I knew that it was alcohol and gotten beaten up even though I realized how it hurt. Wicked were those who pushed bitter liquor against my lips, and worse still those who slapped me until I saw stars. But the worst of them all were those who made me do whatever they ordered but didn't buy the gum. The harder it was to sell the gum, the harder I tried out of spite. I added one more thing to my street survival essentials.

It was gutsiness.

This residential building on one of the Yongjeon-dong streets was where
Sungbong Choi was under the threats of organ trafficking, where he was
beaten and abused, where he took drugs and alcohol, where he hid away
when he had withdrawal symptoms, and where he sought refuge when
he was in danger. The building was a place where characters of all sorts
resided and congregated including gangsters and hookers. Despite all the
ordeals he had gone through in the building, Choi says the building is
very significant to him, and remains very much a part of his life. "It's also
the last trace of my childhood," he says. The building is still occupied by
people but it will soon be demolished. *Photo courtesy of Sungbong Choi.*

Like a Stray Dog, Like a Street Cat

I MADE IT through each day with the two things I had: tact and guts. I didn't know anything save how to live and not to die. For instance, other people had three meals a day, they changed their clothes every day, and they knew that you needed to wash your face and brush your teeth...I'm not sure that I even knew how to clean myself after taking a dump. The only thing I knew was that I needed to eat and sleep. With those two things, I could at least live like a mayfly.

There were three nightclubs in Yongjeon-dong. They were always teeming with people. Once you made it into one of them, it was like being in heaven, where you could make several days' earnings on a single night. But if you got caught by big touter brothers,* you ended up tasting hell right away.

I would wait until the big touter brothers had gone outside to smoke or go to the toilet, then I'd quickly slip in from the entrance to sell gum. If I came out right next to a customer, I could avoid getting beaten to a pulp by the touters or bouncers. After one or two successes, however, there was always a day when I had rotten luck, and on those days, I would get beaten up until I was bleeding and bruised all the previous days' worth.

When the last customer had left, the store sign lights had turned off, and the touters had gone home, I could finally find myself a place to rest.

---

* Young, well-dressed promoters who distribute advertising flyers to potential customers.

The place where I slept the most was nightclub A. It used all three floors of the building, and even though they were above ground level, the windows were blocked off. It was pitch dark inside even during daytime, and the staircases were wide, so I could lie there and sleep soundly. It was warm and soft there because the stairs had carpets.

Even if it wasn't nightclub A, most nightclubs were underground places anyway, and the entrances above their stairways continued to remain open after business had ended. When you descended down to the bottom of a stairway, you would find a shutter in front of a soundproof door, and around the shutter there would be big waiter brothers standing by the counter. The little space behind the counter was a perfect place to curl up and sleep.

The stairs were deep and there were no windows. No matter how bright the sun was shining on the ground above, not a ray of light reached where I was. It was a relief to be able to sleep without being disturbed by glaring daylight, but even if it weren't for the practical reasons, I liked the dark. I went out to the streets when the sun set, and then crawled in to sleep at dawn, so I hardly ever walked around the streets during daytime. Once in a while, when I went out to a main street in the middle of the day, I would find myself feeling terribly embarrassed.

The sunlight was so intense as to make me want to close my eyes, and the street was as wide as a square.
I didn't like brightness or spaciousness.
I liked cramped and dark places.
Like a cockroach.
I didn't have friends, but the darkness was like a friend to me.

When I laid my body on the nightclub stairs, the small and dark space felt like the inside of the rubber tub. I felt peaceful when I thought of the rubber tub. What saved me the first time ever in my life was neither my parents nor the orphanage, but the rubber tub. The rubber tub allowed me to hide myself and to escape. In this way, it made me free. The only thing for which I had at least a morsel of gratitude in those mere five or six years of my life was that rubber tub.

The nightclub was the best place to sleep, but I could not sleep there all the time. When I got caught by a touter or a waiter who had gotten off work early, I wouldn't dare come around there for a while. It was the same on days when I got beaten up while selling gum in a nightclub. Sometimes the entire Yongjeon-dong turned vicious due to gangster battles. At times like that, you just needed to spare your bones and be careful.

When I couldn't sleep in nightclubs, I slept inside terminals. The shutters in front of terminal stairs went down at night, and because they did not put any locks on them, I could crawl in through the space between the shutter and the floor. When I went inside the shutter and climbed to the top of the stairs, there was a flat space where I could lie down. It was a place hidden from people's view.

Then when I got caught by a terminal employee and was kicked out, I slept at an unfrequented public toilet. If nightclubs were the best places ever to sleep, public toilets were the worst possible places. Even if you got desensitized to the smell, you had to close the seat cover and sleep in a sitting position, since you couldn't lie down on the damp, cold floor.

I don't remember whether it was a day when I had gotten pummeled by a touter or whether it was a menacing day because of a gangster battle, but it was one of those days when I could not sleep at a nightclub. I didn't know where to go after selling all the gum I had. It seemed that I'd have to sleep on a staircase in a building. Since it wasn't so cold, it seemed that I wouldn't freeze to death even if I slept on the street. When I was walking up and down the street, somebody called out to me.

"Come here, kid."

It was a street soondae˙ vendor. I'd seen him a few times when I passed by his stall, but it was the first time he had talked to me. I found out later that he was addicted to gambling. Telephone room managers[†] and policemen were his poker mates. His face was red, maybe because he had drunk a shot of soju after work.

"You've got a decent face. Why are you going to sleep on the street?"

I didn't reply. Who cares? And what was that comment about having a decent face?

"Come home with me. I'll let you sleep there."

I sensed him out, and he didn't look harmful. He walked ahead, and I followed him. His house smelled of soondae. He took off his socks and then said, "Go wash up." When I washed and came back, he gave me his clothes. So I got washed up and changed, and I was fed and put to sleep in a warm bed. I thought to myself, "So home is where you can have food and sleep in a warm bed!"

When I got up, I saw another meal laid out there. He looked quietly at me as I emptied a bowl of rice down to the last grain. Then he suddenly blurted out, "So leave now."

I didn't ask him whether I could continue to stay with him. I just put down my spoon and got up from the seat. I'd never heard or learned how to say "thank you," so it goes without saying that I didn't know how to say it. But I was thankful. Even if he had brought me home out of impulsive compassion and then got tired of me the next day when he got back his discernment, it was enough that I had slept comfortably just that one night of my otherwise wearisome street life. I didn't expect anything more. I knew instinctively that I should not want anything more.

There was a time when a customer at a restaurant took me home. When I put a pack of gum on his table, he stared into my face.

---

* Korean sausage.

† Phone-sex parlor owners.

"If my son had been alive, he would have been exactly your age..."

His eyes were full of tears. I looked at him, puzzled, not daring to ask him to buy the gum. He patted me and said, "Let's go to my house. Go to my home."

His house was spacious and clean, altogether of a different league from the soondae vendor's house. As soon as I went in, he started ordering me to do this and that: wash yourself well, put the towel in the basket, wear slippers, sit up straight at the meal table, don't shake your feet, do this, don't do that, blah, blah, blah...As soon as I opened my eyes the next morning, I fled his house.

Sometimes, the manager of the nightclub where I often slept took me to his home. There were two managers: one of them was scary, but the other one was quite kind. The kind manager seemed to feel sorry that I was sleeping at his nightclub, and he took me to his house from time to time. It was an apartment, and it was the most luxurious house I'd ever been to. He had a wife and a kid around my age. The first time I went there, the kid covered his nose and grimaced as soon as he saw me.

"Go away. You're dirty."

I hated that kid. It wasn't because he openly avoided me. I was angry because there was someone who lived with his parents in a nice house while I was living out in the streets. I fought with him whenever I went to the manager's house. Perhaps it was because I didn't get along well with his kid. After some time the manager stopped taking me home. I didn't want to go there either. I didn't like situations where I had to compare my circumstances with those of others. I didn't like returning to the streets with a feeling of inferiority and deprivation.

It was for a very short while, but there was even a time when I lived with several big brothers. They were bullies in their late teens who sold pineapples. I was strolling down the street early one morning when they approached me in a mob and threatened me with a knife to follow them. I wasn't their match either in terms of strength or number. It was kidnapping by any sense of the word, but nevertheless they cooked noodles for me as soon as we reached their place. They told me to eat a lot and to make myself at home. There were around twenty of them living together in one house. The reason they had taken me was so they could sell more pineapples. My role was to stand next to them and plead with a pitiful face, saying, "Please buy one," when they were selling the pineapples. It was something that I did every day, so it wasn't hard at all. After some time, however, I got sick of being with people. I wanted to be alone. I escaped the hideout and avoided crossing paths with them for a while, but later on they left me alone when we ran into each other. So I was free to roam around the streets once again.

I got taken home by various people, but the outcome was always the same.
Either they told me to leave, or I left of my own accord.
The mornings when I returned to the streets, I felt comfortable, as though the streets were my home.

I had to mind the others' feelings when I was at people's homes, but on the streets, there was nothing I had to trouble myself about. Although I didn't have any fixed place to go and sleep, being a kid with a small build, I could squeeze into any dark and narrow place I found, like a cockroach. Or perhaps a bit better than a cockroach. Anyway, my life was nothing better than that of a stray dog or a street cat.

To Those Who Ask Me When Was the Hardest Time in My Life

────────── ✿ ──────────

I WANDERED AROUND the streets like a street cat or a stray dog, looking for a shelter that would keep away the rain and the wind, and looking for food that would fill my hungry stomach. Street cats were my seniors in street life, and I learned my survival skills from them. After seeing the cats digging through the garbage bags on the streets and taking food out from there, I began scavenging garbage bags on days when I couldn't sell gum.

When I found a half-eaten pig's trotters or roasted chicken, I picked the bones clean of leftover flesh. When I was thirsty, I drank rainwater dropping from the edge of a roof or scooped up the water from a puddle on the ground. When I made money by selling gum, I would buy cup noodles. Then I would go into a public toilet and eat cup noodles sitting on the toilet cover. Why did I eat it in a toilet, of all places? Because I hated people— people who beat me up for no reason, people who swore at me, people who used me in any way they wanted because I was young...I hated people, but what I hated more was to have them look at me while I ate.

For some time, I only ate cup noodles. It wasn't a matter of whether I liked cup noodles or not; rather it was because I didn't know how to buy other food. I knew how to buy gum: I could enter a supermarket, pick up the gum, and then pay for it. And when I got hungry, I picked up the cup noodles along with the gum. I thought all buying and selling happened in that way. It took me a long time before I knew how to enter a restaurant and order food.

The next phase after the cup noodles was ramen noodles sold at snack stands. Ramen noodles were a tremendous discovery compared to the time when I ate cup noodles in public toilets, but they were still noodles. Then one day, I ordered something called "kimchi fried rice" at a restaurant. I must have watched someone at the next table order it and copied what they did. That was the way I learned how to do almost everything—watching people from the corner of my eye.

When I had one spoonful of the kimchi fried rice, tears fell from my eyes. It wasn't because I was sad or sorrowful. I felt bitter and angry. If I had known that there was something so delicious in this world, I wouldn't have eaten cup noodles every day. It was spicy rice stir-fried with kimchi then served with a fried egg on top! When you popped the fried egg, the soft yolk spread over the red rice. Oh, the slightly salty and somewhat fishy-tasting yolk, together with the spicy yet sweetish rice! The flavor was one thing, but more striking was how once I was done with the rice meal, I felt full in a way that couldn't be compared with the way I felt after eating noodles.

What I bought most often to eat, though, was jajangmyeon. It must have been because it was the first food I had ever had in Yongjeon-dong, but putting those black and sweetish noodles into my mouth brought all kinds of thoughts into my head. Sometimes I would be taken by feelings that puzzled even me, and I would end up filling the noodle bowl with tears. And on days when I felt sentimental, I would eat a double portion that cost fifteen hundred won, and then leave after placing a ten-thousand-won note on the table.

In any case, jajangmyeon and kimchi fried rice are my favorite foods even today—so much so that I can't reply when asked which one of the two I like better.

When I developed some techniques in selling gum, I remembered that the big brother who had taught me how to sell gum had also sold the Bacchus drinks along with it. So I decided to sell Bacchus drinks as well. Then I began to have a lot more money left over than when I had just sold packets of gum.

I couldn't have known the concept of sets and packages then, but when I tied together a bottle of Bacchus with a packet of Ursa' capsules and sold them for five thousand won, my earnings increased delightfully. From then on my pockets were always full of paper money and coins.

I made money, but because I didn't know how to use it, I would just keep it in my pockets. I didn't know how to buy something for myself, let alone save the money. The only thing that I needed was food. Money, which I didn't know how to use, was just metal pieces and paper. The more I had, the more cumbersome it was.

After filling my stomach, the most painful thing I found was time.
I had nothing to do and nowhere to go.

Since I didn't have any goals to achieve after earning money, when I had made enough money to buy cup noodles, I didn't feel the need to sell gum anymore. When I stopped going around to sell gum, the day seemed to become endlessly long. Then one day I saw a few men gathered on the street.

"This way; this way. No, a little more to the side."

"There, stop there."

I went behind the men. There was a doll inside a square glass box. The men were looking inside the box and urgently ordering something or sighing with vexed expression.

"Got it!"

The men gave out an exclamation of joy when the hook-handed machine grabbed the doll. A melody sounded, and the doll was carried to the opening and then popped out of the box.

After they left, I went in front of the doll-drawing machine. I put in a coin like they had done and moved the lever. I let go of the lever at a spot

---

* Pills that some South Korean people believe will improve liver function.

that felt right and pressed the button. The hook hand seemed to almost grab the doll but missed it every time. I became angry and antsy.

Again, again.

Just as I started to lose count of how many times or how many hours had passed, the machine grabbed a doll. The anger and angst that had built up till then went away like indigestion that cured. I felt as though I was a savior who redeemed dolls. Perhaps I had been so intense about drawing out the doll because I wanted someone to pull me out of the mud pit in just the same way. I didn't really want to have the doll, but because of the pleasure I felt during those moments when the hook hand pulled up a doll, I spent quite a lot of money and time there. As I was just a little kid, it was the only entertainment that I could enjoy.

I ran out of money after drawing out a few dolls. Then I set out again to sell gum. I included a doll in the bundle for customers who didn't beat or swear at me. It was a losing business considering the money I spent in drawing out the dolls, but they were useless to me anyway.

When I got tired of doll-drawing, I went to a bus station. Sitting on a station bench and watching the people waiting for buses, I was curious about where all these people were headed to. Were they going home, or had they left home and were going elsewhere? There must be someone waiting for them at their destination, be they parents or friends.

The people waited for their buses restlessly or in a relaxed manner, looking at their watches or listening to music with earphones plugged in their ears. When the buses came, they got on and disappeared to heaven knows where. It seemed that it would be nice to have somewhere to go. Let's get on when the third bus arrives, I decided. It didn't have to be the third bus. I just wanted to wait for a bus like the others before getting on, as though I had some place to go.

Once I got on the bus, I went to a window seat at the very back. There were not many people in the bus, and the last seat, which was the most spacious, remained empty. When I opened the window, the wind swept by my cheek. The familiar scene of Yongjeon-dong got pushed back along with the wind. The bus left Yongjeon-dong, made short stops in worlds unknown to me to pick up or let out people, and then moved on to farther, more unfamiliar places.

When the bus arrived at its terminal station and the last passenger got out, I left the bus as though that had been my destination from the outset. The scenes didn't really vary wherever I went: old gray buildings, alleys meandering like intestines, single-story buildings clustered together in residential areas...

Walking through an unfamiliar town, sometimes I would see a playground or find a river. When a place I liked appeared, I had the fanciful illusion that perhaps I had taken a bus just to be there. I sat absent-mindedly watching the scene that was spread out in front of my eyes. Sitting for the first time ever at a new place, even the sky, the clouds, and the sunset that I must have seen hundreds of times appeared strange. They were unfamiliar, yet they were not new.

When I met friends, I whiled away my time playing with them. Stray dogs with tucked-up bellies and rashes and street cats that were swollen up and had gunk in their eyes from edema were my friends. I pitied and identified with them. Dogs and cats had streets as their home and were beaten up or driven away by people. Just like me.

I emptied my pockets and bought milk with the money. I warmed the milk and put it in the street corners where my friends passed. I was the happiest person on earth watching them lapping up the milk that I had left. I began to vaguely understand what it feels like to be able to do something for someone. There were times when I got bitten in the hand trying to touch a strange dog, but after some time, most dogs and cats did not avoid me but let me get close to them. I liked them better than people.

Much later when I started to be known, people would ask me whenever I had an interview, "When was the hardest time in your life?" I always hesitate at that question. I get stuck trying to answer because I don't know what "when" means. Because I had no concept of time, I didn't know that I was getting older or how old I was. I have no memory of concepts like "when," "why," or "how." Each day spent on the street was boring and miserable enough as to drain away any need to remember when you did what and why, or when you went where and how.

It's also difficult to understand the concept "the hardest." Since I lived ten years on the streets, how could there be a day set apart as having been the hardest day out of them all? It's like asking someone who is incarcerated in a solitary cell when the most boring day was, or like telling someone to find five grains of the prettiest sand.

There was no concept of "when" nor of "the hardest" in my mind; everything that happened during those days was all jumbled up in one lump.
In other words, the days were all connected to each other: a series of days when I would get beaten up, a series of days when I would be assailed with swear words, a series of days when I would get kicked out of places.

Even out of all those days when one day seemed to be a mere repetition of another, there was indeed a moment that stood out clearly in my memory: it was the day when I again saw the gum-selling big brother who had saved me on the street. He was being dragged by grim-faced men. As he kicked his feet with all his might, a gum container fell out of the box on his back, spilling the contents. The men forced him into their van and disappeared somewhere. The only thing I could do in that suffocating horror was to watch in hiding.

"Anyway, living on these streets, we'll be running into each other often enough."

Those words that he had spoken with a mature look rang in my ears. I had the fearful hunch that I would never be able to see him again.

You Got a Knife? Then Can
You Please Kill Me?

—— ❧ ——

Yongjeon-dong was a scary town. The smallest thing there led to a fight. Men collapsing after getting stabbed by a knife, women who yelled their heads off while being dragged by men, drunkards asleep on the streets, bullies stealing the drunkards' money from their pockets, muggers who took off the bullies—those were the daily scenes of Yongjeon-dong.

Running toward where I heard screaming while selling gum, I would find people fighting in large groups. These weren't minor quarrels but organized gang fights. They would jump up in the air to kick, smash down, and break, in the end brandishing knives to stab and slice...Even when scenes that could only appear in gangster films unfolded before my eyes, I had never thought, "What's wrong with this town?" Yongjeon-dong— where the law of the jungle had absolute reign—was the only world I knew. To me, that was all there was in this world.

Gangs beat bullies to a pulp, and bullies beat kids like me to a pulp. Normal children my age would be eating meals their moms cooked for them and going to kindergarten, but I was at the very bottom of Yongjeon-dong's food chain. Little kids on the streets were the easiest prey in that world. I feared the bullies the most. They were the ones directly above me in the food chain, and the ones who actually beat me up.

When I saw the gum-selling big brother being dragged away, I was consumed by fear. I could also be dragged away at some random moment, and maybe get killed. No one would look for a gum-selling orphan who went missing. Only then did it become clear to me the reality I faced.

A few days later, I was leaving a public toilet after eating cup noodles when some seventeen- or eighteen-year-olds came to surround me.

"Give us your money."

"I haven't any."

They sniggered.

"Only as teeny as rat's balls and already bluffing?"

Suddenly I saw stars, and before I knew it I was down on the ground. They ran in to beat me with their fists and kick with their feet. I clutched my stomach and moaned. When I got up, they had already gone. And, of course, the money in my pockets had too.

Sometimes I would get up after sleeping on the stairs of a nightclub and discover that my pockets were empty; someone had stolen my money while I was asleep. Although on the one hand I was upset, on the other I thought to myself that it was not the worst. After all, there were plenty of them out there who beat you up and then took your money, so those who just took your money were being merciful to some degree.

One day I was wandering around looking for a place to sleep after selling gum all night when a seedy-looking man came up to me.

"Did you sell much gum? Cough it up."

I knew that I wasn't his match in size and strength. Instead of meekly handing over the money, however, I clenched the money in my pockets. He dove at me, aiming at my pockets, but I didn't know how to fight back, so I just crouched there and tried to hold out. When he finally grabbed my wrist and pried out the money from my clenched hands, I flung myself at him and hung onto his arm. He shook me off like it was nothing and turned around. I sprang at him again. This time I hung onto his leg, but a single kick sent me flying backward.

After he disappeared, I clutched my sore belly and laid myself down on the stairs of a nightclub, and that's when resentment, rage, and sorrow all hit me at once. I had spent all night taking all kinds of treatment selling gum, and the only thing I had left on me were empty pockets and bruises.

No matter how well I sold gum or Bacchus drinks or Ursa pills, if life was going to be this way, I wouldn't be able to continue living on these streets. Suddenly I was struck by a thought: remaining passive would only leave me open to further attacks. I should never appear like an easy prey—I couldn't go on getting beaten up and robbed.

Again I thought of the big brother who sold gum. Life was tough anyway. If death meant becoming peaceful as in sleep, it would be better to just die. But I didn't want to suddenly disappear one day like the big brother. Getting dragged away at some unknown time by some unknown people to some unknown place…I wasn't afraid of dying, so why did that make me fear and tremble so?

Perhaps it was because I had an instinctive fear about being handed over to other people. Being born and left at an orphanage hadn't happened according to my will. I was helpless and had to be taken care of in other people's hands. The first thing I did of my own will was to run away from the orphanage. Even though I ended up living like a stray dog or a street cat, it was a life that I had chosen. I didn't want to be dragged away helplessly again by someone.

Gang-fight scenes replaced the images of the big brother being shoved into a van: beating, being beaten, jumping up, rolling, kicking, getting kicked…eventually they would brandish their knives to finish. The long knives with blue edges. Yes, let's get a knife. That was the only way that I was not going to be beaten, robbed, or killed by someone.

One day, I was in a restaurant selling gum when I saw that the kitchen was empty. Even the hall was pretty free. I sneaked into the kitchen, and there I saw a knife lying on the counter. It was a sashimi knife, with a long, flashing blade like the ones that gangsters carried around. I hid it under my clothes and got out of the restaurant.

I covered the blade with a cloth, then put it against my belly and wrapped it around my body with gauze. The feeling of the cold knife pressing against my belly frightened me. That fright relieved me: with this knife, I'll stab those who attack me. Or perhaps I may stab my own neck to end this weary life. Whether the tip of the knife pointed at my enemy or at me, the fact remained that I would be the one holding its handle.

I looked in every nook and corner of Yongjeon-dong to find those who took my money. Anyone who had their money taken from them then did nothing, and could not go on living on these streets. It was time to put the truth I learned in Yongjeon-dong into action: that offense was the same as defense.

It was at night, inside a playground, that I found him. As soon as he entered my view, I dashed toward him like a mad brain. Then with the speed and the weight of my whole body on the knife, I stabbed his thigh. The sharp knife tip went brusquely down some soft spot. I could vividly feel that where it had entered was soft and warm, as if I had tentacles on the blade. I had really stabbed him! Stabbing, just as being stabbed, brought a frightening and intense shock. While I sat in a daze, the guy clutched his thigh and then began leaping up and down. I ran away faster than I came.

I must not disappear like the gum-selling brother—that was the only thought that came into my head after stabbing a person. The fact that he wasn't there anymore meant that I no longer had anyone who could teach me how to live.

The first time he appeared in front of me, he taught me how to live.
The last time he appeared in front of me, he taught me how not to die.
How to live and how not to die—they were two completely different ways.

Not everyone was afraid of a knife. Once I was roaming the streets when some man bumped into me and began muttering with a twisted tongue.

"What you puny thing doing on the street? Go home, quick."

The man with unfocused eyes was barely keeping his balance.

"Why, I haven't a home...Please buy a gum."

"What the heck, this world. A puny kid like you selling gum out on the streets, and me, with nothing but a load of debt and rubber checks…"

"So what? Can't you just earn money? Or just die if you can't."

"Ho…Even a shrimp like you slighting me now?"

The man tried to kick me. I took a step backward. On me I felt the knife that seemed fused to my body.

"I have a knife; don't touch me."

I growled in a low voice. I knew that a knife wouldn't solve every problem. In fact, bullies were far from scared when I brandished the knife and would instead subdue me with their power and throw the knife away or point it back at me. In any case, I was a kid. When someone attacked me with all their resolve, there was nothing I could do. But he did not try to overpower me, nor was he afraid of the knife.

"You got a knife? Then can you please kill me?"

His lifeless, dead-fish eyes suddenly glittered. This was during the 1997 Asian financial crisis.

After I grasped the concept of money, I bought a jackknife (a folding pocketknife) and kept it in my pocket wherever I went. After I made friends with gangsters, I even got knives from them. Carrying a knife around with me made me want to kill a lot of people. The person I wanted to stab most of all was me. I'd stab whoever robbed my money or beat me—the evilest of them out there—and then I'd stab myself. If I killed someone and then killed myself, wouldn't we then become companions to each other? Even the evilest one out there might not be so bad a companion on that last journey.

It comforted me somewhat to think that I could end this life at any moment. The knife was as reassuring as the rubber tub. Sometimes it felt as though I wasn't concealing the knife, but rather the knife was concealing me. The coldness of its blade soothed me like warmth.

I lived with my senses on edge, like the sharp end of the knife. Even now, there are times when I feel chills down my spine or feel my hair stand on end. At those times, I'll quickly look behind, startled and thinking, "Wouldn't someone try to harm me? Wouldn't someone stab my back?"

Everywhere on my body are scars that remain like tattoos: one on the stomach from being stabbed by a gang, one on the knee from a car accident, one on the wrist from having tried to kill myself by slashing it. I cannot remember how all the scars of violence and self-inflicted wounds came about. I have clear memories of exactly how some scars were made, but for some others, the memory of when and where they were made is very dim.

It's all the same with me whether I remember them or not.
The countless scars on my body,
they simply stand for who I am.

The Lowest and Darkest Street:
The People of Yongjeon-dong

IN YONGJEON-DONG, THERE were many people like me who had come
to live out on the streets. Of them all, it was in fact the tteok-bokki[*]
lady who taught me how to speak. Until then, I knew so few words
that I could count them on my hands. The only ones I knew with exact
meaning were those I needed for selling gum, and swear words. I didn't
even know what "annyonghaseyo"[†] actually meant. I understood it as
something I had to say upon entering a restaurant or a bar to sell gum,
and nothing more.

For other words and phrases, I would just get a feel of what they must
mean by listening to people say them. You used these kinds of words and
said those kinds of things, and so on. Since I learned speech by hints and
tact, I hardly knew any words other than the ones I used in daily life.
Retrospective emotions, consideration for others, morality, ethics—I'd
never heard such words and had no idea what they meant. The words I
understood most accurately and used most often were swear words. They
were the commonest speech in Yongjeon-dong.

"What do you want to be when you grow up?" the tteok-bokki lady asked
me.

"When I grow up? I don't know what that means, fuck."

---

* Stir-fried rice cake.
† "Hello" in Korean.

"Then you should say, 'I don't know yet, ma'am.' You need to speak politely to grown-ups. Say, 'I don't know yet, ma'am.'"

"I don't...know yet..."

"Ma'am."

"Ma'am."

The lady paused, stirring the red, mouth-watering tteok-bokki, looked back, and grinned. I didn't like tteok-bokki that much, but I went to see her often. She was also the first person to ask me what my name was. People called me "Hey, you" or "beggar brat." Nobody knew my name, of course. That's because even I didn't know my name.

"What's your name?" the lady asked me when we had become familiar enough with each other over time.

"I don't know that sort of thing."

"Don't know your name? Hm, then how's Jiseong? Say you're Jiseong from now on."

She took out a paper and drew some lines and a circle with a ball pen.

"See, it's written 'Jiseong.'"

I looked blankly at the white paper and the black letters and repeated to myself, "Jiseong, Jiseong." It felt weird. Whenever the lady called me "Jiseong," I would have to answer "yes" because I was Jiseong from then on. I imagined introducing myself in front of others: "I'm Jiseong." Of course that never happened. But anyway, it felt like I had suddenly become a different person. I even felt a bit flattered.

People who are given names right from the start won't know that feeling.
When the lady gave me a name,
I received the very first gift in my life.
The moment I became Jiseong, I was no longer one of the many gum sellers.
I was a boy named Jiseong.

That night when I had stabbed someone for the first time, I went to the lady at the cart bar. She'd been around a long time working on the

Yongjeon-dong streets, so there was nothing she didn't know about the place.

"Have you seen the gum-selling brother by any chance?"

She shook her head. I told her about how I had seen him getting dragged away a while ago. She said to me in a low voice, "Jiseong, be careful."

"Why? Of what?"

"The people who took him away, they are probably organ traffickers."

"What's that?"

"Guys who cut up people's bodies and then take the stuff inside."

An image of the big brother lying with a blue face, his body opened up with the intestines pulled out, flashed before my eyes. No matter how I shook my head, I couldn't make that terrifying image go away. I asked in a fearful voice, "Then what's happened to him?"

"Dead, probably," she answered.

If the tteok-bokki lady taught me everyday speech, it was the "turtle" lady who taught me street swearing. The turtle lady was the owner of Turtle Restaurant. The restaurant opened in the early morning around the time when gum selling ended. So basically, as I was wrapping up my sales, the lady would be beginning hers. When I entered the restaurant, she began swearing at me right off the bat.

"Why are you here, you bastard. You stink, so piss off! Filthy bastard."

Many people swore at me, but the turtle lady was different from them all. I had the feeling that her sticky, copious swearing wasn't actually sincere, that there was yet another heart hidden behind all those swear words.

"Ajumma,* life's so hard. I'm dying of stress," I said to the turtle lady.

After selling gum all night, I would enter Turtle Restaurant, deliberately pulling my face to look more miserable than I really felt.

"I don't care whether a nobody like you lives or dies."

---

* Middle-aged woman.

Even while blurting out comments with an annoyed voice, she would secretly push food in front of me. "Why do you keep coming? I'm so sick and tired of you," she would sometimes complain, while passing me—half dumping, that is—clothes to wear. She had a rough mouth, but she didn't pity me like the others. Listening to her swear, I thought that here was someone who understood me. Of course I never said that to her.

After a night's work, I would find my feet headed toward Turtle Restaurant again and again. The turtle lady was comfortable to be around. She would curse and complain with her mouth, telling me not to come back, but would also toss out pieces of clothing to me, sometimes as though she had been waiting for me to come by. Women didn't beat or throw things at me like the men, but they weren't nice either. Even though they wanted to take care of me because I was such a little thing, they made sure to push me away and to keep enough distance, worrying that I might get naïvely attached to them.

"That bastard brat, got a cutesy face but stares like shit. Eye holes slit right across to the ears, and he raises them all scary."

"What did I do?"

"Fucking bastard, you could kill someone with that glare."

After hearing those words, I studied my face thoroughly in a public toilet, as though I were looking at a total stranger. Only the shape of my face was that of a child; what I found in the mirror was a person who glared back with a fierce and spiteful gaze. I forced a smile. My facial muscles, however, seemed to have forgotten how to smile and twisted oddly.

Among the masses driven to the streets were those who belonged to a different category from the street vendors and gum sellers. They were the gangsters. They were similar to bullies yet different. One day while I was loitering around a nightclub, a gangster man sitting in front of the club waved his hand at me.

"Hey, kid, come here."

I went to him in a flash. It seemed that he was going to give me alcohol. Gangster men often gave me drinks when I did my rounds selling gum.

"Hey, squirt, come and drink this."

Then I would just drink whatever they handed me without knowing what it was. As I drank, my head would start to spin, and my body would sway to the front and back and side even if I tried to stay still. Just as my face began to turn red, I would feel that my feet were swimming in the air. Then together with the feet, my heart would also start bobbing in the air. It felt as though the murderous intent toward myself and others was becoming diluted. My desire to die turned into stupefied abandon. I liked the sensation that my body and heart weren't really mine, and it drew me to alcohol. I already knew then how to drink and went around getting drinks from people almost every day.

What the gangster man handed me in front of the nightclub, though, wasn't alcohol but a brick. I didn't understand what he meant and looked blankly back at him. He looked as though he was dying of boredom.

"Bash my head with this."

"Why?"

"If you do, I'll give you five thousand won."

As soon as I got the brick, I bashed his head. I didn't simply knock him, but jumped up and bashed him using my full weight.

"What the fuck, cheeky bastard!"

He grabbed the brick from my hand and bashed my head. From his head and from mine, blood oozed and trickled. He looked down at me silently and smirked.

"This bastard's got some steel. What's your name?"

"Jiseong."

"Have you eaten?"

"No."

"Let's go."

He took me to a seolleongtang* place. That first tasting of the pale, bland soup wasn't as impressive as it had been with jajangmyeon, but someone buying me food still came as the highest favor that a human being could ever extend to me. The man also ordered a bottle of soju. My eyes twinkled as I watched the bottle.

"Wanna drink?"

I nodded. He filled my soju glass to the brim. The steaming soup and the soju he poured me lessened the throbbing pain in my head.

Living on the streets taught me how to sense people's real motives.
I could make out pretense from sincerity almost instinctively.
Whether it was wit or psychic power,
the fact remained that it was a quite useful skill to have
while living on the streets.

I never opened myself up to people who were fake in their hearts, no matter how they tried to pretend otherwise. This man, however, seemed real.

After eating the seolleongtang, I went to sleep at his place. The next morning he shook me awake. I followed him to the toilet and brushed my teeth with the toothbrush he gave me. In the mirror were his large body and my small body standing side by side. I watched him in the mirror and followed what he did. He brushed his front teeth up and down. I did the same. He held some water in his mouth, and then made a gurgling sound with his head leaned back. I did exactly that. Making toothpaste bubbles and brushing teeth with him felt like a fun game.

He then stuck out his tongue and rubbed it with the bristles. This time also, I copied him and cleaned my tongue. In the mirror, I saw him suddenly stop his motion. For some reason, he was glaring at me with a scowling face.

---

* Stock soup of bone and stew meat.

I stopped brushing. I was just about to ask, "Why?" when he suddenly struck the back of my head.

"What? Why do you hit me?"

"Fucking crud, get the hell out."

He threw his toothbrush with a screwed-up face and left. I also threw down my toothbrush, and without bothering to rinse my mouth, I left the house. I didn't even want to ask him why. He had bought me seolleongtang out of a passing impulse, then wanted me to clear off because he decided he wasn't interested anymore. I still don't understand why, but perhaps it might have been because I seemed to him like a pushover. He had done for me what he felt like doing, and I had mistaken him as having had goodwill.

Occasionally there were some young outsiders who came to our town to sell gum. I could have stabbed them with my knife, but I didn't harm them or drive them out. There were no set territories for selling gum, and being a solitary wanderer myself, I didn't know about territoriality and rules. Some of these gum-selling outsiders were older than me and some younger. They all disappeared to somewhere after two or three months. When I saw the tiny kids, I would feel like taking care of them for no reason at all.

"Should I tell you how?" I would offer them a conversation or buy their gum.

There were times when a panhandler would crawl past me, waddling his whole body with hymns resounding from his audio device. Then I would discreetly drop coins into his bowl. Somehow I wanted to, even if looking after myself was hard enough.

It wasn't pity per se. I was used to it, but disliked being pitied, so I didn't pity anyone. It wasn't understanding either. I'd never been understood by anyone, so I didn't know what that was. What moved me to show even the slightest concern toward them was perhaps a sense of kinship. Perhaps it was whatever it was that had made the gum-selling brother raise me up from dying on a street, feed me, and teach me how to sell gum.

They each had their own reason for being on the streets,
but they all had the same purpose.
Money.
People who had been driven to the extremities of life because of money
stood there selling gum, tteok-bokki, and fish cakes.
To all of us, the streets of Yongjeon-dong were the world's ultimate edge.
Getting thrust out from here meant plunging down life's uttermost cliff.

Swearing and Crying, Falling Asleep Crying, Selling Gum Crying

———— ✼ ————

I MUST HAVE been around ten. I was watching the roadway from the sidewalk. The cars were rushing past with fearsome speed. I'd been watching them for so long that their speed was beginning to feel surreal. The sidewalk and the roadway marked the boundary between life and death. Walking over one step, I could end this life and be at peace. Like a kelpie tugging your ankles down into deep water, the gray asphalt was pulling me in. Several times I would almost put my foot out but wouldn't actually jump into the roadway. I hadn't yet the courage to end my own life.

A few days later at dawn, however, I got run over by a car at an intersection. I hadn't jumped in front of it intentionally. On my way back from gum selling, my mind had been cloudy, maybe because I'd been either hungry or sleepy. I had entered the road half awake, without thinking.

I felt the impact of a massive object that then ran on past me. I felt my body fly up into the air. The moment was instant, but it felt like I was flying for a very long time. I don't think I had closed my eyes because I think I saw the sky and the ground turn upside down. Maybe there had been a faint light of dawn gleaming in the corner of that sky, and maybe I saw the ground turn into a curved surface and then spin around. When I regained consciousness, I saw the faces of several people surrounding and looking down at me. There must have been some busy people on their way to early-morning shifts or people returning home after spending the whole night drinking.

"What's going on, what's going on..."

"A kid got run over."

"Oh dear."

They bustled. But only bustled. No one tried to get me up. I lay there like that for a while unable to move, but the ambulance didn't come. It was already a long while since the car that had run me over had passed out of sight.

I couldn't feel any pain. I wasn't even panicking. "This is the end"—that was the only thought circling in my mind. So this is it: now it's really the end…I had always wanted it to be the end—a day sooner, or right now if at all possible. But thinking there that my life had actually reached its end, an incomprehensible and unacceptable longing that it should not end like this swept over me.

Please help me! I wanted to say. Please help me! The people just kept standing there looking down at me, mumbling. During those times when after a gang fight corpses lay strewn about, I would grit my teeth at the sight of the dead flesh, the extinguished life…and I felt like I had become that corpse. The faces of the people looking down at me overlapped with the image of my own face staring at dead bodies in horror.

I crawled, and got myself back to my feet. Then I left the road, dragging my feet. It was by the East Terminal. Even until I finally got myself into the terminal toilet, nobody tried to get hold of me or ask whether I was okay. As soon as I entered a toilet cubicle, I collapsed on the floor. The pain in my feet was severe, and I wanted to burst with screams, but there was nothing I could do, other than to stifle the screams and cries down my throat.

Somebody who came into the toilet must have called for help after seeing the trail of blood I'd left behind. Soon, an ambulance came and rushed me to a hospital. I couldn't think of anything at first because of the pain, but after the emergency treatment and getting bandaged around the legs, I suddenly woke up to the horrendous reality. I ran away from the hospital, limping, afraid of all the facts that were soon going to be uncovered: that

I didn't have any money to pay the hospital fees, that I didn't have any guardian, so the police were going to come and then discover the fact that I had been going around with a knife and had stabbed someone. Even in the throes of pain that made me scream out at every step, I had to run, run away. I was a little kid frightened of all these things, because there was no one there who stood by me.

When I could no longer continue limping, I started trotting on my toes. When I couldn't trot on my toes anymore, I got down and crawled with my body like the impaired panhandlers. I arrived at Turtle Restaurant that way. The turtle lady was crying, but not because she saw me like that. She'd been crying for quite some time already.

"Why did you come? Motherfucking bastard. Who do you think you are knocking around everywhere? You think you'll sell more gum that way?"

While swearing with her mouth, she was crying in her eyes. She was someone who genuinely wouldn't blink an eye even if I really died. But she looked like she was hurting. She seemed to be hurting as much as me.

I rested there briefly then left again. As usual I went to lie down on the stairs of a nightclub that had closed for the day. I couldn't fall asleep because of the pain, but I hypnotized myself saying, "I have to sleep, I have to sleep," because sleeping was the only way out of the pain. But I would barely manage to fall asleep and would be jolted awake by severe pain, and I would find my face wet from having cried in my sleep. I couldn't figure out what was the matter with my legs, but I couldn't bend or move the limbs. The injury to my knees was so serious that the bone lay exposed. It freaked me out, but there wasn't any way other than to leave it alone, since I couldn't go to the hospital. The best I could do was to imitate what the nurse had done at the hospital and keep it wrapped in a bandage. In the park, in the public toilet, in a remote corner of a back alley, I would feel waves of sorrow flood over me as I rewrapped the bandage all alone. What was sadder than wrapping the bandage around my knees while stifling groans and cries down my throat was unwrapping the bandage.

I still remember vividly the pain I felt on that day. I was sitting on a park bench, crying. I unwrapped the bandage—the gauze had fallen out long ago. The bandage, wrapped right above the wound in a swath, had become matted to the regenerating flesh as the wound healed. Unwrapping the bandage tore off the flesh where scabs had just barely begun to form. From there, pus flowed out, accompanied by a nauseating smell, and from the festering knee, white worms wriggled out. I was angered, aggrieved, embittered by the pain of the tearing flesh...I bawled and bawled, gagging with deep sorrow. As I attempted to walk in that condition, my unwashed, dirty clothes would graze the wound.

Welling up in sorrow, I would burst out crying continually, without end.
At sunset when darkness covered the sky,
as I stood leaning against a dimly lit streetlight,
while walking the murky and untrodden back alleys of Yongjeon-dong,
I would find myself resistless against the abrupt fits of tears.
For a long time after that, I swore crying, slept crying,
and sold gum crying.

Looking back at it now, I think the wound had festered so badly that the leg almost had to be amputated. I didn't have to amputate it in the end, though, whether by luck or tough resilience. Even now, although I think I walk okay, people sometimes comment on how I seem to be limping on my left leg.

It was around that time: I'd been totally drained by the endless crying when one day, I entered a public toilet. I had no strength remaining in my body and barely stood, leaning on the washstand peering at myself in the mirror. My eyes were bloodshot, and my cheeks were blackened with grime, stained by streaks of tears. I bent my head to wash my face then looked up again, disbelieving what I'd seen.

When had it happened? My whole head had turned snow white. I gawked at the whitened hair. How could my hair have turned so white at ten-odd years of life? I was really frightened. Was I turning into an old man even before ever having grown up? I had contemplated death more than a hundred times, but I hadn't anticipated turning old so instantly before it happened. Then I went to the turtle lady.

"Just look at his goddamn hair. That brat, he turns into a bully bastard then dares poke his face back here!"

I couldn't sell gum in that condition. I was no longer a poor little kid but a bully rascal. Roaming the streets with white hair, I'd get beaten up twice instead of once and otherwise suffer all kinds of undue treatment. The turtle lady dyed my hair black again. For a while white hair grew under it, but from some point on, I started to have black hair again.

The car accident wasn't a one-time incident. I don't know why I got run over so often. Was it because I was a kid with attention problems, or was it because working mainly at night, I was always out and about in the dark? Was it because my head was always full of suicidal thoughts? Maybe I was just awfully unlucky.

"Oh dear, I'm so sorry. Aren't you hurt? Where's your mom?"

People would jump out of their cars with alarmed faces at first, then upon discovering that I had no parents, look for the right moment to wriggle out of the situation to finally climb back inside their cars and speed away. Perhaps in their minds, orphans didn't count for responsibility. But those were actually the better ones, because there were people who even went as far as throwing their temper at me and slapping my face.

"Why did you jump in front of a car? Have you gone mad?"

Every time I got hurt, it was the legs. Each step I took caused incredible pain, but I had to get up by myself and walk out of the roadway. I never returned to the hospital after the first accident. I could at least get disinfected if I went to the hospital, but in order to get treatment, I had to write something on a chart. I had nothing to write. I had no name and no age; besides, I didn't even know how to write. They would eventually have to call the police.

During that time, I abhorred all people. It wasn't just those hit-and-run people. There were two kinds of people I met: the beating kind and the pitying kind. If you were to ask me whom I hate more of the two, just as I can't choose between kimchi fried rice and jajangmyeon, I wouldn't be able to answer the question.

People who beat and people who pitied had totally different faces, but the truth remained the same: they were both indifferent. I was a phantom person, blurred out of sight. People who callously went away after running me over, people who looked away when I approached, people who pretended not to hear me even when I tried to talk to them—I was just a dispensable nobody among these people. I could allow myself to get attached to stray dogs or street cats, but never to those people.

I didn't know whether I was going to die that day or the next, but nobody would remember me either way. I thought often about how much I wanted to die but didn't ever think deeply about death. The most I thought was perhaps that when you died, that was the end and you could rest in peace. Neither did I give much thought about the world that would be left without me. No one would grieve for me, and nobody would know whether or not I'd even existed in the first place.

Those thoughts made me just a bit sad. Was the reason I didn't die because of that split second of sadness when I lamented a world in which I no longer existed? I don't know. I think it was because I believed that I could die anytime, whether by stabbing or by car accident, and that belief led me to keep delaying that moment again and again—till today.

What I really can't seem to understand is that through all those weary times, there was a strand that I was holding on to. It wasn't any sort of hunch like "one day I'll be living a different life than now." So I'm quite sure that it wasn't a "dream" or "hope" or anything like that. Then what exactly was it? To this day I don't know, but in any case, it postponed my death. And maybe now is the time to find out what it is.

Whenever I approached people, I heard a voice that said,
"I hope he doesn't come this way."
It wasn't the sound of their voice leaving their mouth and reaching my
eardrums.
Rather, it was the sound of their hearts coming to grate against mine.

One very cold day, that very familiar voice seemed louder than usual: "I hope he doesn't come this way, I hope he doesn't come this way..." Snow fell and bitter wind raged, but the street dazzled brightly. Miniature bulbs glittered around trees, and there were people sounding bells on red kettles. Here and there on the street, foreign songs whose meanings I couldn't make out resounded.

"What day is it today?"

People said a word that I'd never heard before. It was Christmas. I didn't know what that meant. I just knew that today was a special day and that on a day like this, people dreaded me more than usual. The more brightly the streets dazzled and the happier and toastier people felt, the lonelier and colder I was. I learned what Christmas was later when I began attending church. Even now during Christmas time, I can still hear the voice ringing in my ears: "I hope he doesn't come this way..." It must be because I was abandoned shortly after I was born, and Jesus's birthday just feels ever lonelier and colder to me.

Big Sister: The Only Warm Person on the Streets, My First Love

———— ❧ ————

I THEN STOPPED working so desperately at selling gum like I used to. Instead, my days were more often spent running errands for gangsters. Running errands was more interesting than selling gum, and it seemed to make time pass by faster. It also brought me a lot more money, and on some days I'd get treated to food and even drinks—which I liked so much—so it was better than gum selling.

The reason I didn't end up as a gangster was probably because by nature I detested being dominated and oppressed. Gangs are groups that maintain themselves through command and obedience. Minions had to do as they were told, and disobeying brought fearful consequences. Running errands and getting treated to alcohol was more or less the part I was fit for.

However, I couldn't get drinks all the time. There were days when I couldn't run errands for them, and sometimes they didn't buy me drinks even after I did the errands. Once I began to enjoy alcohol, my desire to drink could no longer be satiated only when people treated me.

One day when I was earnestly craving alcohol with no one there to treat me, I sneaked into where gangsters stored their fake liquors. But just as I was sneaking out with two bottles in my hand, I ran right into a gangster. Without my knowing, the liquor bottles slipped out of my hands, then crashed loudly onto the floor. I wasn't against just another gum peddler or a bully, but a gangster, and soon I was going to find myself in the same plight as the bottles that had just crashed at my feet.

I'd become sufficiently inured to getting beaten up, but that was the first time when I felt that I was going to get beaten to death. They weren't the kind who let you off easily just because you were a kid. A brick bashed down on the back of my skull. Sticks and metal pipes struck from every side. When I regained consciousness, I found myself thrown away in an empty construction field. After that I lived half-crippled for quite some time.

Along with drinking, I also began smoking cigarettes. This was through the gum-selling big brother. One day I met him on the street, and we went into a video arcade together. Children and adults alike had their eyes riveted on game screens, busily moving the levers. The big brother didn't sit in front of a game machine but entered a karaoke booth in the corner. He inserted some coins and began singing. The song's title was "Rock Island."

A rock island washed by breaking waves,
An empty place—
Yet even here they began arriving one by one
(…)
Now even the seagulls have left
And though no one remains,
I want to go on living here on this rock island.

Inside the isolated booth, the big brother's voice resounded plaintively. I couldn't understand the lyrics well, but the sorrow in the song affected me silently and bitterly. His side profile as he raised his voice high, and the lyrics he sang, somehow seemed forlorn. His voice quivered. For some reason I had the feeling that that song was going to become the song of my life. After leaving the game arcade, he stuck a cigarette between his lips, lighted it, and spouted a long puff of smoke. Then he handed one to me to try. I put it between my fingers like he did and puffed out the smoke. Since I hadn't sucked it in, there was hardly any smoke, and I stood there fascinated by the big brother, who could spew out so much smoke.

Sometime later I picked up a packet of cigarettes on a street that someone had either dropped or thrown away. I tried smoking alone on the nightclub stairs. This time, I lighted the cigarette then sucked it in with all my might. The smoke filled up my lungs all the way to the innermost capillary. I felt like a hollow shell that had been emptied of its content. It felt good to stuff the empty chest full with something, even though it was only smoke that soon disappeared away.

After the big brother disappeared, it was the big sisters who shared their cigarettes with me—kind and warm big sisters, in karaoke bars. When I entered karaoke bars to sell gum, I would find them gathered in one corner, playing Go-Stop.ˈ In their small, full lips, there were always thin, white cigarettes. The men would be rough and violent, but the big sisters didn't swear at me or drive me away even when I sat there staring at them. When our eyes met, they even smiled at me.

"Do you know how to smoke? Should I give you one?"

They pushed a cigarette between my lips. The karaoke bar was warm, and the time spent smoking a cigarette and watching them play card games was quiet and peaceful. If possible, I wanted to stay by them forever. But just like with nightclubs, it wasn't easy to enter karaoke bars. In terms of menace, karaoke bars could match nightclubs in every way: they also belonged to gangster domain.

There were more than three gang factions in Yongjeon-dong. Since gang fights would start at the drop of a hat, there wasn't the tiniest bit of tolerance or leeway with the gangsters in that town. Among themselves the gangsters knew their domain and rules, but I didn't know such things. I not

---

* Korean card game.

only intruded into their territory in any way I wished, but even went as far as snubbing their orders, not to mention giving them no respect as grown-ups. I talked roughly to anyone I met and didn't hesitate to blurt out blunt comments when I got in a foul mood. There were times when no matter how I tried to stay unnoticeable, I got spotted by high-level managers inside karaoke bars. While I sold gum to the customers, they would slap the heads of the waiters instead of directly slapping me.

"What's that? It brings down the classiness of the bar for our customers. Who let him in? You want to die?"

Still, I went on and barged in anywhere to sell gum and wasn't really scared even when threatened. I'm sure the underlings must have been hugely annoyed to be chewed out all the time by their bosses because of me. After getting to know the big sisters, I became more forcefully determined in entering karaoke bars. There were days when I would feel a particular longing for people's touch.

Days would come when I felt loneliness reaching my marrow.
On those days I desperately needed to hear a kind word from the big sisters
or be offered a cigarette.

It was around that time that I met this big sister. I often saw her alone on the street, and she seemed to be as lonely and solitary as I was. Not really having anything to do or anywhere to go, I followed her wherever she went.

"Hi, Jiseong. Have you eaten?"

She didn't tire of me even when I followed her around, and she would talk to me in a friendly voice. Meeting her somehow made the ends of my lips go up. She was the only person who made me smile.

She was a runaway girl who worked in a phone-sex parlor. Her job was to make moaning sounds into a phone. One day I went in front of the phone-sex parlor because I missed her. She was just stepping out of the building where she worked.

"Big Sister!"

I ran to her excitedly. She spoke to me in a warm voice, as usual.

"Jiseong, would you like to go somewhere with me?"

I didn't ask her where we were going, and I just followed her. I liked wherever it was she went. She stopped on a street and then paced around, glancing about. Moments later, a man appeared. "Who's this kid?" he asked, seeing me stuck at her side. When she explained something to him in a low voice, he nodded his head. The two of them entered a motel. I followed, holding her hand.

That was the first time I had entered a motel. Like the houses of the people who had taken me home, it was warm and had places to wash. And there was an enormous bed. It was similar to a house, but the atmosphere was completely different. Inside the motel, the man and Big Sister took off their clothes and lay down on the bed. While they touched and licked each other's bodies, I sat still on a chair in the corner of the room.

She continued to take me to motels every now and then. And each time there was a different man. I watched her silently in one corner of the room while she sold sex. Thinking back about it, I think she took me with her because she wanted to avoid people's suspicious gaze. A man in his thirties or forties and a teenage girl entering a motel together would have been a dead giveaway to people that they were engaging in paid sex.

But I never in the least thought that she was using me. When the men were finished with their job, they immediately left the room. Then we could be alone in the room together. After the men left, we went inside the bathtub together and washed ourselves. I was almost as tall as Big Sister by then, around five feet and three inches.

After washing ourselves clean, we lay on the bed together and went to sleep in each other's arms. Nothing was more relaxing than getting washed up in hot water and then lying down on a soft bed. What was better than the hot water and the soft bedding was her smooth and snug skin. Big Sister was warmer than the water and softer than the blankets. I was beginning to pass out of childhood and was growing into a young man.

Being with her, I began to figure out what men and women did inside hostess bars, and why opening the door of some rooms to sell gum caused people to shout such curses. The environment that surrounded me was full of promiscuity, but I felt that the time I spent with Big Sister was different from the rest. There was no money or charges that were exchanged between us. Just being together was enough in itself. Like me, Big Sister was also someone who needed a friend.

After some time, Big Sister disappeared from Yongjeon-dong's streets. How many days had I spent looking for her? Then one day I ran into her on a street.

"Big Sister, where have you been all this time?"

"Yeah, well just…Jiseong, would you like to come with me?"

Where she took me was the house of some loan shark. He was a man in his mid-forties with a fierce gaze. He looked me up and down, then said in a husky voice, "Who's this kid?"

Big Sister held my hand tightly and said, "He's my little brother. Please let us stay here together."

"Send him out right now."

"Please. He doesn't have anywhere to go."

He alternated his gaze from her to me with a frightful face, and then said I could sleep over one night and stepped back. The next day, however, I didn't leave; nor did I leave the day after that, or the day after that. Even though I had to stay on tiptoe and bear with swearing tirades, I still didn't leave. But that didn't last long; eventually he grabbed me and threw me out.

I'd never felt that empty and lonely returning to the streets from someone's house. The streets of Yongjeon-dong, which I had considered home, suddenly felt unfamiliar and strange. Just one person had left those streets, but it felt as though the entire street had been deserted.

I didn't even know what Big Sister's name was.
I didn't know her name, but I knew how I felt toward her.
Longing. It was a lonely thing.
I was left feeling desolate, as though one corner of my heart ached with frost.

I didn't want to do anything—neither selling gum nor eating food. Growing indifferent to everything also broke down my guard. It must have been because of this that I got pushed into that van I always feared.

I Cannot Forget Them, Not
Even in My Dreams

A BRUTAL HAND grabbed the scruff of my neck. I was shoved into a van, and the car door shut with a bang. That was the sound of my life ending. Things started to blur in my head. Strange people, a van...Only organ traffickers would do this sort of thing. Now my body was going to get split into two. They were going to pull out all my intestines. I could sense quickly that they were organ traffickers: I couldn't feel the warmth of their bodies. They gave you the feeling of horrifying iciness, so that you couldn't ever believe that there was warm blood circulating in their bodies.

Organ trafficking was the biggest source of dread in my life on the streets. The feeling heightened after I heard that the people who kidnapped the gum-selling brother were probably organ traffickers. I knew, through my street knowledge, how they extracted organs and killed people. Some drugs could turn you into a human vegetable. You couldn't move even if they beat you or cut off parts of your body. Under the influence of those drugs, women were raped and men got their organs removed. The big brother must have suffered that way.

Outside the window, waves rolled. Why a sea? I remembered the story I'd heard from the tteok-bokki lady about shrimp boats. Maybe I had to be grateful that the kidnappers weren't organ traffickers after all but those who sold people off to catch shrimp on an island. Just as I had expected, the car stopped by the seashore.

"He's too young to come to a place like this."

Somebody was saying something like that outside. Once they put you on the boat, that would mean the final end. I tensed my nerves and got ready to escape. While the people were busy talking, I opened the door and bolted out. And I ran as fast as I could.

Out on the streets, I always had to run away from someone. I'd never wanted to be a good runner, but I automatically became one. When I started running, even most grown-ups couldn't catch up. But no matter how fast you could run, you could never be entirely safe. Even if you succeeded in escaping ten times, one mistake could throw you into a fatal situation. But today I absolutely could not afford to make that mistake. I was determined not to fail, come hell or high water. I was going to return to the streets of Yongjeon-dong, alive.

Realizing that there was no one pursuing me, I stopped running. My feet were no longer treading on asphalt road but a tranquil country path. I couldn't figure out how to get back to Daejeon. I was trudging down a dirt path when suddenly an old man spoke to me.

"You are not from here, right? Where's your home?"

When I told him that I didn't have a home, he took me to his. At first he just made me run simple errands, but soon he began using me as a laborer to do farming and all kinds of odd tasks. When I showed that I was tired, he would say with a stern face, "Be grateful that I'm feeding you and letting you sleep here."

After some time, I ran away from that house. I'd been working from dawn to dusk like a cow, but there wasn't even a single coin in my hands. I walked for days and somehow got myself back to Yongjeon-dong.

Why did I keep returning to these streets?
The place where I would return to—after having run away from an orphanage that had fed me and housed me.

These streets where there wasn't really any place to sleep nor hands that fed me were indeed my home.
Other than the people and the alleys I'd grown familiar with on these streets, there was no one or no place I knew.

As soon as I came back to the streets, I went to the tteok-bokki lady. I was famished.

"Ajumma, I'm starving to death."

She glanced at me, put out some fish cakes for me to eat, and then asked, "Where have you been?"

"Well…"

I looked up at her, mumbling through a fish cake. She was putting a skewer through a fish cake with her back toward me. It seemed that she wasn't really interested in finding out. After eating the fish cakes, I went to the turtle lady.

The turtle lady had been running a cart bar after the Turtle Restaurant went broke. When I entered the cart bar, she yelled into my face, "Motherfucking bastard, where you been, poking back only now!"

Only after getting an earful from her did I feel warm inside again and at home. Whether it was in the Turtle Restaurant or at the cart bar, not a hair on her seemed to have changed. Swearing at me like it'd been that way for eternity, she clicked her tongue at my shabby appearance.

Sometime after I had returned to Yongjeon-dong, I was on my way to sleep after exhausting myself selling gum when a sedan stopped in front of me. A young man put his head out the car window.

"Hey, kid, do you live around here?"

I didn't know why he was asking that. He ran his eye over me staring blankly, made a face that said he understood, and then asked, "Have you had any food?" It had been a bad day for selling gum, and I'd gone without food the whole day. When I heard the word "food," my stomach growled. When I shook my head, he said, "I'll give you some food, so get in." He had a comely face and was well dressed and didn't seem like he would harass me like a bully or a gangster. Besides, I was so hungry, and I just got into his car. The car entered a lonesome mountain road and then stopped at an old farm. It seemed like the man lived alone.

The man brought me a small table with food. Kimchi and dry side dishes were all there was, but even that was delicious because I was so hungry. I was stuffing my face with food when I suddenly felt something queer and lifted my head. He was looking at me with a strange smile. I slowly put down my spoon. Then I glanced at the door behind him with the intention to dart out when the moment came.

Was it me who pushed off the table? Or was it him? The table overturned and the plates fell all over the place, and he jumped on top of me. I was forced flat on my face. My pants came off. I screamed like crazy under him, but no one could hear my screams from that isolated house on the mountain. I had no strength to resist the irrational beast, and the notion that he may go on to kill me after the rape struck me with utmost terror: a man having satisfied his lust kills me in some reckless way to clear away all evidence, and then disposes of my body somewhere in the mountains...

I yowled, vomiting all the food I ate, but the man didn't stop. His penis penetrated into my anus. It was an awful, terrible pain. Shortly strength drained from my whole body and I couldn't even move a finger. For a long time then, the man violated me in any way he pleased as I lay there limp like a cicada stuck under a tack. I was looking down at all this wretchedness, having drifted out of my body, or it was at least as vivid as that. If I could end this pain, I would welcome even death. Then I lost consciousness.

When I awoke, the man had disappeared, and I was left there naked on the floor. The pain was severe. I came down from the mountain fearing that perhaps he would come after me and kill me. I wasn't going to let myself be killed by him.

After that happened, I began to fear everyone on the streets. Everyone seemed to be a rapist. Watching men pass by, my eyes would travel below their waist, and every so often I would start up in alarm. If in the past I hadn't liked people, now they'd become the subject of my terror. Meeting the eyes of grown-up men, I would quickly try to read their motives, and if I bumped into any of them by accident, I would scream and run away. My wariness of people rose to its hysteric height.

Then when I was beginning to loosen my guard a little, I sensed a dangerous person. It was a bully I'd see every now and then in town. At first I simply passed him by, but from some point on, I felt him watching me with strange eyes. One late dawn I met him at a narrow alley; I realized that I was in danger. I tried to run away, but it was a narrow alley that led to a dead end.

The place he dragged me to was the toilet on the stairway of nightclub B. The nightclub had ended business, and it appeared that there was no one in the building. He pushed me into a cubicle and then suddenly began battering me. Inside the narrow toilet cubicle, I couldn't escape or move my body away from the blows. The best defense I could make was to collapse onto the floor and huddle down as much as possible. Punches and kicks flew in from all around my huddled body. I'd gotten used to getting pummeled, but his feet and fists were merciless. When blood seeped into my eyes, my sight began to blur. My face must have been covered with blood.

When I regained consciousness, I found myself lying in an empty toilet cubicle. My pants had been taken off. My feelings turned deadly foul. I'd tried to be so careful, yet I'd fallen prey again. I didn't know how many more times this sort of thing was going to happen, and I already feared the unknown future that was closing in upon me with every dreadful second. There were many people I wanted to kill, but there was none I wanted to kill more desperately than that bully and that swine who lured me to the mountain. I combed through the whole town of Yongjeon-dong to find that bully. I even retraced my memory and got back to the farm on the mountain, but there was no one inside. Considering how they could have escaped my search, it has to be fate that apportioned them such long lives.

The people who chased me around the most, and the people I had to run away from the most, were the police. Because of them I'd been to almost every single care facility in Daejeon. I hated the police more than gangsters and bullies. They were the most detestable lot out of all the human beings on the streets. Whenever there was a gang fight, they would begin by picking on me and drag me to the police station.

"Say everything you saw."

The police pressed me, threatened me, and browbeat me. Whether or not they got the answer they wanted out of me, the end was always the same: they would lock me up in jail for a few days and then take me to a care facility. However, I was no longer a five-year-old kid who hid inside a rubber tub. I wasn't that kid anymore who had run away, turning back countless times fearing that someone was coming after him. Running away from the care facilities after having gone through all sorts of experiences on the streets was as easy as a walk in the park.

One day while I was in the middle of an investigation at a police station, I managed to run away before getting sent off to a care facility. I sneaked out the police station's back door while the guard wasn't paying attention, and no one stopped me. For a few days afterward, I hid around thinking that I'd be in big trouble if I ran into the police on the street. Then one day, I ran right into one.

"Have you eaten?"

I'd expected something vicious to happen, but the policeman was simply asking after how I was doing like he really couldn't care less. I quickly nodded my head then went on my way. I felt rotten. I longed for people, so I would go and do anything for those who talked to me, but being asked after by the police simply gave me goose bumps.

Looking back, I'd always been on the run from someone. I know that now there is no one coming after me, but even these days in my dreams, I find myself running away from someone. My heart seems like it'll burst any moment, but my legs don't move as fast as I want them. My legs, suspended in the air, move slowly like in a slow-motion video. Flailing, seized by terror that some invisible hand is going to catch me, I wake up.

Who are the people still chasing me?
Policemen? Gangsters? Organ traffickers?
The person who pursues me in my dreams doesn't have a face.
I don't know the identity of the person who is chasing me.

This is the interior of the same residential building as shown on page 10. The building was like a maze with many entrances and exits. "This building was the very place that filled me with 'malice' and rage against the world, the building that made me who I am now, and my 'home' during those years on the streets," says Choi. *Photo courtesy of Sungbong Choi.*

Cold People without Even
Bodily Warmth

———————— ✁ ————————

It was a good thing that there were alcohol and cigarettes. The stupefying and dizzying effect of alcohol and the white smoke that passed through my lungs and then escaped from my mouth and nose—without these two things, I would have burst out crying and resolved to die more often. What drove me crazy the most when I was sober were the questions: Why am I an orphan? Why do I have to sell gum out on the streets? Why do people hate me? All those countless "whys," answerless "whys," the entrapped, forever-lingering "whys"…

But even the effects of alcohol and the smoke from the cigarettes couldn't help me avoid the reality that confronted me. If only I could, I would have erased those questions—all those "whys"—and clean them off my mind. If I couldn't make them go away, I wanted at least to ignore them by covering my eyes and blocking my ears. Then that opportunity came to me in an unexpected way.

The first time I saw them was on the streets. I'd never seen their kind in Yongjeon-dong before, and they seemed to have icy, rather than menacing, vibes. They had no expressions on their faces, and their eyes gazed sharply ahead. They felt similar to organ traffickers, but these people who called on me were not organ traffickers. They were similar yet different. I approached them, hesitant. They exuded an aura that led you to neither dare disobey nor defy them.

"Take this to room number 302 in that motel over there. We'll be watching you from here. If you try anything silly, we'll go after you to the end of the earth and tear you to pieces."

That was the beginning. I didn't know what the drug smugglers were passing to me. But it seemed that they'd decided to use me as their mule. The process was always the same. When they passed me the object, I delivered it. They would watch me from afar and check on whether the object was delivered well. They were scary people, so I couldn't refuse them or defy them.

Even before I met them, there was a time when I had run strange errands. Gangsters would give me a drug bottle and tell me to deliver it to some place. They told me that they would give me money or buy me jajangmyeon if I did the errand well. I didn't know what that drug was, but I did as I was told. More than getting money, more than eating jajangmyeon, what fulfilled me was the fact that someone talked to me. When I approached people, they huddled away or turned their backs as though they might contract a disease from me. When I talked to them, they swore at me or told me to shove off and pushed me away. The gangster men, like the tteok-bokki lady and the turtle lady, were the few people who talked to me.

One day, a gangster man handed me a beverage and said, "You see that pretty sister sitting there on the bench? If you go give this to her, I'll give you five thousand won."

"What's this? What should I say when I give it to her?"

"You don't have to know, brat. Somebody told me to give this to you because you're pretty—just say that."

I didn't know what that beverage was. The only thing I knew was that someone had talked to me, and that by doing that one errand, I would earn money that I could otherwise make only after selling five packs of gum.

I took the beverage and approached the woman.

"Big sister, someone said to give this to you because you're pretty."

60

The woman looked in the direction I was pointing. The man grinned, raised his hand, and then put it down again. She bent over and looked down at me.

"You look nice."

Soon after drinking the beverage, the woman seemed to sway, and then she collapsed like a dead weight.

From somewhere men began to appear and surrounded the woman.

"What's she doing sleeping here? Hey, carry her on your back."

The men lifted her, and carrying her on their back, began to head somewhere. I held in my hand the five-thousand-won note that the gangster man had given me and looked down the direction they disappeared. It was by the motel zone. Only then did I get the hunch. That errand was a bad thing to do. I'd done a bad thing.

> But who is good on these streets?
> Siding with which group will make you righteous?
> I couldn't know anything.
> Even the police didn't look righteous to me.
> I was neither on the righteous side, nor was I on the evil side.
> I was on the side of people who would talk to me;
> I was on the side of people who gave me food.

The reason I ran errands for people who seemed as cold-blooded as snakes wasn't simply because they came and talked to me. When they said that they were going to come after me to the end of the earth and tear me to pieces, I felt that it wasn't just empty talk. They were the kind who would probably even go beyond. If I felt like it, I would act any way I wanted with the police or even with gangsters, but with them I dared not utter a syllable in reply, let alone defy them, and so I ran the errand exactly as I was told.

"Go ask that person, then come back."

Then I would go right away to whomever they had picked and thrust to them the thing I got.

"Hyeong,* do you like drugs by any chance? Would you like to try?"

There were many things I would deliver for errands. There was something that looked like flour and also something that could be smoked like cigarettes. I grew curious about why they were handling these things with such great care. Seeing how obediently I ran their errands, they would sometimes give me money and even buy me food. I took the opportunity to relieve my curiosity one day when they took me out for a treat.

"What's this? May I try it once?"

At first, they freely allowed me to taste the powder with the tip of my finger. After about two dabs, my whole body floated into the air and heaven opened before my eyes. That powder was a ticket to heaven. I forgot the entire reality that surrounded me. I'd found it at last: the thing that was more potent than alcohol and stronger than nicotine—nay, something that was so powerful that such things didn't even measure up. If there ever was a way to heal my wounds, it had to be drugs. What I saw and heard and felt in hallucination were as transient as an intoxication that soon shattered into reality, or cigarette smoke that soon diffused away. But while I was in that hallucination, I was no longer an orphan boy. And that was enough.

When the hallucination ended and I returned to reality, the misery I felt nearly drove me crazy. There was a difference in the intensity of misery you felt between living in hell not knowing that there was heaven and returning to hell after having tasted one. I began to secretly lick the drugs, again and again.

Doing drugs made heaven appear in front of you instantly. When you returned, though, it was back without exception to the hell of disillusionment. A reality in which the original pain had multiplied several-fold

* The word that boys and men use to address older brothers.

awaited me. In order to break out of the pain, there was no way other than to escape into hallucination. I had become addicted.

Among the errand items, some things were more frightening than drugs. I heard that they were substances that went to organ traffickers, and that by administering them, you could paralyze people and extract their organs. It horrified me to think how the people who took away the gum-selling brother must have used such substances. I wanted to get away from the grip of those terrifying people.

But there was no way. I had thought that after all that time on the streets, running away from someone was one thing I could count on being able to do, but there was no way I could get away from these people. They were methodical: they did not allow even the smallest gap in their scheme. They had to be. Drug smuggling was a grave crime—something that should never get caught. Besides, I'd become enslaved to the taste of heaven from their drugs. I felt anxious and afraid when I couldn't do the drugs. After I got caught licking, they prevented me from touching the drugs.

"Please, allow me just once. Please? I beg you."

"You want it?"

"Yes, I'll just dab it once, just once."

"Then bring money, bastard."

In fact, it wasn't true that drugs were heaven and reality hell. The real hell was the withdrawal syndrome. Once I delivered some drugs to a motel room. The man in there must have been out of stock for a long time and looked totally miserable; he kept dribbling saliva with unfocused eyes, repeatedly smashing his head on the wall. Taken aback, I handed the drugs and left immediately. A little while later, however, I saw him walk out of there looking as vigorous as ever.

When the withdrawal symptoms began, I would run inside some place away from people's sight. My body felt like it was getting twisted all over and itchy. I couldn't swallow my saliva and drooled like a mad dog. It was as though my whole body had become paralyzed, and I couldn't even flick a finger. Some water might have helped, but I just couldn't move. After a withdrawal fit, I would find in the mirror deep, dark circles under my eyes. I was afraid of the smugglers who were controlling me, of myself addicted to drugs, and of the fact that I couldn't get hold of what I craved. Getting caught stealing drugs would mean sure death, but it appeared that I would just have to brave death in order to get some.

Just as they had suddenly appeared one day, so they suddenly disappeared one day. I wasn't sure whether the drug smugglers had absconded or gotten cracked down on, but they disappeared completely without a trace from my life, leaving me a drug addict, left alone with the torment of withdrawal. Reality: the terrible reality—the questions once again whirling inside my head—and the hellish confusion. I felt like I was going crazy. I couldn't do anything, neither eat nor drink.

I began to appear more and more spent as the days passed. Even my heart seemed to have turned into ruin. It was around that time that I met the big runaway brothers. They were hiding in an empty lot doing something. I couldn't tell exactly, but they looked similar to drug addicts. I copied what they did. Something came—that thing that I had craved so much. It wasn't a drug, but it induced a similar state, a hallucination that allowed you to erase off reality. Thus I escaped into sniffing glue and gas.

But I soon stopped doing that, not because I'd realized that it couldn't bring me the minutest redemption, but because of migraines. After waking from hallucinating from sniffing glue and gas, my head hurt like it was going to split. The migraine caused such pain that I began to think that my head was going to explode.

What hallucination ultimately revealed to me was that there was nothing that could lift me out of reality. The only hope I did have was death: only by dying would everything end. I slashed my wrist with a knife. I must have hesitated at the final instant, however, because when I regained consciousness, my wrist was covered with dried-up blood.

It seemed that killing myself wasn't going to be easy, so I found gang-sters and bullies, got them pissed off, and asked them to kill me. Bricks bashed down my head and golf clubs struck every part of my body. Coming around again, though, I would find myself still alive.

When the withdrawal syndrome and suicidal impulses reached their extreme, I ended up throwing myself in front of running cars several times. Yet though I had such an intense desire to die, I could not die. I could not kill myself through any method whatsoever.

> *What had really tormented me weren't the gangsters, or the bullies, or the police.*
> *That my life had been cursed—that I could not die even if I tried—*
> *that I had to force myself to live a life cursed by being rejected by death:*
> *those were the greatest torments.*

The biggest scar remaining on me is not engraved on my body. I still have not been able to completely erase my skepticism toward life. I tried to get regular psychotherapy and to have a positive mind, but the urge to die, which flooded over me many times a day, tortured me still.

Seeing the Naked Face of Hell
from a Mud Pit

CHILDREN USUALLY WANT to do or become something later. For a long time, I had nothing I wanted to do or become. Then when I saw a man selling bung-eo-bbang* on a street, I wanted to become something for the first time in my life.

I watched the bung-eo-bbang man for a long time: pouring flour dough on an iron grill, breaking off a clump of red-bean paste and placing it on the dough, and then quickly flipping around the grill. I never got sick of watching those three motions. The man, thinking me a sort of famished beggar, put one bung-eo-bbang in my hand. What in the world! That taste! The outside was crunchy but the inside was chewy, and when I bit off the bun, the sweet, warm red-bean paste spread all over inside my mouth.

What drew me even more strongly than the taste was the way the man looked, selling bung-eo-bbang in that secluded spot. He wasn't even standing at a favorable and crowded location. He didn't even tout loudly. He was simply watching the people pass by from a vacant street corner. He seemed to show a lonely yet detached attitude toward life. In my mind, I placed myself, grown up, in the spot where he was standing. It seemed that I'd look quite cool if I grew up to be a good-looking adult and made bung-eo-bbang like that. Of course the buns would sell really well.

Then the tteok-bokki lady came to my mind—the one who'd asked me what I wanted to be when I grew up. At that time, I didn't know what I would

---

* A fish-shaped waffle stuffed with red-bean paste.

be, but now I knew for sure. I was going to go the single path of selling bung-eo-bbang. I went to the tteok-bokki lady's cart bar, ready to tell her that Jiseong was going to become a bung-eo-bbang seller when he grew up. She was up to her elbows mixing the tteok-bokki, slicing the soondae, and rolling the kimbab.*

"Ajumma, I'm going to become a bung-eo-bbang seller when I grow up."

She tidied the street stall and half-heartedly replied, "Yes, yes." She'd asked me what I wanted to become, and now that I'd come all the way to tell her...her reply bummed me out.

"Ajumma..."

I looked at the egg and gestured to her that I wanted to eat it. She didn't even throw a glance. An egg cost three hundred won. Sparing one shouldn't have been such a big deal, but we lived in a reality where each was busy with his or her own livelihood. I was on my way out of the cart bar feeling sullen when I saw a flyer on a seat where a customer had just left.

"Ajumma, what's this? What's written on it?"

When I shook the paper in front her, she glanced at it and said, "It says that they are going to start a night school in the village. It's a student recruitment flyer."

I wanted to ask her what night school was, but she was too busy. I left the flyer behind and went outside.

The next time I heard the words "night school" was from a gangster man. He told me to do some errand, so I was riding on his car passing through the street when he looked at a flyer stuck on an electric pole and turned crabby.

"What can you learn from that kind of crappy place?"

"Why? What's that?"

---

* Dried seaweed rolls that look like sushi rolls.

I wasn't sure whether he was talking to himself or replying to my question, but he muttered in an irritated voice. "What? Rediscover your dream through learning with us? Yeah, my ass, crazy bastards."

Yongjeon-dong was an adult entertainment triangle: a triangle of nightclubs, bars, and motel area. Looking back at it now, it didn't make any sense location-wise that they were setting up a night school in that kind of town. The people who created night schools and recruited students were people who lived within the system, with morals and norms, and the gangster man must have begrudged them as a matter of course because we were outsiders.

Since the people around me found night school obnoxious, I vaguely considered night school as a place unsuitable for me to go. They said that they would rediscover your dream through learning, but to me—whose only dream was to become a bung-eo-bbang seller—learning didn't seem like it was going to be of much use.

Winter was approaching. For me, it was the most painful season of all. Passersby on the streets had thick coats on and were totally wrapped up with mufflers and gloves. I was wearing a parka that the turtle lady had given me. Under that parka that was coming apart at the seams, I had only one short-sleeved T-shirt on. I would walk the streets with it zipped all the way up the throat. Even then, icy-cold wind would dig into my clothes.

Just as the day was about to break, I walked toward a nightclub with a square chili paste container in my hand. Crouching on the nightclub stairs, I put some fuel into the chili paste container and started a fire. When the warmth began to spread, I became drowsy. It seemed that I was plunging to sleep, but before long I'd open my eyes again because of the teeth-chattering cold.

The staircase was pitch-dark with its lights turned off. I fumbled through my pocket for the lighter and relighted the fire. But that would only last for a while, and I'd again have to put in a tissue or something to relight it, and then soon it would peter out, then I'd relight it...How many times must I have repeated those steps? I finally succumbed to drowsiness and fell asleep.

Before falling asleep, I thought of the gangsters. When I got caught stealing liquor, I wanted to kill them all and kill myself too, if only I could. Would setting the nightclub on fire settle some of that anger?

"Fire!"

I heard someone's desperate cry. I opened my eyes wide. The sound of ambulances and sirens rang noisily. Right away the police crashed in, and I was caught by the scruff and dragged out. It wasn't me. The person who had set the nightclub on fire wasn't me. Of course, before falling asleep, I'd been burning with anger that was more red hot than the fire inside the chili paste container, thinking about the gangsters who'd bashed me with bricks and pummeled me with sticks and steel pipes, and I'd been thinking that I wanted to set the nightclub on fire. Yet while I was asleep, a real fire had started at the nightclub. The fire hadn't started near the stairway where I was sleeping, but within the shutters of the nightclub.

Whether it was due to a secret feud between gangs or someone's mistake, the one who'd fallen asleep in front of the nightclub with a fire on was me.

"You did it, right?"

"No."

The policeman slapped me across the face.

"You started the fire!"

"I said no!"

The policeman beat me with an electric fly swatter. Whenever the fly swatter touched my skin, it made a buzzing sound like the beating of insect wings. And each time, my body flinched along. Wherever the fly swatter touched, the flesh felt like it was getting incinerated.

"It's not me, fuck!"

When I swore, the policeman recorded it. When he beat me, I swore at him, he recorded it, and then he beat me again, and then I swore at him...I couldn't figure out anything, be it what had happened or what I was doing there. Through all the countless blows, I repeated again and again that it wasn't me. Because it wasn't. I never caused that fire.

"Go."

Finally after a few days, I was released on warning. It seemed that they decided to just release me and not send me to a care facility because they knew that I would run away anyway.

I'd gotten away from the police, but I couldn't roam freely in the streets like I used to. Gangsters who thought that I'd started the fire were searching for me with bloodshot eyes. If ever I were to be caught, I'd be burned at the stake, if not worse. Still, I couldn't just lie around hiding because if I couldn't sell gum, I'd starve to death. Either starving or being beaten up by gangsters—I couldn't tell which would be the more painful death. The only thing I could do when I got hungry was to go out on the streets.

I had to be especially careful when entering businesses like karaoke bars that were managed by gangsters. Since gangsters seldom stayed at business establishments but rather hung around lodging venues,* which were their safe houses, there was a better chance that I could sell gum and leave safely, and avoid getting caught and being beaten to death. But it wasn't so on that day.

"Hey, that brat is here!"

I bounded out of the store as soon as I heard that voice coming from inside. Before I could even climb all the stairs, however, I was caught by a brutal hand. Both in front and at the back were gangster minions. No matter how I tried to look around, there was no gap through which to escape. One of them lifted me up and stuck me under his armpit. The strength of his arm was barbarous. Even though I kicked and struggled like crazy, my body did not move an inch. Two gangsters grabbed my hair and pushed me

---

* Hotels and inns.

into a car. Even after being put inside the car, I continued to resist, kicking the car door as hard as I could.

"Let go! Open the door!"

"Stay still. We're taking you somewhere good."

One of the gangsters looked at me with an unctuous smile. I stopped struggling. Once in the car, it was impossible to escape by fighting them off anyway. I decided to pretend that I believed what they said. It was the sliver of hope that if I were to stay obedient and still, I might be able to avoid getting terrible treatment.

The place where the gangsters stopped their car a little while later was a mountain on the outskirts of Daejeon. They took a shovel out of the car and began digging a hole. I freaked out. I resisted with my whole body, screaming, but I was finally thrown into the pit that had been dug deeper than my height.

Mud poured down from above my head. I tried to crawl out, but the mud on the sides of the pit kept sliding down, and the gangsters stepped on my head with their feet to stop me from coming up. "They aren't really trying to kill me, right?" I wanted to grab onto something, even a piece of straw, but the only things that came into my hands were limp grass roots and pouring mud lumps. The mud reached my waist, my chest, and then my shoulders…It poured down faster and faster, crushing me with an enormous weight. I could not move an inch. When the mud finally reached my chin, I began to believe that they really meant to kill me. Why was it that I would go around doing all kinds of things to die, when at the approach of death, I would struggle so desperately to live?

By this time, mud had poured into my eyes and mouth. I became breathless. I quickly cupped my hand to make a breathing space right in front of my eyes, nose, and mouth. Before long, the mud was covering my cheeks, my ears, and my head. I was completely buried in earth. Each time I'd hold my breath and then inhale again, the mud seeped into my nose, mouth, and ears.

How long would I be able to stand this?
I'd tasted measureless suffering, but this was the first time I'd experienced a
suffering that so literally took away my breath.
Thinking how my life, never once loved but always beaten and taken advantage
of, was finally meeting a lonely end by being buried alive,
I felt so pitiful and victimized.

Soon the sound of the gangsters' chatting ceased. Had they descended the mountain? The space I'd made with my hand allowed me to move from my wrist to my fingertips. I thrashed my hands madly. Buried there in mud, I had to dig and dig to somehow make a breathing hole. I wasn't sure whether the direction my hands were moving was toward the surface of the ground, whether I would really be able to make a hole, or whether I would be able to hold out till then. While I was digging, the mud continued to enter my nose and mouth.

How much time must have passed as I kept digging this way? That time was longer than the length of my whole life put together. It was suffocating, dark, and more than anything, frightful. When I finally escaped the pit, my whole body was drenched in sweat. If the gangsters had really planned to kill me, they would have buried me, then firmly tramped the ground above. But if they had been ordered not to kill me but to scare me properly, they'd carried out their duty consummately, because when the mud poured into my nose and got levelled above my head, I peered directly into the naked face of hell. Once out of the pit, I forced down my cries from bursting out, fearing that there might be a gangster still lingering about, and carefully descended the mountain.

Now I couldn't go out selling gum or sleep inside nightclubs. Simply watching them passing by in the distance reawakened the terror of that moment of being buried alive. I went to the turtle lady's cart bar, eluding the gangsters' notice.

"You bastard, what trouble are you up to?"

I should have been in a position to beg her to help me live or to hide me, but hearing her swear made it impossible to give a mild reply.

"Don't bother yourself; anyway I'm probably going to get fucked up pretty soon!"

"Who you bullshitting? You're a wreck right from your first syllable. You, go and get yourself to learn how to read at the night school. What's the use of always yacking your mouth when you can't even write? It's all for your own good, so go and learn."

"Why don't you go to the night school yourself, 'ma'am'?"

"Crazy bastard!"

Without warning she grabbed my hair and began to drag me somewhere. She was not someone I could master by physical strength. Her arms were thicker than my thighs.

Part 2:
Setting Out into a New and Strange World
Three Years at a Night School

Night School, My First Education, and Escape from Gangsters

GRAY CONTAINERS STOOD lined against the sunset. The five or six containers put together to make into makeshift offices arranged in an L shape looked shabby and bleak in the dusk. The dull feeling I had when I saw the flyer for student recruitment came up again. "What can you learn from that kind of crappy place?" The words of the gangster man circled round my ears.

The turtle lady, who had dragged me inside the container offices, took a glance around. Inside, which was as shabby as the outside, were some young people sitting around chatting to each other.

"Is this the night school?"

One young man, responding to her question, approached.

"Yes, it is. How did you find us?"

"Here, please teach this brat. Teach him how to read and how to have some damn manners."

"Damn it, let go!"

I tried to wriggle out of her grasp, but she stood rock firm grabbing my wrist. From her tough grasp, I could tell that she was certain about shoving me into a night school.

"Leave him with us."

Only when he said those words did she let go her grasp. I glared at her while massaging my wrist continuously. The wrist tingled with pain because she'd grasped it so forcefully. Just then, a man's swearing was heard outside. I looked around me desperately, and then in a whisk, crawled under a desk in a corner. For a moment I could hear "Bastard, blah, blah," and then the voice soon receded into the distance. It seemed that it probably wasn't a gangster. The turtle lady said, "It's because he's being chased by bullies. He's come here hiding, so please take good care of him."

"Are you his guardian?"

"No, I don't know this brat. He's just a street kid."

"Okay, please don't worry, and return home safe."

After she left, the young man began to ask me all kinds of questions. Left alone by myself in a strange place without the company of even the turtle lady, I felt anxious. I wanted to hide somewhere where there was nobody. I went to the toilet, but there wasn't really one; rather the toilet was placed inside one of the container offices.

"Hi. I'm Jaeyong Sohn. Who are you?"

The man I met in front of the toilet appeared to be in his early twenties. As was my habit, I quickly scanned the person's appearance. He was a short and willowy young man. Wearing plain clothes and with a gentle face, he gave a completely different impression from the drunkards I used to see in adult entertainment venues. His air also differed from that of gangsters or policemen.

His small and thinly haired head seemed somehow to resemble a turtle. The person who had dragged me to the night school was the turtle lady, and now even the person I was meeting looked like a turtle. What was it with me and turtles? Whether or not it was because he resembled a turtle, looking at him, I felt as though I'd known him from before. I let down my guard a little and replied, "I'm Jiseong. What d'you do here?"

"It's where you study and also prepare for your qualification exams. How did you come here?"

"Um, 'cause I wanted to study too."

Of course it was a lie. But it seemed a better thing to say than to tell him that I'd come out of fear that gangsters were going to kill me. He readily nodded.

"How much schooling have you done?"

I didn't know what to say. He was the first person ever to ask me whether I'd been to school. I knew that there was a place called "school." I also knew that some people went to school and did something called "study." But it was the story of some distant world that had nothing to do with me. Considering the fact that he thought I had attended school, he was surely a naïve adult who hadn't been around much. I just said something irrelevant.

"I sell gum."

"Gum? How do you sell gum?"

I explained to him briefly about the gum-selling life, of course in crude language with swear words mixed in. It wasn't because I didn't like "the turtle" or was displeased with him. That was simply the only way I knew how to speak.

"You shouldn't talk like that to a teacher, but talk nicely."

"Nicely? How?"

He made a perplexed face, but didn't comment any further about my diction. Even when he told me to "talk nicely," he was trying to persuade rather than to admonish. It seemed as though he was sincerely curious about my life and was listening to my words. I was an expert in sensing humans who were all pretense and nothing else. I let down my guard toward him. You could say that I even took a little interest in him.

"You, Jiseong, can also become an accomplished person if you study here."

"An accomplished person? What's that?"

"Um, what do you want to be when you grow up?"

I thought of the bung-eo-bbang seller. But I didn't want to tell the turtle whom I'd just met about such things.

"I don't wanna become anything."

I didn't feel like speaking anymore, so I shut my mouth.

He took me to the first container office I had entered earlier. It was the "teachers' room." The people who were there before had left. On the desk were some sweet potatoes. I was hungry. When I stared at the sweet potatoes, he said to me, "Are you hungry? Do you want to eat this together?"

I didn't feel like eating something with a stranger. I took a sweet potato he gave me and went to a corner. I peeled the sweet potato while crouching there, and bit off a mouthful. The dry, crumbling sweet potato had already gone cold, but it was the first thing I had eaten after a long break. Since I'd been avoiding gangsters and couldn't sell gum, I hadn't eaten anything for days.

While I was eating the sweet potato, people started trickling in one by one. There was one who looked like my peer and also some middle-aged women and men. There were also some grannies and grandpas. It was around the time when ordinary people would be leaving work and returning home, or around the time when they would be crowding around Yongjeon-dong's red-light district and drinking. I couldn't understand why these people were coming to these shabby makeshift offices at such a time.

"You said you were Jiseong, right? Eat slowly, then come in also," the turtle said.

The turtle and the people moved to one of the makeshift container offices that was being used as a "classroom." I ate the sweet potato and then went to attend the thing called a "class." When I sat on the chair, its legs squeaked loudly. The desk also had mismatched angles, and it wobbled. I peeked into the book on the desk. There were some of those rare words I did know, but most were unintelligible.

By the grace of the tteok-bokki ajumma, I could speak enough to not have trouble in carrying on day-to-day life. But I had a tiny vocabulary and couldn't understand anything well other than everyday conversation. When she said "crisscrossing emotions," I first had to think, what's "crisscrossing," and then what's "emotions"? When she said, "Our communication doesn't work," I would hesitate because I didn't know the word "communication."

Even during conversations, my only resource was street wits, which I had learned and refined while living on the streets. I would remember what the tteok-bokki lady had said about something, and I would use that word on encountering a similar situation. But reading and writing were two different things. Not only was it difficult to learn only by wits and tact, it was also simply useless to me. At that time, I didn't think that I had to learn anything other than what was helpful to my survival.

I peeked over people's shoulders to observe what they did. They were all holding their pencils and writing down what the turtle was writing on the board. When the turtle explained something, they nodded their heads intently and listened to him. I closed my book and left.

Looking in a book, explaining something, writing on the board, taking down things in a notebook…Even though I didn't know exactly what they were or why you had to do them, one thing I could figure out soon enough was that they were extremely boring things.

I returned again to the teachers' room in the container office. The classrooms and the teachers' rooms were makeshift structures that looked like deserted offices. The only difference was that inside the classrooms there were desks and chairs, and inside the teachers' rooms there were sofas; that was about it. But whether desks or chairs or sofas, they were all the same in the way that they were all worn out.

I sprawled down on the black sofa that was torn here and there and had fillings sticking out. At the foot of the sofa was a blanket that looked almost like a piece of rag. Mold had spread over the gray cement wall without wallpaper, and the floor too was just rough, bare cement. I looked up at the ceiling. The low-intensity white light blinked now and then. Shifting my gaze to the corner of the ceiling, I could see spider webs. One spider was climbing the wall along its web. I looked at the desolate interior for a short while and then sprang to my feet. I'd had my fill of food; I'd rested my body. There was nothing else to be gained by being there, so I left the makeshift offices without a second thought.

Once again I set out on the streets.

I wasn't unafraid of the gangsters, but after having filled up my stomach with food, the confidence sprang that I'd be able to make my way around, away from their notice.

I bought some packets of gum and walked toward the red-light district.

That was the only place for me to go anyway.

The night school: where Sungbong Choi spent three years.
Photo courtesy of Sungbong Choi.

The Normal, yet Unfamiliar
Country of Yours

❦

I HID MYSELF at the entry of the street corner leading into the red-light district. I checked to see whether there were gangsters among the passersby, then set out on the streets. I didn't have the guts to strut about in the middle of the streets like before. From behind parked cars to behind electric poles with flyers, from an unilluminated alley corner to beside a cart bar, I advanced little by little, hiding myself here and there like a kid playing hide-and-seek.

I entered a beer bar. There were gangsters sitting in the corner seats. I quickly turned away and exited the bar. But the gangsters were approaching from the end of the road. I entered another bar nearby. I watched gangster minions walking down the corridor noisily and ran outside again.

I had audaciously returned to the red-light district, but I could not go around the streets or sell gum this way. Not being able to walk around the streets meant that I was no longer free. Not being able to sell gum meant that I had lost my means of making a living. But it wasn't only that. I'd also lost a place to sleep. Sleeping on nightclub stairs would be like walking into a gangster hangout with my own feet.

What could I do? While I was repeating the tedious hide-and-seek, deprived of gum-selling, night had passed and dawn was breaking in the distance. I was overcome by sleepiness. My eyelids closed. Now that I no longer had my nightclub pad, the only places I could go were terminals and public toilets. It bothered me that anyone could come and leave terminals and public toilets. If I were to be seen by gangsters again, this time I wouldn't simply be dragged to a mountain and carelessly buried.

Then I remembered the night school—and the black sofa where I had lain just a few hours ago. Even though it was a ragged and broken sofa, it provided a place to sleep, and that took away all my hesitation. So I returned to the night school. Fortunately, the window to the teachers' room wasn't locked. I locked the door from inside and lay on the sofa. An indoor space, a place to lie down, being able to lock the door—when those three things were met, my heart began to relax and languidness flooded in.

The tattered blanket provided almost no insulation, and the broken sofa was sunken here and there, but still it was far better than terminals and public toilets. Other than those times when I had slept in other people's homes, it was also the first time I was sleeping indoors. The fact that it was a place where I wasn't going to be caught by gangsters relieved me more than anything. For the first time in a long while, I fell into a deep sleep.

From the next day on, after classes ended and people returned home, I hid inside the night school. Worried that people might kick me out if they found me, I stayed there like a recluse, keeping away from people's notice. I got out of the night school before the teachers and students came for classes, and then went back in after they left. I also didn't touch any of the equipment there and left them in their original condition.

When the night school facility began to get better equipped, however, I couldn't just hide around anymore: they had installed a lock system with passwords. I went to find Mr. Jaeyong Sohn, the teacher I had met on the first day at the night school. When I called him turtle teacher, he took it like a veteran who had already heard those kinds of remarks plenty of times. He looked like one, so it must have been his nickname.

"Turtle teacher, I have nowhere to sleep. Please lemme sleep here."

When I rather awkwardly played the baby, he graciously went ahead and told me the password. And so the night school became my abode.

One night, when I entered the teachers' room to sleep, I saw a skinny man with a moustache occupying my sofa and drinking soju. "What's this? Why is he sprawled out on my sofa?" He looked like a homeless man who had stolen into the night school looking for a place to sleep. It wasn't just that his body was even thinner than mine; you could tell from the way he looked drinking soju by himself and the stench of his breath whenever he spoke that he was surely a homeless person.

Then I found out that he was actually Mr. Hong, a teacher who taught math at the night school. Although he was a college student, he gave off a similar air to the people on the streets whom I was so familiar with. Put nicely, he looked like an ascetic, but put badly, he looked like a tramp. He was on friendly terms with the bullies who prepared for high school qualification exams and was indifferent to having economic sense or knowing what was going on in the world. He drank every day inside the teachers' room and went to teach drunk. You almost couldn't figure out whether he was teaching how to do math or how to drink.

"Why ya sleeping here? Don't you have a house?"

"It's in Yuseong."

"But why?"

"Just like that. But how about you? You have no house, no parents, and no school?"

As the nights we both slept at the night school began to overlap, Mr. Hong and I naturally became roommates. As we spent long stretches of time together in one space, we would speak a bit about ourselves from time to time, but that didn't mean that we opened ourselves up to each other or were on good terms. We basically ignored each other, and I disliked almost everything about him. I didn't hate him, however, for one reason: he'd stood by my side a couple of times when the other teachers disapproved of me sleeping in the night school and scolded me for being rude. Only because he had been on my side and because to me that felt like a great favor, Mr. Hong was someone I could not hate, although he appeared strange even to a kid like me.

I'd solved the problem of finding a place to sleep, but then I didn't know what to do about feeding myself since I wasn't able to sell gum. So I decided to ask the people who came to the night school for help.

"I'm starving, so gimme some food."

There would be boys around my age who would take out snacks from their bags, and also ajummas who would take me to restaurants and buy me meals. There were also people who would offer me the fruits and kimbabs that they had packed to eat themselves. This story might come across to you as one of "a poor gum-selling orphan meeting good people and living a warm life with the help he receives." That wasn't the reality, however.

Of course when I told them I was hungry, they gave me food to eat. If they had food, they would give, and if they didn't have food, they wouldn't. When they gave, I ate, and when they didn't give, I couldn't. That was all. There was an invisible line between them and me, and they didn't try to cross that line. I was no different from them: I also did not know how to cross over that line to approach them.

Apart from asking for the minimum amount of food, I didn't know how to talk to them. I knew I would be rejected if I were to ask them for anything other than food. Even then, I wanted to tell them something about myself.

"I'm hungry. Gimme some food."

"Can't you say anything other than that you're hungry?"

"Fuck, I lived out on the streets. Every day I got beaten up by people."

"Oh...oh, okay..."

The conversation between them and me did not continue any further than this. Eventually I gave up trying to tell my story and went back to the way things used to be.

"I'm hungry. Gimme food."

Those were the only words that people responded to.

Night school life was difficult in a different sense than street life. The people there were of a kind that was too unfamiliar to me. The inclination to learn and accomplish something, the desire to live a better tomorrow—they had something that I had never had in life, something called will. Was I the only one who didn't know while everyone else was living that way, doing what they wanted to do, learning what they wanted to learn, and thus endeavoring for a brighter future?

For the first time, I came to see my life side by side next to normal people's lives.
That, in a sense, was more tormenting than living on rough streets,
because I didn't know how to cross over to their world.

The people I knew until then were all bottom class: orphan gum sellers, runaway youths, girls who worked in phone-sex parlors, karaoke bar hostesses, touters, smugglers, gangsters…I did know that other kinds of lives existed in the world, but the majority of lives around me were of such kinds, and I was more or less "normal" within that category. There was no chance for me to approach real, normal people and to witness their lives.

The people I met at the night school had houses and families. Moreover, they had the will to learn and the hope to live better lives. If I had the mere desire to live and survive, they had a desire that had evolved further from that basic need—a desire that I had never dreamed of. When I compared what they had with what I had, I was overwhelmed by a sense of deprivation and rebellion. I wanted to grab any random person and throw a temper, pick a fight, and unleash a swearing tantrum. Had puberty set in? If the reason I was so evil was because puberty had come even to a kid like me, then it was actually something to be grateful for.

I was nasty to everyone I met at the night school. I swore at the people who didn't give me food. Even if they were people who had given me food before, I swore at them if they went back to not giving me food. I walked into classrooms in session and got clamorous and violent. Regardless of whether they were adults or children, I provoked them to quarrel with me. Even then, in one corner of my heart, somehow I had the childish wish that they would treat me nicely, but they just moved farther and farther away from the bad-tempered boy. Even those who had initially provided me with food out of goodwill would leave their seats or look elsewhere when I approached them. From some of them, I could hear the voice of the hearts that used to whisper whenever I sold gum: "I hope he doesn't come this way."

When my relationship with people turned foul, I couldn't find the means to feed myself anymore. At those times, I would see the turtle teacher as my easy way out. With the most pitiful face I could make, I would open out my two palms toward him.

"Turtle teacher, gimme one thousand won."

After being ripped off a few times, even the turtle teacher was no longer so free. When I asked him for money, he pried into all the details of why I needed it and what I was going to buy.

"Poor Jiseong has no money for his meal."

Then he would sigh and open his wallet. Inside the leather wallet, torn and with bursting seams, there would only be a few thousand won bills.

"First just get something to eat with this…"

Sometimes it was a thousand won, and sometimes it was two thousand won. That was all that the turtle teacher had to give after taking out his bus money. It wasn't a lot, but I could get at least a packet of cup noodles to eat. On weekends when he didn't come to school, I had to starve for two days straight.

No matter how often I went through it, hunger was something I could never get used to.

When my sight began to turn faint and my mind dizzy,
when my empty insides began to throb,

nothing would come to my mind other than that I had to find something to eat.
Hunger was cruel and persistent, and other than by putting food inside,
there was no way to calm it down.

Even when I had just eaten, if someone offered to buy me food, I would follow them and stuff food down my throat. Even though the food that had been forced down seemed to be coming back up my throat, I didn't let go of the spoon until I had finished all my share of food. If I had to vomit, let me vomit later! I simply couldn't refuse the food laid out in front of me when I thought of the pain of hunger.

On Mondays following such hungry weekends, the turtle teacher would willingly let me rip him off. But later on, when I whined to him about giving me money, he would gesture to me like he was too tired to even reply. Still, I would pester him to give me money whenever I saw his face since he was the only source where money came from. I wasn't sorry either to the turtle teacher or to the night school students. I considered them decent folks and thought it was obvious that they should help me.

In retrospect, they weren't people who owed that kind of obligation. They weren't economically well off nor socially successful. The teachers, including the turtle teacher, were college students who were serving on a near-voluntary basis. The students, instead of going to a qualification examination academy, had crowded the night school that offered free tuition. They were middle-aged people and elderly who had missed their chance at education. The children my age were probably also attending the night school because they couldn't afford to go to school.

I didn't know it then, however. To my eyes, they didn't look hungry or lonely like me. I demanded without hesitation and felt no guilt about my demands. Inside my heart, I was always crying out, "You people need to compensate me. I have nothing and am always hungry."

I Suddenly Wanted to Start Reading One Day

❦

THE OFFICIAL NAME of the night school that I attended was "BBS Jae-Il Night Elementary/Middle/High School." It belonged to the Yongjeon-dong administrative zone and was situated one block from the red-light district and right in front of the motel area. I would eat and sleep at the night school yet stay away from the actual classes. It was partly because I couldn't communicate with other students, and also because I wasn't too keen on the idea of learning itself.

Ordinary children get used to life and to people through their parents' guidance and teaching, but I was different. Since there was no one who taught me how to live, I had to learn the ropes by colliding and smashing into things with my whole, bare body. I was resistant to the fact that I suddenly had to learn something from another person. Even then, the turtle teacher tried for quite a while to teach me.

"Jiseong, do you know how to read this?"

"Nope."

"If you don't, I'll teach you how."

"No. It's not fun."

"But you came all the way to the night school, so shouldn't you be learning how to write and come inside the classrooms?"

When the turtle teacher tried to teach me how to read, I would resist or run away. Then if I needed food or money, I would latch on to him and ask him for this and that. Was it because he wasn't like the other teachers who openly ignored me that I thought I had the liberty to treat him like that? He could neither subdue nor neglect me. But even the meek and benign turtle teacher didn't like how I would turn affable only when I needed something. So I would always just end up never studying but arguing with him.

"Why do you talk like that? Why do you talk like you're quarreling? I feel like blowing up just talking with you."

"Try living like me. Then you'll become like this. Teacher has a comfortable life. It's because you're like that. That's why you don't know what it's like to be in my situation."

"What do you think you know about my life? You think you know everything, right? You're just an old young and a sharp spoon.*"

He knew how to speak logically. I knew how to rile a person to the uttermost. When he tried to argue things logically, I would goad his temper with invidious and sarcastic remarks. Yet even though we argued, he was someone who would lend me his ear, and though he couldn't teach me how to read, he let me know that I was an old young and a sharp spoon.

I was basically illiterate but was able to come around to reading a tiny bit at the night school. It was the same method as how I got to know words by listening to the tteok-bokki lady—in other words, through wits and tact. For instance, I would commit to memory how people would pronounce letters of such a shape in such a way and then grasp the rule that this kind of letter sounds this way and that kind of letter sounds that way. I couldn't write, but I was able to at least combine the shapes and sounds of the letters I had remembered and achieve something close to reading.

---

* Old young and a sharp spoon: According to the Naver dictionary, "old young" refers a child who looks or behaves like an old person. It is not used to criticize someone but more as a tease or mockery. According to the Naver dictionary, "sharp spoon" is defined as a person who seems to be knowledgeable (usually because of his or her high academic background or knowledge-related career) but who does not know what he or she is supposed to know or fails to make the right choices in real life.

When the red-light district became out of bounds for roaming, I needed another place to kill my time. As it happened, there was Hannam University not too far from where the night school was. The night school teachers, including the turtle teacher, were mostly Hannam University students. I killed my time doing things like walking around the campus and lying on the grass. Sometimes I would meet the teachers there, and then I would get treated to a snack or a meal.

One day, I came across one of the night school teachers on the campus, Ms. Mihwa Yoon. Feeling glad, I ran up to her and began complaining.

"Teacher, I'm bored."

"What shall we do? I need to go to class..."

She glanced at her watch then took me to a building. It was the library. She made me sit in front of a computer and quickly typed on the keyboard her student ID number. When the computer turned on, she pointed to a blue *e*.

"See, this is the Internet. You click the left mouse twice like this, and the Internet opens. Then if you click on the address bar..."

After telling me how to use the Internet, she went away to somewhere in a hurry. When she had gone, I clumsily dragged the mouse around and peeked into some random sites. The Internet provided a game that was of a different dimension altogether compared to doll-drawing or bus riding. It was as though a new world was unfurling in front of my eyes.

From then on, I spent most of my time web surfing at the Hannam University library. The Internet was a vast and inexhaustible world, but being unable to read, I couldn't enjoy even that world. If I knew how to read the words, I could be having so much more fun on the Internet...For the first time, I began to regret that I didn't know how to read.

I went to look for the tteok-bokki lady. She was hectically filling in letters and numbers into what looked to be either a sales statement or a housekeeping book.

"Ajumma, teach me a bit how to write."

"I heard you're going to a night school. Go and learn from there."

As she said that, she wrote down something rapidly with her hand. I gazed over her shoulders at the letters she was writing. I knew roughly from what I saw at the night school that there were consonants, vowels, and final consonants in the Korean script. I also knew that you wrote according to what you heard. I was completely lost, however, when it came to figuring out how to combine everything.

"Teach me a little; me too, ajumma. Yeah? Yeah?"

"Ugh, you're confusing me. Go away."

"Then I'm not going to come here!"

"Whatever you like. I'm too busy with my own life anyway."

What she said was true. Although she was the one who had taught me how to speak and had given me my name, she was not my mom or family. She could be really cold sometimes and would never willingly give me an egg or a skewer of fish cakes.

I thought perhaps I should try the thing called studying, but I couldn't get rid of my pride. I couldn't stomach the fact that I would have to bow my head to the night school teachers and students and obediently learn something. Though I was an orphan street kid—and *because* I was an orphan street kid—I had a strong sense of pride. I didn't know how to respect myself, but I thought that at least I shouldn't look contemptible to others.

Before going to sleep, I lay on the sofa and leafed through the dictation book on the desk in the teachers' room. It was the book used by the elderly students at elementary level. I held a pencil and copied down the letters written in the book.

Gah, Nah, Dah...It made me laugh to be writing down those things.
I'd always thought the elementary-level elderly students were funny.
"What difference does it make to be learning such things after you've grown old?"

I would openly mock them.
Yet now I was trying to learn the letters just like those elderly students...

For me, however, there was a reason called the Internet. Desiring to know all the words that appeared on the Internet, I taught myself every night how to read Korean.

The Story of Two Big Brothers, Involving Church and Pepero* Sticks

———— ❧ ————

THERE WAS ONE place I used to go to other than Hannam University: the church. One of the night school students who would sometimes give me food was a young man named Yehjong. His parents were missionaries, and he had come to the night school after having attended an international school in order to prepare for a qualification exam. Whether or not it was because people who went to church were just naturally nice, he seemed sincere and cared about me, unlike the other students at the night school. Whereas they would simply drop the food in front of me when they offered it to me, Big Brother Yehjong was someone who would say, "Jiseong, I bought this for you."

"Do you want to go to church with me?" Yehjong asked me one Sunday. I knew that there was a small church behind the night school but had never once thought about going there.

"What's the use?"

"I'll make you something nice to eat."

As soon as I heard that, I sprang out of my seat. When it came to food, even traveling far distances was nothing, so there was no reason that I should not go to the church that was right behind the night school.

I followed Yehjong to the worship service. When the pastor gave a sermon, people listened to him intently with meek faces as though they were little lambs. Perhaps I'd been overwhelmed by that atmosphere. Even

---

* A cookie stick dipped in chocolate, manufactured in South Korea since 1983.

though I was hungry, somehow, enshrouded in a holy environment, I did not complain. So I followed right along and listened to the sermon with a nice face.

Even before going to church, I had believed that God existed, be it a one and only God, the Buddha, or the three gods of childbirth. Although I'd never had the light of peace shine on me or heard words of prophecy, I searched for God during painful moments. Whenever something befell me that I could not bear alone, I would desperately hang on to someone in my heart. Since that someone wasn't a person, I must have believed in the existence of some absolute being, however vaguely.

> *I did not pray to please let me live.*
> *I prayed to please let me die because it was about time.*
> *The greatest blessing that God could give me was to put an end to my life*
> *and to thus free me from the shackles of pain that bound my ankles.*

The sermon was very boring. Not only was it boring, but it was full of stories that I couldn't agree with. Although the pastor said that God gave us holy peace, my life was overcast by violence and pain. He said that God prepared the way in front of us, but having lived a life that was no better than death, I didn't know which way I had to go. When I heard that God would provide us our daily bread, I went beyond being unable to understand to being downright irritated. Then where was the food that I was supposed to eat? When I couldn't sell gum, I had to even steal in order to eat. Why didn't God prepare me my food before I had to start stealing?

The person who gave me food that day wasn't God but Yehjong. He made fried rice with loads of sour kimchi and ham inside.

"I only know how to make this kind of thing..."

"I fucking love kimchi fried rice."

97

"You shouldn't use words like that at the church."

"Okay."

The fried rice he made me was so delicious that it brought tears to my eyes. He watched me empty down a plate with a satisfied face. I didn't want to become good before a God whom I had never even met. But I wanted to become good before Yehjong. The really holy being wasn't some God that only existed inside sermons but Big Brother Yehjong, who was right there in front of me.

I only followed him to the church a few times. Later on, I would go to church by myself, and my heart would feel holy when I met God and listened to sermons—yeah right, 'cause that got me food. Somehow it felt like I shouldn't just ask for food at church. Although I went there mainly to eat, each time I went, I would also attend the worship service.

One day as I was leaving the worship service, I saw a lady staring at me. I knew right away what was in her eyes: disregard or contempt.

"Which school do you attend?" she asked.

"I don't go to school."

She laughed. She laughed unpleasantly. It was a sneer, meaning that it was just as she had expected: Why would a thing like me ever be at a place like this?

"Fuck, am I not human because I don't go to school? Why are you sniggering like that and bullshitting around?"

"My, kid...you need to watch your mouth when talking to adults."

"You've heard about how when they hit you on the left cheek, you should also give them the right cheek, right? Do you want to be hit exactly like that?"

I referred to what I'd heard at the sermon that day. She turned pale. From some distance away, Yehjong found me and came running. Even after I got dragged out of the church, I continued to pour out curses and fume with anger.

After that day, I didn't go back to the church. Yehjong didn't make an effort to take me there either. When I got estranged from the church, he and I also grew distant. When we met at the night school, we would only exchange greetings with awkward faces.

There was another kind big brother like Yehjong. I can't remember his name, but he was my favorite person at the night school, and I remember him as "Pepero brother." Pepero brother was in his mid-twenties and was preparing for his high school qualification exam.

"Jiseong, you've been hungry, right? Let's go."

Whenever he saw me, he asked me whether I was hungry and bought me tteok-bokki. I didn't really like tteok-bokki, but I would enjoy just about anything that he had bought for me, including that.

I had never thanked the people at the night school after demanding and receiving something from them. Far from being thankful, I felt dissatisfied that they weren't offering me something more. Through Pepero brother, however, I discovered for the first time what it meant to be thankful. He didn't simply fill my physical hunger by buying me food. Sharing a plate of tteok-bokki with him as we laughed and chatted loudly together, I would feel as though my empty heart and the hunger of my soul were filling up.

When I found out that November 11 was the day for giving Pepero to someone you liked, he was the first person who came to my mind. Through the small gesture of handing him Pepero, I wanted to express my gratitude toward him. I bought the Pepero with the money I'd ripped off from the turtle teacher. I, with a bashful face, giving the Pepero to him, and he taking the Pepero with a brightly-lit face—I giggled and grinned at the thought of that scene.

Although it was raining, my steps were light as I made my way to meet him. It was as if my feet were flying in the air. I fluttered down the street, half-running, half-flying. Then lightly and quickly, I climbed the overpass.

When I was about to reach the top of the overpass, I missed my step on the wet stairs and slipped. Before I knew it, my whole body was rolling down the stairs and I landed underneath the overpass.

When I regained consciousness, I found myself lying on cold and damp ground. I moved my body around. My arms and legs ached and hurt, but it seemed that there wasn't any place that had broken or seriously gone wrong. I limped back to the night school. I lay on the sofa and waited for the pain to subside. I felt urgent. It felt like Pepero Day was just going to pass by. I got myself up and came out of the night school. It seemed that healing could wait until after I met him.

When I returned to the overpass, the rain had thickened. This time, I walked slowly up the overpass. Standing on top of the overpass, I became curious all of a sudden about what happened to the Pepero. I took the Pepero out of my pocket. The soggy box had torn and squashed out of shape. The Pepero sticks inside had also broken, and their chocolate coating had fallen off, making an ugly sight. I couldn't give that kind of thing as a present. But I didn't have the money to buy another one either. I threw the Pepero on the ground and trudged down the overpass.

Was I the kind of kid who was incapable of giving even the smallest thing in the world to someone he liked? I thought, watching the guardrail of the overpass. The guardrail had flat steel plates that connected together like slides. It was a path that allowed cyclists to drag up their bikes. The raindrops fell on top of the plates and then scattered away. They looked slippery. I thought about how slippery the plates must be, and all of a sudden I had the impulse to go up there. When I pulled one foot up and the other behind it, everything turned fuzzy before my eyes. I slipped and tumbled until I hit the ground. Then I lost consciousness.

How long had I stayed that way? It seemed like quite a long time had passed. When I came back to myself, people had gathered around me and an ambulance had come. The people tried to put me into the ambulance. I shouted, "Please go to the night school; please! It's right behind here. Just please don't take me to the hospital!"

But they wouldn't listen. I fought away the hands that tried to get me on the ambulance and ran away, insensitive to the pain. It was only after I had returned to the night school that I got the chance to take a look at my body. A scraped and bruised and broken body—my body was no different from the Pepero that had crumbled and had been thrown away on the overpass. Tears fell from my eyes. I couldn't figure out whether it was my body or my heart that was hurting, but the tears wouldn't stop.

"Where did you get hurt?"

The turtle teacher plunked a first-aid kit next to me. He was about to leave the school when I came in and detained him. He glanced at his watch and then said, "It's almost time for the last bus...Jiseong, take care and put on the medicine well. I'll be back tomorrow." Then he ran out. It was midnight. Now, Pepero Day was over. I groaned all night thinking of the Pepero, the torn and smashed and broken Pepero that must be getting spattered by the endless rain.

Years later, I didn't get to meet all the people from the night school, but I did have a reunion with Yehjong. He was living in the United States and was soon going to graduate from Berkeley College. When we met again, he said to me, "You've become nice," still with that meek, benign face. He probably remembers the time when I was pouring curses on the woman at the church.

There was a time when I disliked everyone I knew. I also disliked what they remembered about me. If possible, I wanted to erase them from my memory and also erase myself from theirs. Although there weren't many, there were some pictures I'd taken with people during our time together at the night school.

Not wanting to remember, nor to be remembered,
I had torn up even the few pictures that I had.
Yet now, I'm the one who is searching for the people.
If nobody could remember me,
it would be like existing without really existing.

Learning to Dance: Movements to Shake Off Anger and Rage

ONE DAY, I was surfing the web in the Hannam University library as usual. I peeked into a couple of sites and then clicked on some foreign videos with dancers. At that instant I felt them speaking to me with their whole bodies, which were moving in rhythm to an intense beat. I stopped the mouse and fixed my wandering gaze. Watching them dance, I could hear a silent language, and my heart understood the message they were delivering: communication. I felt that the dancers, in their faraway countries, and I, in the Hannam University library, were connected by a cord called dance.

I seldom trusted what people said. The tongue spoke lies and laid out sugar-coated words. The body was different, however. The body was more honest than the tongue. And I felt that just as they were talking to me with their bodies, I would also be able to talk to people with my body.

Memories related to dance came up in my mind. The very first one was the nightclub: people who would shake their bodies in time to the music that seemed to pound on your eardrums. I could also remember a touter brother I had met on a street, a dance lover who would often sway his body to the music that came from the external speakers of nightclubs or from carts that sold cassette tapes. He taught me how to dance too. Like this, like this, shake your body like this. When I moved my body intensely, it felt like the pent-up anger inside my chest was gradually dissipating. Maybe that's also why the touter brother had been dancing at any random place, at any random time.

When I returned to the night school that evening, there was something I'd never seen before lying on the turtle teacher's seat.

"What's this?"

"It's an MP3 player. Something you can listen to music with. Do you want to try?"

He turned on the MP3 player and then plugged the earphones into my ears. When I was left by myself in the teachers' room, I tried moving my body in time to the music. My movements were awkward, but when I moved my arms, legs, and hips, it felt like light bulbs were lighting up one by one inside my head. Whenever I moved my body, it seemed as though frustration, sadness, and anger were all falling away.

I'd never set my heart on learning something, but it was different with dancing. I wanted to dance well. I made a search about what I had to do to learn how to dance. I had some trouble typing in the words but was finally able to type "learning how to dance" into the search box. And thus I succeeded in finding a dance academy in Daejeon.

The room was surrounded by mirrors. Every surface, from floor to ceiling except the entrance and windows, was covered with mirrors. I could see some students dancing in front of the mirrors. The loud music, the sharp smell of sweat, the heat given off by people—I could feel the energy. The dancing room, which I was visiting for the first time in my life, had a special something that excited me.

"What brings you here?"

One of the men who was dancing saw me and walked toward me. I answered him by asking with hopeful expectation, "To learn how to dance. You teach dance here, right?"

"The lesson fee is eighty thousand won."

"What?"

I was startled by the unexpected words. It was my first time hearing the words "lesson fee." I obviously didn't have eighty thousand won with me. But I had to do as they asked me to do. For the first time in my life, I had found something that I wanted to learn. But I was anxious that things might go wrong if I told him that I didn't have money.

So I began selling gum again. I went to the red-light district every night. I was afraid of getting caught by gangsters, but I had to make eighty thousand won somehow. Hoping to make the tuition fee as quickly as possible, I sold the gum doggedly. That didn't mean that I could let down my guard. I couldn't afford to be dragged away by gangsters and be buried underground even before I had a chance to learn how to dance. Desiring to do something gave me hope to live.

When I finally got together the eighty thousand won, I went back to the academy. The first dance I learned was poppin'. First I learned arm pop. It was a movement where I had to hold out my arm and then jerk it. After arm pop, I learned leg pop. I also learned that the "pop" in "poppin'" had the meaning "to pop or to bounce." Doing a pop made the muscles feel like they were waking up with a yawn. It was as if I could hear what my body was telling me.

After mastering the basic level for poppin', I also learned the choreography for television shows. Becoming one group and making the same movements with other people gave me a sense of belonging for the first time in my life, and I would sink into a feeling of oneness as though I had become one entity with them.

After I became somewhat used to dancing, I danced at events with other students. The first stage I went to was an event in an apartment building. An audience crowded around. Girls my age looked up at me and cheered for me. People were watching me. People had always turned their gazes away from me, had sworn at me and hated me, yet unbelievably, here they were watching me and sending me applause.

Whenever I went to an event, girls followed me around. I didn't know why, but among all the dancers who did the events together, I was the most popular. Girls would follow me around or send letters—goodness, this was really happening to me! It was also a strange situation for me that the guys who danced with me were tossing sarcastic remarks such as "I see you're quite popular!" in a quarrelsome tone. I, whom I had considered a lesser creature than others, had now become a subject of envy.

Dance shattered the shell that had entrapped my ego.
As I concentrated all my energy into dancing,
I felt the strength in me.
I was beating my wings to fly outside and into the world.
I did not cry anymore. Instead of tears, I now shed sweat.

While other students would only practice two hours or so, I remained in the practice room from ten o'clock in the morning when the academy opened until ten o'clock at night when it closed. In other words, I was dancing twelve hours each day. There was nothing I wanted to do other than to dance, and anyway, I had nowhere else to go. The practice room was both my stage and my world. While I danced, I felt no sadness nor distress.

When I returned from the academy, I would throw myself on the sofa. After dancing all day, I went to sleep instantly. Before starting to dance, I'd seldom slept deeply. On the streets, I'd have my nerves set on end even while I was wandering in a dream, because if danger were to hit suddenly, I would have to get up from sleep and run away. I suffered helplessly from insomnia as those days ran on. After starting to dance, however, I could fall into deep sleep.

My whole body would be covered in sweat after practice, but since there were no shower booths in the academy, I had to wash at the kitchen sink at the night school. Washing meant barely putting some water on my face and neck. It was impossible to shower at the small pot-and-pan sink. Perhaps because I was getting soaked in sweat every day and always wore the same clothes for the lack of any others, from some point on, my skin began to crack like the soil of a rice paddy during a drought. I had had skin diseases several times while living on the streets because I couldn't wash properly. Now, having contracted another one, I was fed up.

When I got a skin disease, my skin would chap and crack until one day blisters would appear and my whole body would start to itch. When the itchiness began, I felt like going crazy. Scratching here and there turned the skin red with infection, and when the condition worsened, the flesh turned black as though it were rotting. And it must have been because I had a lot of sweat on the soles of my feet; one day, I saw that my soles had been covered entirely with blisters. Dancing in that condition while hardly ever changing socks and with only one pair of shoes meant that my hygiene was very poor.

I should have at least washed my feet often, but that thought didn't cross my mind. Or perhaps it was because I just couldn't bother. Since it was the soles that were covered in blisters, whenever I walked or ran, the blisters would burst and fluid and blood would squirt out. The blisters would even come up to my ankles. When things reached that extent, even I would shudder at my own body. I got disgusted with anything gross, and the fact that the gross thing was my own body was really horrible. But since I couldn't go to a hospital, I just had to wait until it healed naturally, making sure to wash a bit more diligently from then on.

At the time, I was five feet three inches tall, and my weight was thirty-eight kilograms. I was always skipping meals, and even the food I ate was insufficient, so my body was no different from the shape of a chopstick. I was almost certainly malnourished.

Living practically every day inside the dancing room made eating meals even harder. I had to sell gum or ask the night school people for food, but now I couldn't do either. At times when I went to visit the cart bar lady, I would find appetizers that people had left behind.

"Ajumma, I'm clearing all this."

I would bring the leftover appetizers in some foil. They were things like roasted mackerel, soondae stir-fry, and gopchang.* I put them in a plastic bag and carried them to the academy. Without rice, the appetizers were too salty, and some were on the verge of rotting, but those were still my packed meals. While dancing, my vision would often turn white; I frequently became dizzy and sometimes fainted.

Dancing was the only way I could communicate with the other trainees. Sometimes some of them would ask me to eat with them. Then I would tell them, "Today I'm eating with my mom and dad." But I would just go to the night school and eat the food I had brought inside a plastic bag.

I was still clumsy at socializing, but the students took good care of me, calling me by my name. It was partly because I was the youngest among them, and also because they seemed to find it commendable that I was applying myself to practice from morning to night. We would sometimes drink together in places like the playground after practice.

The disposition I had developed while living on the streets, however, didn't get corrected easily even after I became friendly with people. I was way too outspoken. While I could express negative things clearly, I couldn't express positive things too well. Also, petty fights would happen sometimes. After quarreling, however, I would be the first to apologize. That couldn't have happened with my former self, but I wanted to learn how to dance even if I had to swallow my pride. Dance was the only thing that I loved to do and wanted to do. It was the only thing in the world for me.

A month passed. And the day came when I would have to pay the lesson fees again. Dancing alone was already taking up every bit of my time, and I didn't want to go out again to sell gum while trying to be careful not to displease the gangsters. When I returned to the night school, I found a part-time teacher who was also an office employee and who taught twice a week.

---

* Fried intestines of cow or pig.

"Teacher, please gimme eighty thousand won."

"For what?"

"I need to learn how to dance. Please, ummmm?"

His forehead scrunched up.

"I haven't got eighty thousand won on me."

"You have a house and are well off. I have nothing. Give me just eighty thousand won. I can pay you back later."

"Ugh, I'm not really that well off either. I don't have it, seriously."

I pleaded with him in all sincerity, but he refused coldly. I was furious, and I wanted to pour a swearing tirade at him. It may sound strange, but until then, I'd been living without having to worry about money. As long as I could eat, I didn't need money. I didn't understand why people around me went floundering around, saying money, money. I simply thought, just use it if you have it and earn it if you don't. Then for the first time, I realized that if you didn't have money, you couldn't even do the things that you wanted to do.

From a Gum-Selling Kid to a Thief

—✾—

I STORMED OUT of the night school and walked on, not knowing where to go. I felt all blocked up in my chest. My heart was furious. I felt like going crazy because I was so angry at the teacher who had refused to lend me money. Chilly wind blew all over my body. Had the wind cooled the anger inside me? As the anger subsided, I realized that the reason for my anger wasn't the teacher. No, I wasn't even angry; I was despairing at the fact that I could not dance anymore.

I was trudging down a residential area when I suddenly felt the urge to go to the toilet. Just then, I saw the gate of a house that was left ajar. Through the opening, I could see a child playing in the yard.

"I really need to use the toilet. Could I use the toilet in your house?"

The kid pointed toward the entrance. I hurriedly ran inside the house. On my way out after relieving myself, I saw a wallet that had been placed on top of a stationery chest. Without a second thought, I opened the wallet. There was money inside, at least a hundred thousand won by rough count.

I heard the voice inside my heart that would rationalize my actions every time I begged the turtle teacher for money and demanded that people give me food.

You people have houses and families, but I have nothing.
Therefore it is only right that you should help me.
I responded to that voice:
Yes, I can have this.

I took out the money from the wallet and put it inside my pocket. When I came out to the yard, the kid was still playing alone.

"Thanks for the toilet."

As soon as I got outside the gate, I started running. I knew that no one was following me. But I had to run away—from that moment of a gum vendor's downfall to becoming a burglar.

I returned to the dance academy. Dancing from morning till night, I would shake off life's sorrow and despair, together, of course, with the guilt that I was dancing with stolen money. The fee payment day came regularly like an unrelenting usurer. Each time, I would go around looking for an empty house.

As I walked down the residential area that was in the vicinity of Hannam University, I could sense that some houses were empty or unlocked. Curiously, whenever I went to such houses, I'd find that the owner wasn't in, or that there was a window open, or that the key had been placed inside a milk bin or a mail box. Upon entering a house, I would first go through the closet. In some houses, there were bills placed under bras, while in others, they were placed between folded trousers.

Sometimes I felt anxious that something might go wrong while I was at it. While searching the Internet, I found out about security cameras. The security cameras, which used to be totally invisible when I was getting pummeled on the streets, were suddenly more than conspicuous after I became an agent of crime. There were cameras installed at every possible place: on the streetlights in dark residential areas, at the entrances and corridors of apartment buildings, and inside building elevators. Now what I had to escape from wasn't gangsters or bullies; it was the hidden eyes of the cameras.

As I began to steal more frequently, I began to have money left over even after paying for the lessons. Repeating the experience muted the feeling of guilt, and I still didn't have any sense of economy. Whenever I had money, I spent it right away. I never once thought about how I'd be able to steal less if I had saved the leftover money to pay for the following month's lessons. I had not moved on, not even a step, from those times when I would waste what little money I had on doll-drawing, and then simply sell gum again upon running out of money. The only difference was that now gum-selling had been replaced by stealing.

Whenever I had money, I would visit a game room after finishing practice on my way back to the night school.

"Would you like to be my friend?" I would ask any boy who looked my age, approaching them at random and putting coins into their game machines. When I succeeded in winning their favor, I would then ask, "I'll buy, so let's go eat together." I didn't know how to make friends, so I had to find people to eat with me by using money. There was a time when I disliked having people watch me eat, but by this time, I disliked eating alone. Eating food with stolen money somehow wasn't appetizing. It felt like the rice grains were getting stuck inside my throat. It may have been that although my heart was insensitive to guilt, my body was suffering from guilt in that way.

There was an old apartment building near the night school. It was a security camera blind spot. When there was a house that felt empty, I would put my hand into the round hole for receiving milk at the bottom of the entrance, and often I would find the key there. If after putting my hand into the hole I sensed someone's presence, I would run away. If I did not, I would open the door and enter inside. There was a time when a woman came in while I was rummaging through the house.

"Who, who is it?"

I ran away frantically and escaped being caught red-handed. That was when I was still somewhat lucky.

A few days later, while I was roaming in order to rob an empty house, a policeman grabbed me by the scruff of my neck. While being forcefully dragged to the police station, I racked my brain about how the police could have found out. As the number of robbed houses in the town increased, the Yongjeon-dong police might have been flooded by reports. Having had all kinds of ill-fated encounters with me, they might have thought of me as a primary suspect. Perhaps I had been caught on a security camera without my knowing. When I reached the police station, a man who was a victim of the theft looked at me, appalled.

"A kid like this…"

"I'm sorry. I've done a terrible crime. Please forgive me."

As soon as I saw his face, I started to beg humbly, rubbing my two palms together. Although he was still grimacing, he didn't hurl insults or beat me. Looking at the deep wrinkles around his eyes, I could tell that he was someone who, given a different situation, would smile a lot. I decided that here was a compassionate person and begged him to forgive me, bawling out all the snot and tears I had.

"Please don't punish me."

The victim seemed to see a poor orphan boy in me. The money I stole wasn't such a big amount either. Even the police looked at me pitifully.

"If you do it again, we'll send you to jail."

The police threatened thus and sent me to a children's shelter. Running away from the shelter was a piece of cake. The police had told me that they would send me to jail if I did the same thing again, but there was nothing I could do to not do it again. I had to learn how to dance.

I resolved time and again to quit stealing. I even roamed around the karaoke bars at the red-light district thinking that I would go back to selling gum. But after being pummeled by gangsters who approached me saying, "Long time no see," I realized that now I wasn't even in a position to sell gum anymore.

Besides, it was much easier to enter an empty house and to walk out with money than to sell gum while getting slapped by someone or suffering all kinds of verbal abuses. Selling gum also became harder as I got older. When I was a tiny kid, I could easily attract people's pity, but after I grew taller and bigger, people did not open their wallets easily. So I attended the dance academy for one more year by robbing empty houses. I lost count of the times I got taken into custody during that one year.

Just once more.

So I thought to myself. Let's just steal big one last time, then stop. I was really going to do that. I really could not stand being taken to the police station and looking at the faces of the victims anymore.

Then on purpose, I went to an apartment that I had never robbed before and stood in front of an entrance. I pressed the bell. I was going to run away as soon as someone came out. I pressed it several times but no one came out. I tore off a beat-up security grille on a window facing the corridor and broke into the house. There was money there, inside a drawer, about one million won. Perhaps the God of fortune was helping me out because this was going to be the last time.

But no. Fortune was never on my side anyway. A few days later, I was dragged to the police station. I changed my strategy; instead of provoking their pity, I feigned innocence.

"It wasn't me!"

"Hey, it's all recorded in the CCTV here. Look, this is your face, right? You'll be in the slammer this time."

It was the security camera inside the elevator. Uh-oh, I thought; the amount I stole was considerable, and this wasn't going to end simply with them sending me off to a children's shelter. If I didn't return the money, I was inevitably going to be dragged to a youth detention center. Youth detention centers weren't as easy as children's shelters. They were places to stay away from. The victim said that he would settle the case if I just returned the money, but somehow, there was not a cent left of the one million won or so that I had stolen.

The police inquired into my identity. Although I was a minor who had not yet been issued an identity card, evidently the orphanages I had been at when I was little seemed to have registered my fingerprints, and some data came up about me.

"You've got a father."

"Huh? I'm an orphan."

"No, you've got a father."

The police must have somehow gotten confused about something. Perplexed, I watched a policeman dial up a person called my father.

"Huh?...What?...Then that's too bad."

He spoke those three things into the phone, and that was it.

I didn't know how things turned out, but after some time, I was let out of the police station without being sent to a youth detention center or getting punished. They told me that things had been agreed upon.

"Agreed? But by who?" I asked the police.

"Your uncle paid up."

Some of the friendly gangsters used to tell me to call them "uncles." Had one of the gangsters paid the money? No, they couldn't have. None of them could have walked in voluntarily and willingly paid that kind of money for me.

Both "uncle" and "father" were strange words to me. I thought that the police must be mistaken about something. Thinking otherwise seemed to drive me crazy with confusion.

I was an orphan.
All my sins and misfortunes had happened because I was an orphan.
But if I wasn't an orphan...
Then why did I have to live like this?

I was hungry. I couldn't go on stealing money anymore. But if it was food, wouldn't that be okay to steal? I saw a cart bar that had its lights turned off. I pushed away the tent and entered inside. Inside the fridge, there were some uncooked chicken gizzards. I didn't know how to turn on the gas stove. I turned on the gas and tried lighting the fire with a lighter. It didn't light easily. Meanwhile, some tissue must have been set on fire while I was having trouble lighting the stove. When I saw it, the fire had burned up the tissue and was spreading to other fixtures. I picked up the dishcloth lying next to me and madly swung it around. The motion that was meant to douse the fire invited disaster instead; the dishcloth caught fire and blazed up in flames.

"Fire!"

I don't remember whether it was me or someone else who cried out like that. I was simply out of my mind. People came running, and water was poured all over the cart bar.

The fire was extinguished only after the fixtures and a part of the cart bar had been burned down. The owner of the cart bar had been among the people who had crowded the place. He alternated his dumbstruck gaze between the cart bar and me. A cart bar owner couldn't have been so well off. How hateful must a kid, who obviously didn't seem able to compensate for the loss, have appeared to him?

His rough palm struck my face. The sound of the palm striking my cheek rang as loud as thunder. Before I had a chance to lift my face, fists began flying in. Even after I lost my balance and collapsed, he continued to beat me and kick me with his feet, wailing.

The only place I could return to clutching my hungry stomach and a body full of bruises was the night school. When I entered the teachers' room, I saw the turtle teacher.

"Where did you go to get beaten up like this?"

Without answering, I laid myself on the sofa. I was hungry, ached where I had been beaten, and felt like crying, yet even tears refused to come. The turtle teacher gave out a sigh. He wouldn't be able to solve anything. I had a hunch, or rather a conviction that I wouldn't be able to dance anymore. It was the first thing I had ever loved, and the only thing I wanted to do. Instead of tears, a feeling of emptiness flooded over me. Once again, I was just an orphan boy with neither dream nor hope.

Sungbong Choi: The Name I Found to Be Mine at Age Fourteen

AROUND THAT TIME, they had an academic board meeting every day at the night school. The meeting agenda was about what they should do with me. The teachers were divided into two groups: one that wanted to have me out, and the other that could not allow that. The teachers who wanted to have me out said that I was influencing the other students at the night school in negative ways. Moreover, I would often throw stones at windows when classes were in session, run away after hitting the back of the teachers' heads, and behave in other perverse ways. The insistence of the teachers who said that I should not be sent out was comparatively unconvincing. The only counter-argument they could make was to ask how the school could ever eject a child who didn't have anywhere to go.

While the meeting was on, I had to stay outside the teachers' room. I clung to the door and perked up my ears to eavesdrop on what they were saying inside. They weren't talking about just any story but a story about me. I suffered through the wait impatiently, curious and anxious about what conclusion they would come to. One day during the consecutive meetings, the turtle teacher told me to go to the dong* office.

"The dong office? Why?"

"Let's try applying for basic livelihood security."

"What's that?"

---

* The smallest urban submunicipal administrative region that has its own government office and staff.

118

"It's when the country gives you money. The society helps you out, in other words."

I was enticed by his words and followed him along. At the dong office, however, we couldn't find out about anything. I didn't know who I was, and neither did they. The turtle teacher suggested going to a police station to conduct a background check.

"You said you were going to help me, so why are you taking me to a police station?"

When I heard the words "police station" or "the police," I almost broke out in a rash. The turtle teacher persuaded me. It wasn't because I'd done something wrong that we were going there; we just had to find out who I was. I dreaded the idea of going to the police station when I hadn't done anything wrong. But after knowing that I wouldn't be interrogated or handed over to a children's shelter, I changed my mind.

The police checked whether I was a missing child, and if so, whether I had been reported missing, and then ran a background check with my fingerprints. Who was I? I'd never thought of such things when I was living on the streets. I was little, and surviving on the streets alone was already overwhelming. When I got a bit older, though, that question would crop up in my mind now and then. Who was I? I was an orphan. I was Jiseong. But there was something dubious about that answer. Was that all? The background check result came up on the monitor.

"His name is Sungbong Choi. Born in 1990."

I was at a loss for words. An unfamiliar name, and an age that was only now ascertained: I couldn't believe those words described me. A greater shock came, however, from what they said next.

"And...he has a father."

It was the same thing I'd heard at the police station when I was arrested for stealing. They had not been mistaken then. The first time when they said that I had a father, I did not believe them; I could not believe them and did not want to believe them. The second time I heard it, however, I could not simply deny it. I was not an orphan. I was not even Jiseong.

"Then how about his mother?" the turtle teacher asked. He too looked surprised and taken aback.

"Nothing comes up about his mother."

The police looked at the turtle teacher and me, as though asking whether we had anything else we wanted to know. I did not want to know anything anymore. I was afraid to know more things. I half escaped from the police station.

It was a long time later that the turtle teacher came out.

"I tried to contact your father."

I didn't say anything. I simply looked down.

"We couldn't reach him."

There was a small stone lying there. I kicked it with the tip of my foot. The stone rolled forth dejectedly then stopped. The turtle teacher said that I had an uncle. He couldn't contact my father so he called my uncle instead, and the only response he got was to not contact him anymore in the future. While he spoke, I continued to look down on the ground. I should have been consumed in wrath. I should have gotten angry about why they had abandoned me. I should have demanded to know what those people had been doing while I was living out on the streets—how they could ever have done such a thing when they were my own family and relatives. But I remained calm. I didn't feel anything.

According to what I had just found out, I was fourteen years old, but my life had already drifted too far down an irrevocable direction. While all those things were happening to me, neither my father nor my uncle appeared in my life. They did not pity me, not even as much as the people who bought gum from me on the streets. Neither did they show me as much compassion as the people who invited me to sleep in their homes for a night or two.

So I didn't care anyway.
Whether I had a father or an uncle, the only thing I had to do was to continue
living alone.
As I had always done, just like it had been in the past.

While listening to the turtle teacher speak, however, I did think for a very brief moment about how I wanted to meet my father, not because I wanted to see him but because I wanted to kill him.

Returning to the dong office and going through the livelihood security application process was boredom itself. The turtle teacher and the dong office employee exchanged the following conversation:

"He can't apply since he has a father."

"The father has given up on providing for him."

"We can't register him because he has no address."

"Then please put down our night school address."

"We can't, because that's a municipal estate."

We can't, we can't: that's the only thing they said. We can't, because of this; we can't, because of that. Then when they were done with the "we can'ts," the "whys" began. Why are you trying to make him a security recipient? Why did his father give up on supporting him? Why doesn't the kid have a house? Why does the kid live on a municipal estate? The process was tremendously stressful. Even the turtle teacher seemed to be disheartened.

I didn't give up but continued frequenting the dong office for another few days. As I could no longer sell gum or steal, I wanted to become a security recipient despite the seemingly endless "nos" and "whys." Yet why did they have to ask so many questions I couldn't answer, and why were there so many documents they needed? The more I found out about the process, the more it felt impossible to become a security recipient. The biggest obstacle was the fact that I had parents listed on my family register. To the people who trusted documents, the parents who had abandoned me were still considered my parents.

I now forgot the moment when I had confirmed the existence of my father, as though burying the memory of that moment would also erase away the person called father. If I suppressed the memory, would I then be able to live as if I'd been an orphan all along? But I felt that there was a being who would jump out abruptly and scare me no matter how deeply I had buried him inside my heart. That specter-like being was my father.

Sometime later, I passed by a record store. A song was resounding from the speaker installed in front of the store. It was a man's voice: a simple, unaffected voice, which despite that, had the power to pull at your heartstrings. It was melancholic yet consoling. I halted my steps without realizing.

As the streetlights light up one by one
and another day wanes over a dark red sunset,
everything somehow feels to me like a dream.

Amazingly, the streetlights on the street where I was standing began lighting up one by one. The day was waning over a dark red sunset. I stood stock straight like a streetlight, at a loss with an intense emotion that burned like the sunset.

What was my image reflecting on the glass looking for?
Even though I try to say something and remember something,
I see only listless eyes looking back.

I looked at the reflection of my face on the record store's windowpane. Just like in the song, there I saw a boy with listless eyes. The moment when I'd found out about my father's existence, I'd remained more or less apathetic. When I heard that song, however, emotions that I had not been able to feel while at the police station exploded—emotions that I had tried to ignore with great effort, emotions that I had no choice but to suppress because they were simply unbearable. I was not okay. I wasn't fine. I was angry, sad, resentful, and begrudging; I wanted to burst out in tears and to yell and scream.

I'd always been alone. I'd become so used to that fact that I didn't even feel like I was lonely. When I listened deeply to the lyrics, however, the fact that I was alone suddenly seemed to shroud me in dark gloom. While the song resounded, lights lit up one by one in my gloomy heart, just like the streetlights that had lit up one by one before my eyes. If there was one person in the entire world who understood the dark gloom in my heart, it was this man who was singing the song. And he was also the only person in this entire world who lighted a lamp in my heart. The feeling that this man was telling the story that I could not express in my own words, the feeling that he was consoling me so…Tears flowed down my cheek. This man, as I found out later, was the singer Gwangseok Kim.

That night I lay on the sofa at the night school and sang a song to myself. It was "Rock Island," the only song I knew. "A rock island washed by breaking waves, an empty place." Perhaps I was indeed an old young, like the turtle teacher said. The song's lyrics, which probably wouldn't be too popular among my peers, were embedded deep inside my heart. Songs bring up memories that are tied to them. Singing "Rock Island," I would automatically think of the gum-selling brother, the person who had saved me, the first person ever to have sung to me. Wherever and however he may have died, as long as I continue to sing "Rock Island," I will never be able to forget him.

Carrying on from the memory of the gum-selling brother, one instance during the gum-selling days arose in my mind. It was one of those days when I entered a nightclub to sell gum. A man who had been invited as a special guest was standing on the stage. He had a voice that was different from ordinary people, and the song he was singing was also an unfamiliar one around the nightclubs. Although he was in a nightclub at Yongjeon-dong's red-light district, it felt as though he couldn't have been farther away from that nightclub teeming with people.

It looked like he was the only one who existed in a different world.
I didn't know which song it was, but I felt a strange sensation.
It gave me goose bumps, as though I'd been thrown into cold water.
My whole body quivered as though it had been electrocuted.
What if I could also sing like that...

Like him, I wanted to sing songs that didn't fit in with nightclubs or the Yongjeon-dong red-light district. I didn't want to simply become a singer. I wanted to stand somewhere that was completely removed from the things that surrounded me—at a higher place, and a very faraway place.

The following day, I began searching on the Internet. Relying on my memory from a few years ago, I began searching for the song that I had heard at the nightclub, and about what I needed to do to be able to sing like that. And I discovered the thing that had made my body vibrate through and through was called vocal music.

Knock and It Shall Open unto You:
An Encounter with a Benefactor

It was at some Internet café that I found an ad that said, "We give voice lessons." It was a college community café that shared information about singing and streamed music. I decided to call on the person who had placed the ad. I didn't know that you needed a lot of money to learn how to sing. I only had an indefinite hope that they might teach me if I pursued them and pestered them.

The place I went to after looking at the notice was Pai Chai University. Inside a practice room of the College of Music building was a young man with swarthy skin and big, bright eyes. He was the person who had put up the notice; and this was my benefactor, Mr. Jeongso Park. At that first encounter, I was instantly conquered by the charisma he exuded. However, I felt that I shouldn't be intimidated. While I may be shabby, I had to appear confident.

"I'm Sungbong Choi. I would like to learn how to sing."

I spoke confidently, but as respectfully as possible. I was still unaccustomed to my real name, but I also couldn't say, "I'm Jiseong" without a surname. The teacher looked at me with a hint of doubt.

"Really? Let me hear you sing."

It was something I hadn't in the least expected to hear, and it threw me off a little. Inside my head, I was wildly turning over the list of songs I knew. The first ones that came to mind were "Rock Island" and "On the Street," but they didn't seem like appropriate pieces to sing in front of a vocalist. I sang a pop song that I'd heard on the turtle teacher's MP3 player.

It was a song by Flower. When I began to sing, his expression wrinkled up a little.

Uh-oh, maybe not like this. All kinds of thoughts came to my mind. He looks busy; perhaps I've disturbed him by coming here. I don't want to cause him any inconvenience. What if he tells me to just go back? I stopped singing and told him honestly, "I don't have any money."

I tried to be confident even while saying that. It seemed that it would be useless to act pitiful like I did when I was selling gum. On the other hand, I remembered the time when I had to quit dancing because I had no money.

"Then discuss with your parents and come again."

"I haven't any parents either."

The teacher asked me things about myself with a dubious face: how I was doing, where I lived, why I wanted to learn to sing. I told him candidly about my story. He listened to me silently, then gave out a sigh. His eyes seemed to show that he was shaken. He remained silent for a long while, then said, "That's good for now."

On my way back to the night school, I thought about what "That's good for now" meant. It was a comment that was neither positive nor negative. Yet to me, even that ambiguous answer felt like hope. At least he hadn't said no. And if it wasn't a forceful rejection, there was a chance that it could be changed into the affirmative.

The next day I went to see him at the school.

"Hello. I'm here."

He looked at me with an undecipherable expression. But even then, he did not kick me out or say anything negative.

"Go and watch the people practicing there. That's the kind of singing we do here."

I found it pleasant to listen to the Gyeongsang-do[*] accent mixed in his speech. There were many small rooms with pianos in the music college. Inside those rooms, people were singing with that unique vocalization that had so captivated me. I never got tired of listening to that voice. And I had sung a pop tune after coming to a place like this...I blushed at the thought of the previous day's events.

I went to a secluded spot in the campus and tried to produce a voice similar to theirs, but even merely trying to imitate proved to be difficult. I tensed up my throat to the max, but nothing changed. It seemed that I needed to have a completely different method to sing like them. I desperately wanted to know what that method was.

The next day, I went back to the school again. Perhaps Mr. Park had been taken by my determination to learn; he asked me to take him to the place I lived. His girlfriend—who is now his wife—also went along. There were no classes scheduled at the night school at that hour, and the place was empty. I showed them the teachers' room, where I slept. I turned on the lamp, but the spent tube light blinked for a while, then finally gave out.

"This is where I sleep..."

He looked around the teacher's room and asked, "How do you sleep when it's so cold?" When I replied that I swathed myself with a jumper and slept with just my nose poking out, he let out a tiny sigh.

"In a place like this..."

I became nervous about what he might say next. Worrying that he might say that a kid who lived in a place like this could not learn how to sing, I waited for the next comment. He did not go on with his comments but instead asked, "Where do you wash?" I took him to the kitchen and showed him the sink. He went up to the sink and turned the faucet. The water had frozen due to the cold, and the faucet ran dry. Again, he didn't say anything.

---

* Gyeongsang Province.

Having stepped out of the kitchen, the teacher and his girlfriend turned around. I followed him out, then stopped myself. I didn't know what to say to the back that was facing me. He had just confirmed that what I had told him weren't lies. Was he then going to trust me, or pity me? Did he perhaps consider it unreasonable that I, in these circumstances, would consider vocal music? He looked back at me. For some reason, his eyes were red with tears. He said in a subdued tone, "Let's start with your lessons. Twice a week, and come to the school."

The teacher had told me twice a week, but I went to the school every day. First, I learned vocalization. When I learned how to vocalize, I could make similar sounds like the others even when I practiced alone. But it was difficult for me to pronounce the lyrics of foreign songs when I didn't even really know how to read Korean; sheet music was new to me, let alone the piano.

The teacher was busy because he was in his graduating year and there were quite a lot of people other than me who were taking lessons. I learned vocalization method and the places on the keyboard I had to press when practicing vocalization, and then I practiced alone. That room was the teacher's private practice room. Nobody disturbed me there.

I went to Pai Chai University every day. My day began with music and ended with music.

"Practice."

When I went there, the teacher would always say that to me. I would be practicing alone, and when the teacher was teaching other people, I would watch over their shoulders and learn along. The teacher didn't stop me from being next to him.

"Do this. How come it's not working? You try, Sungbong."

In this way, he would sometimes make me do something while I was watching by the students' side.

"Go inside and practice, Sungbong."

128

Those were the words that I heard most frequently from the teacher during that time. Although I used to never follow anyone's advice or requests, I didn't argue with what the teacher said. When I had spent around five to six hours alone singing inside a practice room, the teacher would pass by the room and then open the door.

"Have you eaten?"

When I shook my head, he would invite me to eat with him and take me to a restaurant or order jajangmyeon. At the music college—which for me was synonymous with music itself—I was treated to a meal almost every day by the teacher. Amid all that, I watched and listened and used my wits and tact, progressing thus in learning vocal music.

Mr. Jeongso Park was a devout Christian.

"Sungbong, would you like to sing in our church choir?"

When he asked me that question, I remembered the lady who had sneered at me. But because I wanted to be an obedient kid at least to my teacher out of all the people in the world, I submissively agreed. I'd seen a church choir when I had followed Yehjong to church. But would it be okay for someone like me to fill such a position? It seemed that it would be okay, because it was something that the teacher had told me to do and because it was about singing.

On Sunday morning, I washed my whole body thoroughly at the night school sink. I didn't have any change of clothes; I washed my clothes at the same time while washing my body, then put on the wet clothes and went to church while drying them in the sun.

The church that my teacher attended was many times bigger than the small church behind the night school. He was the conductor of that church's choir. When I entered the choir practice room after him, I saw a piano and unfamiliar adults who wore choir gowns. The teacher gave me a gown too. When I stood there wearing the same clothing as the others, I felt a strange feeling of kinship.

"Who's this?" one of the choir members asked.

"He's my student."

Pleased with the word "student," I quietly looked up at my teacher. He assigned me my place among the choir members and said, "Since you have a tenor register, Sungbong, go stand in the tenor section."

Around that time, I had learned how to play simple solfège on the keyboard and was practicing vocalization by myself. Even though I had followed Mr. Park half-heartedly to the church, I realized that I could actually learn more from him by practicing with the choir there.

The teacher was dedicated in teaching the choir members. The songs that were sung in ensemble under his baton were beautiful hymns, which could all be sung in vocal singing style.

I liked the fact that I had a part in choir singing—
that the sound I made harmonized with other people's sound.
Breathing together and creating the same sounds as the others
seemed to mean that I was communicating.

When we sang the songs that we had diligently rehearsed at the worship service, people's attention would focus on the choir, and I would feel like a vocalist performing in front of an audience. Some people found it odd that a young member like me was singing amid adults, but I was more than contented to bask in their attention while singing for that short span of time.

While practicing at the school and the church, I also came to know by wits and tact how to read sheet music. On sheet music, the pitch and duration of the sounds made on the piano were marked with symbols called musical notes. When I became sufficiently fluent in reading sheet music, I also began to enjoy playing the piano alone in the practice room at the school. I sang all day while playing the piano.

I didn't know what the choir people thought of me, but I went to my teacher's choir every week. When I went to church, I didn't just practice, but also worshipped and listened to the sermon. I also came to know about religious doctrine and the existence of God little by little. I couldn't say that I began to have faith, but through singing praises, I began to be faintly influenced. Messages of praise tended to console my heart that had been through so many difficulties in life. The song that I especially liked was a gospel song called "I."

> *Though I have no treasures, no knowledge,*
> *and no health that others have, I have something that no one has:*
> *I have seen something others haven't; I have heard a voice others haven't;*
> *I have experienced love that others haven't;*
> *and I have realized something that others know nothing about.*
> *My fair God gifted me with things that others don't have.*

These were lyrics written by a disabled person named Myeonghee Song, who was born with cerebral palsy. The "I" in this song was no other than I myself. I had no treasures nor knowledge. I might come across as perfectly normal, but my legs were in bad condition; I couldn't hear well, and I also suffered from mental distress, so I wasn't even in good health. I sang this song whenever I had the chance. I even developed the faith that if God was fair, he would certainly also gift me with things that others didn't have.

School Qualification Exam: An Entrance Ticket to Becoming like the Others

A LOT OF things had improved compared to the past. I had a fixed place to sleep and somewhere to wash up roughly too. I didn't have to wander through the streets to sell gum or be chased by gangsters or police. Most important of all, I had music.

I decided to get a part-time job. I couldn't afford to lose this opportunity by stealing or getting chased by someone like before. I'll work and save money, I told myself. I'll take care of my own meals and lodging and get proper lessons. Making such resolutions alone made me feel like I was preparing for the future. Rather than struggling through life with only the imminent today in mind, I wanted to draw a big map of my life.

After looking at a room-and-board ad, I went to see an electrician. When I arrived, I found him drinking.

"What? You're a kid. How about school?"

"I don't go to school. I need to work. Please hire me."

The drunkard man climbed ladders to the top of telephone poles to fix streetlights, and I assisted him from underneath. It was the first part-time job in my life, but I had to quit before long.

"Since I feed you and let you sleep here…I don't have to give you money, right?"

What I needed wasn't just food and lodging. With those things, I might be able to live through today, but I could not prepare for tomorrow. I quit the work and went to a supermarket.

"Please let me work; please?"

"First bring a family relation certificate. You need that in order to work here."

The fact that I had to work because I had no family but couldn't work because I had no family made resentment well up inside me. The next job I found was newspaper delivery. I went out at 2:00 a.m. and inserted flyers between newspapers, and when I was done with that, I delivered the newspaper. The agency manager was considerate of my young age and assigned me an apartment in an area that was relatively easy to deliver to. Nonetheless, after pulling around a hand cart piled with newspapers and delivering close to four hundred copies, I would be completely wiped out.

Even though I had begun to work, I scrimped the money I earned and continued to hit up the turtle teacher. In contrast to those times when I sold gum or stole, earning money through labor made me chary of spending; I would save up what I had earned and ask someone for money to cover my living expenses, like I used to do.

"Turtle teacher, I need to go to Pai Chai University to learn how to sing but have no fare."

"You were learning how to dance, and now it's singing?"

"It's true. I'm learning how to sing."

When the turtle teacher gave me one thousand or two thousand won, I would buy noodles with that money, then walk the long distance to Pai Chai University. Eating with Mr. Jeongso Park at the school took care of another meal. Mr. Park wielded his power as a student president to allow me to enter the school, use his practice room, and learn music, even though it was over other people's shoulders. And to add to that, he treated me to meals. He bought mostly jajangmyeon, but it was okay because it was food that I liked.

I wasn't a kid who had owned a piano from an early age, nor was I a kid who had received music education by playing Beyer and Czerny. The reason I was able to like music was perhaps because I had grown up in an environment that couldn't be farther removed from music. The environment that surrounded me was so distant from music. Yet precisely because of that, I felt fulfilled when I was in music.

Many things were now beyond comparison with how they used to be in the past. Despite this, or rather because of it, I realized that I wasn't up to par. I was different from the other kids. The issue wasn't just with the environment. My ignorance was the biggest mark of difference between them and me. By this time I had gotten to know a lot more things than before, but the more knowledge I gained, the more ashamed I was of my ignorance.

My peers who had received lessons for the entrance exam sang songs with foreign lyrics really well. I, on the other hand, had to write down the pronunciations I heard of the foreign words in Korean under the lyrics, and sing an imitated version. I wasn't just ignorant of foreign songs. There were too many things in the world that I could not catch up with simply with what little I had studied on my own at the night school. I could not enter conversations with other people and wasn't familiar with the issues that they were interested in. I felt like I was the only person who was still green and the only one who was unable to mingle with others.

Wouldn't things change if I studied in school like the others?
I had ended not being able to become friends with my peers at the night school,
but what if I took the qualification exam and went to school—
attended the same school as the others and obtained the same conditions and
status as them?
If only I could mix as their equal…

I was around middle school age, so it seemed that if I did the qualification exams one by one, starting from the elementary level, I would be able to attain the level of education and go on to high school.

"Turtle teacher, when are the qualification exams?"

"Why? Are you going to take one?" he asked me, looking doubtful.

I had always run away out of boredom whenever he had tried to make me stay and study, so it was hardly surprising that he was puzzled by my question. Still, without hesitation, he told me the test dates. One Sunday, I went to a middle school in Tanbang-dong to take the elementary school qualification exam.

Until then, the only classrooms I'd seen were the ones in the makeshift container offices of the night school. Grandmothers and grandfathers sitting densely packed together at desks and on chairs that looked as though they would break down any minute was the image I had of a classroom and school. It was my first time entering a proper classroom, so I expected the place to somehow feel unfamiliar and special. The only thought that came to my mind upon entering the examination room was, "So this is the place where my peers study."

Though it was much more spacious than the classrooms at the night school, this place felt smaller and more cramped for some reason. The thought of how kids around my age would be sitting in that room crammed with desks and chairs was simply suffocating. I turned my head and looked at the window. If there had been bars, this place could pass as a prison.

"Uh-oh, I can't remember anything I've memorized…"

The grandmother sitting next to me was on pins and needles even before the exam started. With a nervous face, she rubbed her palms together on her pants, fidgeting restlessly.

"Have courage. You've lived much longer and know more than elementary school students."

When I said that, she nodded her head in agreement.

"Right, I've lived much longer than them. Of course I know more than little children."

What I said to her was also what I said to myself. Because I'd lived a totally different life from other children, I believed that I had learned things not by rote memory but through hard knocks in life.

The test began. I was right: the questions were multiple choice with four choices, and I could easily pick out the right answer. A score of sixty and above was a pass, and my score was over ninety. I'd passed it in one go—maybe I was a genius! The middle school qualification exam, however, immediately told me otherwise.

At the first middle school qualification exam I sat for, I only managed to pass Korean with some luck and failed the rest of the subjects. It was mandatory to also pass English, math, science, social studies, and an optional subject, but I'd never learned such things on the streets. Only by passing all six subjects could I finally receive the certification.

When I returned to the night school after I had finished my singing practice, I would now pick up the study materials that were kept in the teachers' room. It would be great to pass all six subjects in one go, but that was impossible for me since I knew no basics. I decided to target one subject and to pass the exam one subject at a time.

A noona* I got to know at the church helped me with my studies. I was receiving private lessons for the first time in my life! Well, she tried to teach me a couple of times, but finally gave up because I lagged behind so much on the basics. So I took the money I had saved, for which I had sweated my guts out, to enroll at a qualification examination academy. It was my hard-earned money, so I had to pass the exam, at least for the money's sake. That's how I ended up taking the exam—offered twice a year—five times in total. Within two and a half years, I barely scraped through the middle school graduate certification exam. I was now a middle school graduate, with a scholastic achievement that all the other kids who were my peers already had. I felt that I'd finally become somebody, like them.

Not long after I had passed the qualification exam, I had an enormous fight with my roommate at the night school, Mr. Hong. My aggressive

* The word that boys and men use to address older sisters.

demands for money from the turtle teacher were the root of all evil. I had just behaved like I had always done in the past, but Mr. Hong lashed out.

"Why do you talk in that way to turtle teacher?"

"Because no one's helping the poor little lamb!"

Since going to church, I often used the expression "poor little lamb" when I received money or food from people. If I wasn't a poor little lamb, then who else in this entire world could be one? What I said was also nothing different from the usual, but Mr. Hong got crimson in the face and yelled, "Stop playing that tune about the poor little lamb, for heaven's sake!"

Those words and the irritated voice with which he said those words touched something inside me. My twisted, convoluted heart grew more frustrated, and I felt like hitting the ceiling with anger. I argued loudly with him. The thorny words only made us angrier. We battered each other with our bodies.

The anger did not subside even after he went out. I broke the mirror and furniture. I was sick and tired of the night school, sick and tired of the people…I wasn't the least bit grateful to the night school nor the people there. I wasn't even sorry. Had they ever accepted me wholeheartedly? Had they had even the slightest compassion or affection toward me? I smashed up whatever was within my reach and then flopped down on the sofa. I buried my face in my hands. This too shall pass…A phrase I'd heard somewhere crossed my pitch-dark mind.

This too shall pass…

The night school was trying to forsake me, or perhaps it was I who was trying to forsake it. Feeling that I was going to be forsaken, I was perhaps trying to forsake it first. I'd lived without the night school until now, so who cares? After uttering "who cares?" to myself, however, I was caught up by the disillusionment that "ultimately, my life is a no-go." The time had now come for me to admit that I could neither live in harmony with others, nor stay in one place like some built-in fixture. However, everything shall pass: in the dark tunnel whose beginning and end remained unknown, this moment shall be yet another passing phase...

The faculty meetings resumed. The topic again was me. I wasn't in the least bit curious about the meeting results. I knew exactly how things would conclude. I went and erased every one of my traces that was still left at the night school. There weren't many in any case: a few photos I'd taken with the night school people, a few daily necessities...I cut out my face from amid the people in the photos. A hole gaped at the place where I used to stand. I wanted to hack the cut-out face to pieces. I ripped my face to shreds, then threw the pieces into the trash. I was going to leave now. On my way out of the teachers' room, I looked around me for one last time.

It looked the same as when I had first arrived. The gray cement walls, the cobwebs hanging in the corners of the ceiling, the fluorescent lights with broken connections, the worn and torn black sofa, the ragged blanket...Yet all those things were different from how they used to be at first. All those things now carried the odor of my life; clinging on them were my memories, feelings, and the countless days and nights I'd spent there.

The night school was a precious place that had provided me with food and bed when I'd had nowhere to go. Because it was precious, it was the only place where I could rebel and throw my temper. I discovered here that I stood at the lowest bottom of society, where I should be properly envious of people who had neither money nor scholarly attainments, and who complained about how hard and difficult life was. I also discovered another fact: that like water and oil, people and I could not mix, that I only knew how to fight and not how to reconcile.

The times I'd lived at the night school flashed past my mind.
I'd thought that there was nothing to be grateful or be sorry about.
So then why was it that there were so many people I felt grateful for and sorry to?

No one will remember me as a good person.
I would forever remain a troublemaker in their memory.
Perhaps the reason I wanted to erase my traces
was because I wanted to erase the bad me from their memories forever.

I put my hands in my empty pockets and stepped out into the street. It was chilly outside.

Part 3:
Would I Be Able
to Live like the Others?
School and Music

Is This What They Call Home?
A Roundabout Arrival

I HAD NOWHERE to go once I stepped out of the night school. I delivered papers in the early morning, sold Bacchus drinks at night, and then in the afternoon, went to school where Mr. Park was. I considered asking him whether I could sleep in the school practice room, but didn't dare ask him. He had his graduation coming up, and I didn't want to say some useless thing and be rejected even by him. It appeared that there was no place for me to sleep at the newspaper agency either. I just had to sleep in the streets like I had done in the past. However, when I tried crouching and sleeping in the fetal position on a vacant stairway of a building or in a corner of a college campus like I had done as a little kid, a sense of shame flooded over me: Is my life a repeat sign? It keeps going back. And I'm back to the beginning.

I wondered how the basic livelihood security application was getting on. Having discovered that there was a system where I could receive help, I wanted to desperately depend on it. I went to the dong office and pleaded for them to help, and badgered them to please process my application. The social welfare representative had promised to help, so why wasn't there any news? I began to worry that after the inspection they'd made at the night school to confirm whether I was really living there, it might be a problem for them that I'd left the night school.

I was sighing and wandering in the streets when a hyeong I'd often met in town told me to follow him to his house. That house had a huge number of computers, and many hyeongs were playing online games. They all had sunken eyes and looked burnt out.

"You try it too."

When the hyeong who'd taught me how to play the game saw how adroit I was with computers and how I was able to quickly adapt myself, he cracked up silently and said, "Hey, you have nowhere to sleep, right? Sleep here. One thing, though: play this game all day."

I teamed up with three hyeongs and played the game. I would make quick hunts by driving items to one character, or run three computers alone to develop game characters. It was fun in the beginning, but only for a short while. Soon it was no longer a game but hard labor. Apart from the time I spent delivering papers, I was having to run the computers from morning till late night. Later I found out that the items and characters collected through that game could be exchanged for money. After spending a few months there and having discovered that I was earning hundreds of thousands of won for them per day, I demanded, "Now give me some money too."

"Dude, we feed you and give you space to sleep."

Their words were the same as the drunken electrician's. I wasn't living simply to eat and sleep, but had to save up money to learn how to sing. I didn't want to drift away from singing like this forever. I instantly ditched gaming and left the house. The winter, however, had grown deeper. I could no longer stomach having to sleep on the streets.

That's when I found out about gosiwon.* The cheapest room was so narrow as to be completely filled up when I lay down my body, but it only cost a hundred and fifty thousand won per month. I made two hundred thousand won by delivering papers, so it appeared that I'd be able to live in a place like that, albeit on a tight budget. After worrying through the matter, I finally registered at a gosiwon. It was the warmest lodging I could get

* Special accommodations for exam candidates.

with the money I earned. I then looked for another job to make up for the lack of living expenses.

Among the jobs that I could juggle together with newspaper delivery was hard labor at construction sites. Since I was a small boy, I couldn't carry heavy loads and didn't have any lucrative skills, but by arranging materials and running around busily at the construction sites as they ordered, I could make something like forty thousand won a day. Work wasn't available every day, but I actively went to visit the human resources office and waited for work, and when I got a site to work in, I went and worked there with all my might and came home with my daily wage. On days when there was no hard labor available, I distributed flyers. Running around posting them on telephone poles, giving them out to people, and putting them into each house, I would earn twenty thousand won a day. When I returned to the gosiwon after making money that way, I'd be completely done in.

Although the gosiwon provided a warm place to sleep, it wasn't a comfortable place to rest because I got into fights with the people living there almost every day. The people I would bump into while cooking noodles in the kitchen would regularly smack my head.

"A tiny thing like you, not even greeting grown-ups?"

To hell with grown-ups! I wasn't the type to bear with condescension for being small; moreover, I'd defended myself alone until then, so I did not yield to them an inch.

"We pay the same money to live here, so why should I greet?"

Saying that always led to fights. I was never the one who provoked. A kid around my age would provoke me saying that I had a beggar's eyes, and the grown-ups with faces worn out by hardscrabble lives would say abusive things to me at the slightest opportunity. Once, that particular grown-up who wasn't at all like a grown-up began to provoke me again in the kitchen by rapping me on the head.

"Hey, squirt, are you really not going to say hello? You got no manners or what?"

In terms of having a jinxed life, I couldn't possibly come second to anyone. I pummeled that buster with the pan I was going to use to cook noodles, madly hurled dishes at him, then sat on him and strangled his throat. I wanted to kill him. I'd gotten beaten and hit on the streets almost every day, but I'd always taken revenge later. I was angry at how the society and grown-ups who had not done anything for me were treating me like I was nothing. I can't remember anything about the time at the gosiwon other than having fought like that. It was the first lodging I'd gotten in life with my own money, but to me, that place was merely a part of the comfort-less world.

Doing both newspaper delivery and hard labor at construction sites followed by practicing singing at school made me so tired that I became dizzy. Sometimes during practice, things would spin before my eyes and I would collapse, or coming back from delivering papers, I would silently crumple on the road while on the way to the gosiwon. Even now, if I stand up suddenly or exert myself slightly while running, things turn black in front of my eyes and I lose balance. I was scared of going to the hospital, because I worried that if I were to go on that way, I might not even be able to work, so I made a visit to an internal medicine clinic in town.

"I often get dizzy and collapse."

The doctor peeled my bottom eyelid open, drew out my blood and examined it, then said with a grave face, "You're anemic and dystrophic; you seriously lack iron."

I didn't know what anemic and dystrophic meant, but I used to fall down easily on roads during my gum-selling days, and that had probably also been because of those reasons. The doctor told me to eat a lot of beans. Of course, being someone who always just ate noodles in gosiwon, there was no way I could eat a lot of beans. During that time, I weighed less than forty kilograms. I went on living that way, then when I collapsed again, I had to get injected with Ringer's solution.

Ringer's solution cost a day's worth of hard labor. It appeared to me that I would easily end up turning in all the money I earned to the hospital. I looked for nutritious foods, but they were all pricey. The best I could do for myself was to merely put eggs into the noodles I cooked and to drink milk now and then.

Around that time, I began to have problems in my right ear. I didn't know whether they were aftereffects of car accidents or symptoms of anemia, but my hearing would come and go, and I would hear a continuous whooshing sound. But I needed my ears to be sensitive in order to continue with music. Even though I knew that it could develop into a fatal problem later, I couldn't do anything other than to leave it alone. It only made me a bit uncomfortable, and I didn't collapse or anything. I didn't have any money for treatment anyway, so there wasn't anything I could do. Perhaps the only consolation regarding my health was that I'd almost never brushed my teeth since I was little, and yet none of my teeth had rotted.

Despite all the health problems, on days when I had no hard labor after newspaper delivery, I would go to Mr. Park's school and practice there all day. But the school would soon be out of bounds to me once Mr. Park had graduated.

I'd never thought about what I was going to do with my singing.
But while I sang, I could forget everything.
I could escape from my daily life.

Then one day, a piece of good news came from Mr. Park, who had graduated from school.

"Sungbong, I didn't go abroad to study. I've opened an academy instead. Would you like to come and help out a bit?"

The general music academy that Mr. Park had opened with his wife was a place where they provided instruction geared for school entrance examinations, gave vocalization lessons, taught students who wanted to study music as a hobby, and offered opportunities for applied music. Charged with the hope that I would be able to continue singing at his academy, I ran there as fast as I could.

There were plenty of things I could help out with without having to look for them. I helped out by sticking soundproof sponges that looked like egg crates on practice room walls and cleaning the messy academy thoroughly. The experience I had of working as an odd-job worker at construction sites came in handy; the experience I had from delivering newspapers and distributing flyers also came in handy. There were around four thousand student recruitment flyers to distribute, but Mr. Park's younger colleagues at the academy were too slow and would tire easily. And it didn't look right that Mr. Park was distributing advertisements himself. I snatched the flyers from his hands and ran outside.

I ran wildly from place to place, plugging the flyers into the postbox of every house, sticking them on telephone poles, leaving them on building staircases, sticking them on notice boards in apartment buildings, and handing them out to passersby. My body, trained by all the delivery work, moved by itself. To be honest, as a part-time flyer distributer, I had sometimes given away bunches of flyers to grannies who went around collecting discarded paper, but I didn't throw away a single sheet of Mr. Park's flyers. My feet, running around carrying the flyers, and my hands folding and inserting them into postboxes, felt light at the thought that I still had the possibility to learn and practice singing. Even Mr. Park complimented me for working so well.

"Where are you living these days, Sungbong? Are you still at the night school?"

"No, at a gosiwon..."

He thought for a while and then said to me, "Don't pay money at gosiwon, but come stay here. Let's go, let's get your things."

We went straight to the gosiwon to move out. The man who always used to fight with me continued to provoke me even as I stepped out.

"Is the cocky brat finally leaving?"

When Mr. Park heard that, he glared at him angrily.

"Who are you to be talking like that to my student? Come here, you!"

On the outside, I stopped him from fighting on my behalf, but on the inside, I was both excited and encouraged. "My student"—there was nothing in this world I could depend on like those two words from Mr. Park.

That's how I began to live at his academy. I ate jajangmyeon with him, got washed up in the veranda, sang in the practice rooms, and then slept on the plush sofa placed in a corner of the lobby. Even though it was not a residential space, I felt that I was finally, and for the first time, living like a proper human being.

I Want to Meet Friends and Go to School

A MESSY INTERIOR, with an old sofa and a small steam stove, a small faucet in the veranda, but a place where music never ceased, where I could sing to my heart's content, and where there was someone who called me his student and had taken me in: that was my teacher's academy and my sweet home.

Mr. Park's academy started out with a few kids in town. Until it became well established in the neighborhood, he actually lived there and devoted himself to gathering students. Apart from the time I spent delivering papers, I also helped out at the academy. Mr. Park was not so skilled at using the computer, so I gave him assistance on things that could be done on it and even taught the elementary kids what I knew. I was careful that quarrels would not break out because of me and endeavored to maintain good relations with people, at least at the academy. I didn't have to try so hard, in fact, as I easily got close to the people I met through music.

Some students at the academy started calling me hyeong and oppa.* Living in that environment infused me with the hope that I would be able to get along well with people, and that perhaps I was now capable of communicating with them. Along with the hope, I also began to have an ardent desire: "I also want to meet friends and go to school!"

"Mr. Park, I have a dream I want to fulfill."

---

* The word that girls and women use to address older brothers.

"A dream? Tell me about it."

"I would like to go to high school."

"Why school?"

"I want to experience wearing a school uniform."

"Which high school?"

"I don't think I'd be able to adjust if I went to a normal high school; I'd like to learn singing at an arts high school."

He rubbed his forehead for some time.

"Arts high school would be a challenge even once you got in…"

After some time, however, he said, "Okay, that would be the right way. Let's give it a shot. Even if you don't make it, there's no one to criticize."

I didn't think that I wouldn't make it. Even now, when I want to do something, the idea that I will not be able to make it never crosses my mind. It's not confidence or anything. Perhaps it's because I'd never had the experience of weighing out things by measuring situations front and back. Realizing the desire to make friends with my peers and to wear a school uniform shouldn't be such an impossible thing.

"Wouldn't I be just like the others once I wear a school uniform?"

That was the biggest reason that I began to have hope. I'd heard that for the arts high school entrance exam, your family needed to be well off if you were in the instrumental division, because it was important to have a good instrument. It was a world where it was inevitable that out of two people with the same amount of talent, the one with the more expensive and higher-quality instrument would win. So it was greatly fortunate that I did vocal music. Even if I had no money, it was possible to simply rely on my voice and to go for the challenge.

Mr. Park and I immediately began to prepare for the entrance exam. He looked up application announcements and found that I had to sing two songs for the audition to pass the exam. The songs that he chose for me were the Italian art songs "Sebben Crudele" and "Non t'amo più."

"You'll need to know the sorrow of love in order to sing these songs well."

I thought of the noona I had to part with when she went to live with a loan shark: she was my first love on the streets.

"I probably know about it better than you."

Even after noona, I'd suffered plenty of heartaches. Mr. Park gave me lessons that focused on vocalization technique, breathing, and diction to sing these songs. That was when I first discovered diction. It's a narrative skill; in other words, it concerns where to put the accents when pronouncing the lyrics, and how to express them in order to deliver the story and the meaning finely and precisely. When I learned one thing from Mr. Park, I would return to him with ten more questions. He too felt my determination and helped me as best he could. I had to put in ten times—no, a hundred times—more effort to catch up with students who'd studied music systematically since childhood. I sang the audition songs more than two hundred times per day in the narrow practice rooms of the academy. It was my first head-on challenge in music.

In this way, I spent almost one year preparing for the audition, singing diligently and doing part-time jobs. Nonetheless I felt restless as the audition day approached. I'd practiced singing for only a short period of time compared to the others. I became more and more worried about whether I'd be able to beat outstanding students who had studied singing for a long time and succeeded in the audition. I really wanted to make it through the audition, so I stoked my competitive spirit. A few months before the entrance exam, I pressed Mr. Park for lessons, even though he had become busy with his work at the academy.

"Our dear Sungbong will be taking a school entrance exam. Please keep him in your prayers especially."

When Mr. Park told the church about me, they included my name during the prayer time set aside for examinees. The deacons at the church also treated me many times to nutritious meals.

"You need to eat well to sing well. Eat lots."

Then the audition day came. When I arrived, I saw cars lined up in front of the building where the exam was held. Students carrying instruments stepped out of the cars and well-dressed parents took their children to the audition room. As I had expected, there were many of them who showed the air of privilege. Having humbly clumped to the audition room, I tried hard to keep myself from becoming dispirited.

"So what? When I pass the audition, they'll all just be my friends."

When my turn came, I went and stood before the audition panel, and discovered, to my dismay, how much I was trembling. I tried to be confident, but as the teachers' questions went on, it became more and more difficult to keep my composure.

"Did you take school qualification exams?"

"…Yes."

"You have no parents?"

The resident register document I had brought had no parents listed in it. I answered yes, barely holding myself back from asking why they were asking that question. It wasn't my fault that I didn't have any.

"Let's hear you sing."

I barely managed to suppress my nerves and sang the songs I had prepared. The sound seemed to ring well, but my intonation was off quite often. To add to that, my voice vibrated with a quiver because I was so nervous. Like the bleating of a goat, extreme vibrato seemed to be happening automatically. I'd thought that I wouldn't be trembling with nerves, but there, I'd bombed it.

"Please go outside."

When I finished the two songs, the teachers on the audition panel ordered me out without any expression on their faces. There was no way to tell from their expression how my singing had gone. I had to wait two suspenseful weeks for the results to be announced. Mr. Park told me to keep up my hopes, but he didn't look that hugely hopeful. The total score was the sum of my middle school academic grades and the performance score. I felt ever more anxious since I had barely passed the middle school qualification exam—at the 60 percent cut-off line—and couldn't place great hopes on that.

Then came a day when the anxious wait was replaced by a parade of joyful events. I'd hit the jackpot.

The first reason for joy was my sudden acceptance into Daejeon Arts High School. They selected thirteen students, and I passed as number thirteen. Was my way into the world possible only by barely getting in? It felt like I was dangling by a thread, but anyway I'd made it. I'd passed!

"What? Really?"

When I broke the news about my acceptance, Mr. Park looked at me incredulously. Had he been doubting my success? When I repeated the news to him several times to prove its veracity, he finally smiled brightly.

"My dearest Sungbong, you made it!"

Before the joy had a chance to subside, a second and an even better thing happened: I'd found my own room! How could I ever express the thrill I felt then? I'll never forget the time when I set out with Mr. Park to find a room. He searched for information about several houses, then met a landlord, lowered the deposit, and signed a contract for my room. He and a deacon from the church got together the deposit money for me. The room was a half-basement studio apartment. My heart began to ache as I watched that empty space fill up item by item with the household furnishings brought by the church deacons and deaconesses. For a long time, I had never shed tears easily, but my heart reacted by itself. The computer brought by Mr. Park adorned the finale.

"I know Sungbong likes this."

My pots, my plates, my desk, my room, and my computer. Was this a dream? Well, I soon knew that it wasn't a dream but reality, because that room was in fact being shared by an enormous number of cockroaches. When I awoke at night and turned on the lamp, I would find that the walls had turned completely black—they were covered with cockroaches. They moved in swarms, and they fell on my face while I was sleeping, tried to crawl into my ears, and even flew up and stuck on my face while I was doing business in the bathroom. I didn't mind it too much, though, as I finally had a place I could call my own.

Last but not least of the joys was that I had become a recipient of the basic livelihood security. The dong office made me a youth identity card, and when I opened a bank account, the security began to come in regularly. I could pay my monthly rent with that money.

As part of the security recipient benefits, I could receive state support for the high school enrollment fee and school meals. In other words, all problems with food and lodging had totally vanished. I'd had no answers as to how I'd be able to pay for school, and how I'd be able to get my meals once school started, so the timing couldn't have been better. I was no longer an abandoned orphan boy living out on the streets but had the affiliation and identity as one of Korea's official high school students—and in school for the captivating study of singing at that!

I'd been living in dark despair without even a name for over ten years, and three rays of light had come to shine on me all at once: a space all for myself, a minimal but sufficient budget, and school.

I went to get fitted for a school uniform, which, for the longest time, I'd longed for. The gu office¹ also gave me a fifty-thousand-won gift card to use for buying the uniform. Never once had I bought my own clothes since I was born, and clueless about how I could buy them, I badgered Mr. Park

---

* Borough office.

to go shopping with me. Our school uniform was in formal style. When I tried on a pair of dark-navy trousers and a jacket, I found that they fit me well even though they were off the rack. I wore a dress shirt inside, which was one of the two that a church deacon had given to me as presents. The necktie I bought was in zip style and I could tie it simply by pulling a strap—I didn't even have to worry about how to tie it. I came home in the uniform and kept wearing it at home, and every so often, I went to look at myself in the mirror. "Finally I'm wearing it too!" That night when my dream came true, I was boundlessly happy.

Classroom Days: Musical yet Cruel

SCHOOL FINALLY BEGAN. I put on my uniform and headed to school, as though it was something I had always done. Although it was cold, my heart felt warm. There were a lot of girls my age at the school. Around ninety students were music majors, and classes were divided into two groups of forty-five students, forty of whom were girls. Voice majors accounted for thirteen of the total freshman class. Hopeful about the upcoming life at school, I was in a flutter throughout the entire entrance ceremony.

The excitement ended there, however. Perhaps I'd had too high an expectation about school. When I entered the classroom, the atmosphere was quite different from what I'd expected. The other students knew each other because they were classmates from elementary or middle schools. They also made friends easily with each other because they had the same teacher. I hadn't really worried about making friends, but despite having taken qualification exams, I couldn't really join in their circles. Some of them exuded the privileged air of having lived in good homes without major ordeals in life, and the other students also seemed to have had mostly easy lives and had reasonably good looks. If I had to compare us, I'd say that I was like an alien that had crawled up from some bottommost plane far removed from them all. We all shared our identity as Koreans, and although I'd lived just a bit differently from the others, I felt as though I were sitting alone in a foreign school where I couldn't speak the language. The only ones I felt the slightest kinship with were the kind with something of the bully spirit. I comforted myself that the distance I felt was just an issue in my heart and not the actual reality; I made an effort to be friendly. From the start, however, friends paired up among themselves to accompany and sing, so it was difficult for me to even find an accompanist.

"Do you think you could accompany me?"

"Why should I?"

"Because I want to be friends with you from now on."

"But then what's wrong with your eyes? They look scary."

"They're just like that. I'm not a scary kid."

What was the matter? Did my eyes seem strange? I went to the toilet and looked in the mirror. My eyes looked perfectly cute to me.

I also had serious problems with my speech. Oftentimes when someone told a joke, I would be the only one to take it seriously; likewise, when someone said something serious, I would take it as a joke and laugh it away. Perhaps it was because I'd lived in a different environment from them. I didn't watch television, so I couldn't understand any of the everyday slang they used. As things progressed this way, I became more and more bewildered. For instance, when someone playfully pushed me, I spontaneously blurted out, "What the hell do you want?" And when someone asked, "Sungbong, where did you go for middle school?" I replied, "You cracked or what?" My intention was to express myself in as friendly a manner as possible. "Oh, why doesn't it work?" I felt frustrated by my own confounded self.

"Why do you always have to pick a fight the moment someone says something?" kids would ask. When the situation sank to a point where resentful feelings began to crop up, friends began to fear or dislike me.

During lunch break, I would set out alone to climb the hill behind the school and get lost in delusive thoughts.

"If I were to get close to a girl, her parents would come and pour curses on me and beat me up awfully, right?"

The other students had respectable backgrounds, and it seemed that a guy like me—who was mixed among them, and hiding the fact about having no parents and being one year older than the rest—wasn't going to be tolerated. I would feel comfortable around the kids who came to Mr. Park's academy or the men I met on the streets, but the wall that I felt separating me from my peers was larger and harder than I'd expected. As such days went on, people's random whispers began to sound like gossip about me. "He took qualification exams before coming here." "He's lost one year of school. Don't act like you know him." There was no way that I could check whether people were actually saying such things, but the excitement I'd felt about meeting friends my age vanished instantly, and I became wrapped up in an inferiority complex.

"Maybe school is one of those things that will end up not working out despite setting my hopes on it."

I had to murmur even those words in the rear hills. And alone.

The classes were a problem as well. I'd never sat for such extended periods of time other than, say, on the plush chairs in Internet cafés, so sitting on hard chairs and having to look to the front all the time seemed impossible to get used to. Then I had to study subjects like Korean, English, and math that I'd not studied step by step from the basics. Studying these subjects was like taking me to some space exploration. Then too, having to face the same prison-like atmosphere I'd felt when I went to take the qualification exams weighed heavily on my heart. If the streets I'd lived in were a world where physical stabbings took place, school appeared to be a world where mental stabbing took place.

It came as a relief that I was attending an arts high school where they at least had classes I liked. At least during music classes, I paid full attention with my eyes wide open. During sight-singing classes, I practiced vocalizing on the [a] vowel, and in music dictation classes, I trained to hear and identify pitches. My right ear continued to have ringing sounds, but I strove to concentrate with my good left ear. I got to know exact things about sheet music that I had only learned about over other people's shoulders in the past, and was eventually able to write down music as well. They were things that I'd always wanted to learn. The harmony and counterpoint I learned during music theory classes were a bit of a headache, but they were definitely not things that could be learned by wits and tact, so I studied them with focus. There was also choir class. Since I'd been in a church choir, choir class felt familiar, but it was challenging at the same time. I still had the hope that it would be possible for me to have intimate relationships with people through the mediation of music.

"I also do classical music like you all."

What awaited me, however, was a humiliating experience in performance class. When it was my turn to stand in front of the other students, those who were swearing looked at me with a skewed gaze. "Do I need to sing in front of those guys?" I opened my mouth with an unpleasant feeling, and my voice was off.

The teacher yelled. "I can't hear you well. Try again."

I collected my wits and sang again. This time I was in tune, but I struggled with low intonation. My emotions must have begun to work up because my voice began to break.

"You'll have to give up pretty soon. You might influence the other kids."

His poisonous comment made me hot on the back of my neck. Then I went to Mr. Park's academy and practiced with boiling spite: "We'll see what happens—I'm going to be better than all of you." After repeated practice I made a great return at the next class. The invective teacher finally gave a nod.

"You have a nice sound—quite good quality. Good vibrato too. But you lack a lot of basics."

Blasted basics! Among the thirteen voice major students in my class, some had parents who were singers and some had already learned singing for five to six years, starting with children's choir during elementary school. I had learned singing over other people's shoulders, so there was no way my basics could be as solid as theirs. It seemed that I was going to be the perennial worst student in the whole class.

When it came to music, I had the will to escape always being the last one in class; so I devoted myself to practicing performance and ended up finishing the freshman year with the fifth-highest score in performance. Later, I even went up to being the one with the third-highest score. I never once received the lowest score in performance during all my years in school.

"You sound quite good."

When the other students gave comments like that, I was really proud of myself. During technique classes, however, I was definitely differentiated from the others. Since I'd had no money to pay for lessons, I couldn't learn technique from outside teachers. Wasn't the school supposed to teach everything? There wasn't anyone I could turn to to ask that question. Sitting alone in a practice room with neither a teacher nor an accompanist, I recalled a comment Mr. Park once made: "Arts high school would be a challenge even after you got in. It's so expensive..."

With no money to learn music and no basics, I felt like the only thing in life I'd been given plenty of was my inferiority complex. The rich get richer and the poor get poorer. "Who am I to be doing classical music anyway?" Vocal music just seemed too extravagant.

The two songs I'd sung for the audition—"Sebben Crudele" and "Non t'amo più"—felt as though they had been predictions of my life.
Music seemed like a cruel woman
who rejected my love and went on to mock me.
Did it then mean that I shouldn't love anymore?

My inferiority complex twisted and turned upon itself and finally transformed into violence. The least provocation led me to fight.

"What you looking at?"

"How dare a mere freshman say that to an upperclassman?"

"What do you mean 'upperclassman'? Fuck!"

Thus beating up others and getting beaten up, I grew weary of school life. I let out a sigh, lying in the corner of my room, where cockroaches—undefeated by exterminating chemicals—were dominating the space like some symphony orchestra. I probably appeared like a cockroach too to other people: they seemed to be grossed out by me. It felt like the bully kids among my classmates who sometimes visited my house were also merely using my place as a hideout to drink and smoke. When the train of my thoughts led me to such notions, I decided to stop myself there and quit school once and for all. I was sorry to Mr. Park and didn't want to tell him about it. He'd sent me to school and had even found a house for me, and I couldn't possibly cause him any more trouble.

I went to the homeroom teacher and carefully confided in him my worries.

"So I'll quit school."

"Okay. Quit."

When he consented so easily, I felt sore all of a sudden. Even he seemed to be thinking of me as some extraneous being rather than understanding who I was. My pent-up frustration exploded like a bomb. Upon leaving the teacher's room, I broke the first window I saw. The crashing sounded like my heart breaking. That was how I stormed out of the school.

Helping Hands: Children's Foundation

And even if your beginning was small, your end will be very great.

(Job 8:7)

WHILE I WAS skipping out on school and worrying in the corner of my room, a Bible verse I'd heard at church came to my mind. It seemed commonplace enough, but it was a message that I wanted to depend on. I hoped that those words were stronger than the reality of this irrational world, where the rich got richer and the poor got poorer.

I shut myself in my studio apartment, thinking over things: if I dropped out of school like this, the state aid I received as a welfare recipient would stop and the house would also have to go. At the same time, I would have to give up on music, which I loved so much. But if I were to go back to school, I wasn't going to be able to adapt; and besides, I had no money.

So I was just whiling away my days under blankets as I had no solutions for either, when one day, my chronic illness—encephalomeningitis—came back. It was an illness that came at least twice a year. Then, like before, I had a temperature that went up to forty degrees centigrade, and I lay in my room day and night in that feverish condition groaning in pain. My decision not to go to school had been a decisive one all right, but now even if I wanted to, I couldn't change my mind because I was sick. I became half-conscious with a high fever.

When I could begin to move again somewhat, Mr. Park, having heard my news, came to pay a visit.

"Sungbong, if you want to at least become like the others and build a foundation that gives you a chance to change your life, you'll need a diploma. So just be patient and sit tight."

"I really can't adjust."

"Hey, just remember how much you'd wanted to go to school and be patient."

After he left, my homeroom teacher from school also came by and tried to convince me. Students from ordinary backgrounds might give up on their dreams when they couldn't afford lessons, but I didn't want to be a loser.

"Yeah, I'll just earn the lesson money myself."
I made up my mind to try one last time and kicked away the blankets,
trusting in the Bible verse that my end would be great.

When school ended at 6:00 p.m., I went to work at part-time jobs: washing dishes at a Japanese restaurant and doing night shifts for parcel delivery services at a convenience store. Later, I also worked early mornings sorting items at the distribution center of the parcel delivery service company. I had to earn the darn lesson money.

Washing dishes put heavy strain on my back, and having found washing gloves uncomfortable, I just used my bare hands, which got them swollen. My soles got swollen too because of running around doing delivery errands. Unloading the parcel boxes from vehicles that poured in endlessly from the distribution center, sorting them, then reloading them, I would sometimes end up covering my whole body with medicated patches. As a novice, I would always end up carrying the heavy boxes. When I became a bit more used to the work, I developed the sense to know whether a box was heavy or light just by looking at it.

Working that way all night at part-time jobs made me crave for sleep at school. During regular subject classes—not music—I would make up for the sleep I missed. Being an arts high school, they had a bit of a liberal atmosphere, and while some teachers banned sleeping in class, others left me alone.

No matter how hard school was for me, one thing I liked about it was that they gave you lunch. I got the lunch money as welfare aid, so the fact that I didn't have to worry about meals helped me to overcome my fundamental worry. At the distribution center they gave you food at 3:00 a.m.; you basically filled up your stomach sitting on cardboard paper laid out on the dusty workshop floor. It wasn't anything like really eating, but being able to have a meal alone was a thing to be grateful for.

The parcel service work ended at around 6:30 a.m. Afterward I would come home, rest a bit, shower, and then go to school, and that settled into a pattern. Working two part-time jobs at night deprived me of sleep, and I was often late for school. I got interrogated about tardiness, getting my nipples twisted and all by the homeroom teacher, but I was able to get a monthly salary that way. With that money, I too could start receiving private lessons from a teacher.

One lesson cost one hundred thousand won; so just receiving two lessons per week for a month would amount to eight hundred thousand won, which was an enormous sum. In addition, I had to pay forty thousand won per hour to the piano accompanist; and having to go to the lesson teacher's place incurred costs for transportation and meals, so I had to earn a lot of money. The budget wasn't just tight; it was way over what I could afford even if I were to put in all the money I made.

I'd walked all the way to school to save on transportation cost and had deprived myself of sleep in order to work, yet I still wasn't able to get lessons properly like everyone else. That made me crestfallen each time I went to attend a special lecture class. I searched for places where I would be able to get some more help. The basic livelihood allowance that came in from the dong office was barely enough to provide for the very basic necessities.

"Sungbong, the money you take is three times the amount for normal recipients."

They always said that to me at the dong office because of the expensive arts high school fees. Things being the way they were, I felt ashamed to ask them for more help.

Then one day, I heard this from Mr. Park: "Sungbong, I got in touch with the children's foundation, and you might be able to get support from them if you're lucky. Try writing down your story nicely in a letter and send it to them."

Although Mr. Park was busy with his work at the academy, he made every effort to help me. So I wrote, though poorly, a frank letter about the story of my life, and about how I wanted to study music but that I was pinched with poverty. The saying that every cloud has a silver lining must be true, because upon receiving the letter, the children's foundation contacted me and asked me to meet up with them. Ms. Gyeongeun Kim, a social worker at the foundation, confirmed some facts about me, then told me that she would definitely connect me with a sponsor.

"You've been through so much. We'll help you now."

If Mr. Park was like a father to me—so much so that he would be asked by the church people whether I was his accidental love child—Ms. Kim from the children's foundation was like the mother I never had. Other people had parents, whereas I had parent-like guardians. I had only known what to hate about the world and not how to be thankful, and there had been no way to find out. Finding hands that were able to lift me up helped me to realize that once you had the will to live, you no longer had to be alone.

After that, I started to receive encouraging news from the children's foundation: that they'd found a few sponsors and that they were going to make me a welfare recipient as a child head of household. Once you became a child head of household, you received another government subsidy in addition to the basic livelihood allowance, and you could even get scholarships given by companies or other support organizations. If that came true, then I might be able to afford the lessons. I couldn't make up for all the expenses of studying music through the social welfare system, but if I were to combine it with my part-time work, I would have a thread of hope.

Finally, after Ms. Kim's exhaustive effort running around city hall, the gu office, and the dong office, I was able to receive aid as the child head of household. But the fact that I had parents on the family register and the doubt that a kid like me could ever exist had remained obstacles. Those parents were forever mere hindrances to my life! I found out later on that my father had remarried a foreign woman and had children. When I discovered that, I felt rage in my heart.

"Please help me meet my father."

I made an appeal to my social work guardian. Having reached that point in my life, I could no longer hold back my desire to meet my father, to question him and contend with him.

She searched for my father's residence through the dong office and then went there with me. It was in Jeollabuk-do,* and I was depressed the entire journey. But that was nothing compared to the wretchedness I tasted upon arrival.

We had traveled a long way, but when she got in touch with him, the person called Father said, "I can't meet up, so just go back."

I wasn't curious about what my father looked like. I just wanted to know why he'd done what he'd done, and found it simply absurd that he wouldn't show up. On my way back, not having succeeded in meeting him in the end, the guardian asked, "Are you okay…Sungbong?"

"I'm okay," I said calmly.

---

* Jeollabuk-do: North Jeolla Province (*buk* means "north" in Korean; *do* means "province").

"Don't be too shocked…Everything will go okay now."

I wasn't shocked. The desire to kill him and to kill myself simply kept crisscrossing in my heart. I was on the verge of exploding, having been abandoned yet a second time. It was as though the first time hadn't been enough. However, after going through all the complications and finally being offered aid as a child head of household with the help of Ms. Gyeongeun Kim, I couldn't show my temper in front of the people who were helping me. So I decided to hold it in.

Now I could manage to hold things in little by little.
I was now a child head of household, responsible for myself.
Since I had no such thing as parents in my life,
the only thing that mattered now was music…

I recommenced my lessons. Circumstances had improved since I received aid and sponsorship, but I continued to work in order to balance the tight budget, to pay for lessons and living expenses. Welfare recipients are not allowed to work, but gritting my teeth, I went on in order to have more lessons.

Music and reality: no matter how cruel they are, I will continue to hold up. I pulled myself together, thinking of the lyrics of "Sebben Crudele" that I had sung for my school audition. I remembered the meaning of the Italian words that I had memorized to express the song's emotions. Perhaps what had drawn me to vocal music from the very start was the fact that it allowed me to express things that I could not express through words.

Sebben, crudele
mi fai languir,
Sempre fedele
ti voglio amar.
Con la lunghezza

del mio servir
la tua fierezza
saprò stancar*

I thought of the words over and over again while practicing that song, and I was determined not to lose faith that my end would be very great.

It was around then that I went church shopping all over downtown Daejeon. The Daejeon Joongang Church I had attended with Mr. Park always took good care of me, but I wanted to be less of a burden to Mr. Park and to be a bit more independent. So I visited the church attended by the deacon who sponsored me through the dong office. I also went looking for a church with an atmosphere or sermons that felt right for me. I'd returned from not having succeeded in meeting my father. Feeling ever lonelier, I had perhaps wanted to find a place where there were people who would love me, so that I would be able to respond to and be affirmed by their love.

I continued to serve in the choirs at the other churches. They took me in when I told them that I was a voice major at the Daejeon Arts High School. Though I tried going from one church to the next, being there alone was hard wherever I went. I made several circuits, then finally settled back at the Daejeon Joongang Church where Mr. Park went.

I felt uneasy to be dependent on human love and God's love.
Would a day ever come when I would be able to embrace love wholeheartedly?
Love just seemed so difficult to me.

---

* Although, cruel love,
you make me languish,
I will always
love you true.
With the patience
of my serving
I will be able to tire out
your pride.

Singing despite It All, Because It's the Way I Had to Go

I MET MANY lesson teachers. I tried to seek out different kinds of teachers in my search for the right teacher, and to get ample, all-around instructions.

"To do vocal music, it'd be good for you to put on some weight."

That was the most frequent comment I heard. I continued to be of slender build. Even though I didn't do any physical exercises, not getting enough sleep and working rigorously gave me no chance to put on weight.

The next most frequent comment I got was that I had a good voice, but that my musicality was wanting. It showed that I had not received basic, step-by-step music education.

"It's just imitation—things aren't really organized."

I took such comments as a matter of course. Vocal music wasn't just about singing a song in any way you wanted to, but was undeniably a branch of classical music. To be a vocal musician, it was necessary to learn all the basic details. I relearned things like singing in tune, being in rhythm, and applying correct diction from the beginning.

"Where does the difference between voice and instruments lie? In the delivery of rich emotions through lyrics."

My lesson teachers taught me music and technique in many different ways. There was a teacher who focused on fixing my singing posture, and then there was another who told me exactly how to make a staccato or legato, which adds variation in the expression of the musical beat of individual notes. I also learned how to use my breath by stretching the diaphragm with the right amount of pressure. Overall, however, they were

170

the things that I'd learned from Mr. Park. I was frustrated that I had to learn the same things over again from other teachers, but I considered it as making a thorough review to master the basic skills that I was said to lack.

When I began to master the basic skills through those lessons, I began to awaken slowly to the world of vocal music. Students from good families received lessons from expensive teachers, but after hearing them during performance classes at school, I felt they sang a bit less well than I did. Well, that was, of course, my subjective judgment. I thought that because they didn't have to pay for the lessons with the money they earned, they were probably also not as desperate when it came to learning. Such thoughts allowed me to engage in practice with the confidence that I would be able to get ahead of them in the future. While working part time, I would practice during spare moments the squat jumps and the breathing method—whereby I had to pant like a dog on a summer day—that the teachers had taught during lessons.

Having met many teachers, I soon realized that there were good teachers who were right for me, and those who weren't.

"Who taught you that way? You'll just have to get rid of everything and learn from scratch starting with vocalization technique."

During those times, I was really offended because it seemed like they were belittling Mr. Park. Some teachers wouldn't teach anything but just yell at me the whole time. When I sang light because they told me to sing light, they would yell at me because it was light, and when I sang heavy because they told me to sing heavy, they would yell at me because it was heavy. Then there were teachers who wouldn't teach properly but spend a lot of time talking about how I didn't know the basics in breathing. A university professor whom I went to visit with great resolve didn't instruct me himself but simply dumped me on his student-cum-manager. I'd gone through much ordeal to earn money to take those singing lessons, and yet the teachers, not the least bit mindful of how desperate I was, lacked sincerity in their teaching. I felt mistreated and was sorrowful.

Among them, there was a master-class teacher from whom I learned a lot. He was a renowned first-generation tenor hero, nearing his seventies and living in Seoul. Listening to his high notes would unconsciously send vibrations throughout my body. Without any plan or idea, but driven by the desire to learn music the right way, I boarded a train to Seoul and headed for his apartment. But he wouldn't even consider taking someone from high school like me as his student.

"This is so unexpected…How are you ever going to manage coming all the way here from Daejeon? No."

"I can manage. I will not go back until you take me as your student."

I knelt outside his apartment and waited. I sat there all day, but he didn't take me. I went back to his apartment the next day and knelt before the door, and seeing how sincere I was, he decided to accept me as his student. The first lesson with him was severe.

"Are you really a music student? Your intonation, for one, is terrible. It's a wonder how you ever got into an arts high school."

He was flabbergasted listening to how I sang, but he took me up to a whole new level through his teaching. He played the piano himself and sang together with me most of the lesson with an overwhelmingly powerful voice. His lessons were also at an entirely different price level, but they were worth it in every way. They cost one hundred thousand won per ten minutes, so I only took ten-minute lessons. I traveled from Daejeon to Seoul just for those ten minutes. It took around four hours to get there and back, and I would spend the journey with my music sheet in front of me, listening to music and going over the parts that he had pointed out. Then when I came home, I would put his concert video on repeat mode on the computer and strain with effort to follow along.

Having to handle lessons, school, and part-time jobs all at once, I was outrageously deprived of sleep. But I remember the teacher's compliments about how great my determination was, and how I seemed to finally understand a little bit of what singing was about, so I was able to bear with those grueling days.

It was one of those strenuous and exhausting days when an accident finally happened. I was working at the distribution center early in the morning, and on that particular day, the place was packed with a high volume of items, including heavy things like rice. I was very busy and was sweating profusely. It might have been due to fatigue, because I was having a hard time staying awake while at work. My mind would blank out every now and then. I was sorting things on a rail, the highest elevated place in the warehouse. Numerous boxes were passed in front of me, and I continued to move my body drowsily. I must have eventually dozed off, because I lost my footing and fell from the top of the high rail. It felt like a long time before my body landed on the ground. The moment I hit the floor, an enormous pain rose from my knee, and I let out a scream.

I was immediately rushed to the emergency room. They told me at the hospital that the cruciate ligament on my knee was ruptured. They said that it would actually have been better if a bone had broken when I fell, but because my joint had twisted instead, the injury was more severe. I had to be hospitalized for over a month. I had no choice but to stay in the hospital, but that meant I could neither earn money nor take singing lessons. What kind of disaster had befallen me now? It felt as though my will to ride the wave and do my best had been snapped like the injured knee.

Lying on the hospital bed staring at the ceiling with nothing to do, I was visited by an unwelcome guest from a long time ago: the state of mental panic. My determination and resolve about music had completely disappeared, and I didn't know why I was singing. All I could do was to ask myself what use there could be living such a hard life.

The hospital bills were also an issue. I was a Class 1 recipient of the National Health Insurance, so the government was assisting with the medical expenses for the items covered by the insurance. However, the amount that was not covered was considerable, adding up to three million eight hundred thousand won. It wasn't an amount I could afford. I just had to hold out and tell them I didn't have money, and that they should just cut open my stomach.* I even went up to the hospital rooftop, contemplating suicide, but the door to the rooftop was firmly locked. Then the hospital took the trouble to find a support fund of three million won that I could receive as an aid recipient. But I still could not make up for the shortfall in medical bills. The hospital seemed to take pity on my circumstances, and the staff suggested a measure.

"You said that you were a voice major, right? There is going to be a benefit concert at the end of the year at the hospital. Would you be able to sing for the occasion?"

Singing? Although I didn't have the desire to, I participated in the event and sang. The event title was "Benefit Concert for Disadvantaged In-patients." Quite unexpectedly, through that concert, I realized my singing could benefit someone in practical ways. The people who attended that concert liked the songs I sang, and the donation collected that day was sent to a poor island boy who was suffering from a malignant brain tumor. Suddenly I was reminded of the gum-selling big brother, and the unconditional help from Mr. Park and the social work guardians. When I began to see myself as someone who offered help to another person—and who had offered real help—the mental panic that had come from being hospitalized subsided a little. It was a strange experience.

Because of that concert, an article about me was featured in *Daejeon Daily*, and my story was also broadcast over radio. After the article, titled "The Dream to Become a Vocalist—Is It Too Great an Ambition?" was published, I received encouragement and support from many people, telling me to stick with my dream and work toward becoming a successful vocalist. I received ten kilograms of fresh oysters from someone as an encouragement, and another sent me chicken. There was also someone who sent me scholarship money to supplement my medical bills. There were too

---

* A Korean expression that means "Sue me. I have nothing left."

many fresh oysters, so I shared them with other people. At that time, I decided to contact Mr. Park and the social work guardians from the children's foundation, Ms. Kim and Ms. Hyeonjung Yoo. They were upset with me for not informing them about the accident. "You got hurt; why did you try to settle the matter yourself?" Despite being scolded, I was encouraged. I was assured that if something ever happened to me again, there would be people who would step forward to offer their help.

After I was discharged from the hospital, I wanted to somehow repay the people who had supported me through the children's foundation. They were always giving me something, but this time I wanted to give something back to them. I volunteered to participate in the Christmas party that they had held at the foundation. It was to be attended by the sponsors affiliated with the children's foundation. I couldn't sing well, but my sponsors were happy when they heard me sing.

I'd always only received things from them,
so it brought me humble satisfaction that as a musician I could give something in
return, however small it might be.
If the reason I did music until then was simply because I liked it, from that point
on, I began to believe, however vaguely, that singing was the way I had to go.

Dreaming of Becoming a College Student like the Others

――――――― ❧ ―――――――

THANKS TO THE hospital event, my story was featured in the newspaper and broadcast media. This shifted my status in school, unfortunately not in a positive direction. The things that I had been hiding so well had been debunked. I had deceived my friends in schools, telling them that my parents were in the United States and that they were professors. I had made up all these stories because I wanted to narrow the gap between us. However, my real story was now finally exposed: that I was a kid who had been abandoned at an orphanage, that my parents had given me up, and that I was a social-aid recipient surviving on welfare benefits and barely scraping a living. The classmates with whom I was already on bad terms thereupon began to glare at me as if they were making an interrogation, and whispers began to sound wildly behind me: "So he's an orphan?" "He's a bluffer." "Just as I thought—he doesn't really fit in with the rest of us." "'Professor's son' is a fib."

The secret cord that had allowed me to keep my head up among them had disappeared. Ashamed, I immediately stopped going to school. I resolved that I was finished with school forever.

Having heard my news, Mr. Park paid another visit.

"When people get hurt, they sometimes also tend to become weak hearted. Just consider it as going through a slump, and let's overcome it quickly."

"It's not a slump. It's the reality."

"You only have half of your time left to go. You've come this far, so you can hold out for the remaining half. Let's just get the diploma, yes?"

"No. I can't do it anymore."

When I remained adamant about dropping out of school despite his persuasion, Mr. Park lost his temper.

"What do you mean you can't? Think about everything you've gone through so far! Darn it, do as you like, young man!"

I'd never seen him get so mad before. When he left, guilt and sorrow filled my heart to the brim. Just as my head felt like it was going to burst with worry, the children's foundation guardians also came by.

"Sungbong, what's wrong?"

"Can't I transfer to a different school? Not an arts high school but just a regular high school?"

"We've looked things up, but the admission deadlines have passed."

"Is there any other way?"

"There aren't any alternative schools that suit you either. Couldn't you just continue attending your school? You need to study music."

Aaargh, darn it. Music—yes, of course I need to study it. I went back to worrying again and again, but finally, that word moved me. There was no way other than to give up being obstinate and to return to school. It was embarrassing, but half of me felt sorry to my guardians and the other half felt that I had to go on with music no matter what people said. It was perhaps more embarrassing that my resolve to pursue my path in singing had broken down so easily.

When I returned to school, I put more distance between my classmates and me than before. I returned to the daily schedule of working day and night and taking lessons. It was tiresome and exhausting, but when I held out patiently as Mr. Park had told me, time passed by calmly and in an orderly way.

In my sophomore year, I found out about a system at the Land & Housing Corporation through which they lend deposit money for leasing a house to child heads of household. I was able to obtain a house where there were no cockroaches, where bright sunshine entered because it was above ground level, and where I could be rid of the burden of having to pay monthly rent. Maybe because I had gotten a housing upgrade, my body also began to grow rapidly. I ate big meals to deliberately fatten my body, and I ended up weighing eighty kilograms at the end of sophomore year and up to one hundred kilograms in junior year. I believed then that having a big body would allow the voice to vibrate in a bigger physical chamber and carry greater power. When I put on weight, it felt like my voice was becoming more powerful. At the same time, my determination to pursue vocal music became stronger and greater.

When my school uniform didn't fit me anymore and I had to get it made three more times, that was when I entered my junior year. I begrudged spending money on clothes, but there was no choice other than to buy new pants whenever they tore in the legs due to my weight gain.

Toward May of junior year, the school gave only morning classes or classes twice a week with time set aside for lessons. This was because of the college entrance examination. My classmates were absorbed in preparing for their entrance exams. I couldn't help but think of going to college too, just like everyone else. It must have been because of the atmosphere. But considering my circumstances, I didn't have the conviction that I could make it to college. I received performance lessons anyway, like everyone else did, and prepared steadily. I didn't seek counseling from my guardians or receive their help on career matters; I wanted to work them out on my own.

When the college entrance season came, I sent applications to three universities. Among them, Hanyang University was where the teacher from whom I really wanted to learn taught; I also applied to two other universities.

When I went for the auditions, I realized that I wasn't as desperate or nervous as I'd been during the arts high school audition. Then, I'd trembled like a leaf because that was the first time I'd sung at such an important place. But perhaps because I'd experienced the stage continuously while in school, I was in fact able to take the college audition calmly.

I found out about the entrance and tuition fees after taking the exam. It was a formidable amount of more than ten million won. My College Scholastic Ability Test score was level nine, the lowest level. Although I thought I stood a chance of getting in since the universities placed a lot of weight on performance, it appeared that the fees would make it impossible for me to enroll even if I did pass.

Whether or not I should consider myself lucky, I did make it into two of the universities after all. The moment I confirmed my name on the universities' websites, I rejoiced for about three seconds, thinking, "Wow! Did I do well in the performance?" Then immediately I thought, "Shoot, now what? I have no money," and I became annoyed. But after a while, I began to simper. A billion won wasn't an amount that I could get together within a few days. I wasn't even eligible for loans, so even if I were to manage to pay the tuition fee right then, how would I be able to get together such a big sum of money every term? I had no confidence at all that I would be able to afford it. It was obvious that it was going to be a repetition of not being able to practice because I would start work again and then have days when I would be stressed out with music because I couldn't practice. I'd already experienced what college was like when I used to practice at the university where Mr. Park studied. As I thought ahead about how I was going to have difficulty getting along with people and adapting to the university like in my days in high school, my heart sank.

"Who do I think I am, going to college and all? Let's work toward success through singing alone. Anyway, I didn't make it to my first-choice university."

I decided to search for master classes where I could continue to learn how to sing without having to pay tuition fee. Anyway, it wasn't like I had a complex about academic achievement or anything.

Graduation day finally arrived. But I was busy with part-time work and couldn't make it to the graduation ceremony. Looking back at my school life, it seemed that I had persevered well: I'd had many troubles with class-mates, I'd tried to drop out several times but had decided to harden myself and return, I'd attended classes for the first and last time in my life, and I had considered quitting but then hadn't quit, and caused numerous worries to Mr. Park and the social work guardians...

Suddenly I didn't want to return to society. Other students were enter-ing society, but I was returning to society. It was true that my life was more like that of a manual laborer than that of a student, but if I were to leave school, I would end up living my life as a wanderer. Losing the sense of belonging was as frightening as when I had left the night school.

I still have my uniforms from high school.
I'd like to preserve that sense of belonging, though it had only been that once.
It was a place that I hated, but also a place that I missed.
It was while putting away the several school uniforms of different sizes
that I realized how I had grown from a child to an adult.
I think I also felt some sort of a chill.

To a City of Hope in Search
of a Life as a Singer

―――――――――― ❧ ――――――――――

THERE WAS A lesson teacher whom I got to know around that time. I had tried to have fun with voice; he suggested several ways to make my voice harmonize within music. Many famous singers had taken lessons from him. I went all the way to Daegu, the city where the lesson teacher lived, to get lessons, believing that he was the teacher who could guide my musical growth. I completely gave up my ambition to enter college, contacted him, and explained my situation.

"I'm not able to go to college; I'd like to try just going on with music."

Having listened to my complaints and appeals, he blurted out right away, "Really? I'll take responsibility for your life, so come down to Daegu."

It was a considerably worrisome proposal. If I went to Daegu, the entire foundation I had built in Daejeon wouldn't be there anymore, but it was a very tempting proposal. Was he serious? But what did he mean by "take responsibility for my life"? I had my doubts about him. He was, however, not a charlatan but a teacher who taught me music. Besides, I thought it couldn't be so easy for an adult to say such words about being willing to take responsibility. It was also the first time in my life that someone had said he was going to take responsibility for me.

I worried for a couple of nights and decided to discuss it with my social work guardian.

"No, Sungbong. Then you'll lose your welfare housing and also all your foundation sponsorships. I'll look for more information so that you'll be able to go to college next year. Just spend one year getting ready for next year."

Mr. Park was of course against it.

"What do you mean Daegu? Why all of a sudden? How are you going to manage after you land in a new place like that?"

My heart, however, was moved more by the wish to carve out my own future than by their opposition. I had now become an adult. Finally, I decided to stand on my own feet.

That day, with a huge bag loaded with my personal belongings, I put myself in a bus heading for Daegu. My heart was resolutely determined.

"May Daegu be my city of hope!"

The reality, however, was totally different from what I'd expected.

"Sir, here I am in Daegu."

"Why in Daegu?"

"What? Well, to get lessons from you…"

"Oh, really? I'm busy with other things now…I'll give you a lesson later."

But that couldn't be! The teacher who had told me that he was going to take responsibility for my life when I came to Daegu was suddenly telling me that he wasn't even going to give me lessons. This was awful! In order to come to Daegu, I had borrowed money from a church deacon who had sponsored me previously, and I had paid the housing deposit and all the moving expenses with it. I had to pay back the money soon; then again I was boiling with the desire to learn singing. Things were driving me nuts. Was the teacher thinking something like "I just casually threw some words at him, but oops, he's really come!" I didn't really understand the situation, but I felt cheated and at a loss as to what to do.

For now, I had to start work and pay back the money I had borrowed. I also had to start eating and living in Daegu. I looked for work here and there, and found work in a factory. It was an unfamiliar city to me, so I didn't really know much about the employment situation there, and because I just had to do whatever work there was, I'd gone to the first job placement agency that had caught my eyes. When I started working at the factory, I discovered that the pay wasn't very much. It appeared that I wasn't going to be able to earn enough with just one job, so I found another factory where they had night work. They gave 3,360 won per hour during the day and 4,600 won per hour after midnight when they had night work. Those were the minimum wage levels. From nine to four, I was at a factory that made chocolate snacks, and in the evening, I was at a factory that made cotton and blankets. I decided to work in the factory in the meantime, while waiting for the teacher to be done with his busy situation until he was able to meet up.

My body was getting conditioned to the laborer's life, and I adjusted to work after a short while, but working at two factories was really hard. When I returned home in utter exhaustion, I lay down and slept like a corpse. When I opened my eyes, it was off to work again. It was hard making a hundred chunks of melted chocolate per day. It might look like things would be light at the cotton factory, but the cotton lump that came out pressed was extremely heavy. Three people had to get on it to lift it. Returning home after having carried, opened out, and ironed these things, my body would become as heavy as the cotton lumps.

Within four months of working in Daegu, my weight, which used to be over one hundred kilos, dropped again to the sixties. I hadn't had any separate diet regime, yet I had lost something like ten kilos per month. Even though I burned the fat off my body through working in the factories, the money I made didn't add up to much. The wages I earned from the two factories added up to about one million five hundred thousand won. After paying for living expenses, my monthly rent, and a loan installment, there was hardly anything left. Far from being able to save up for lessons, I was barely making ends meet.

I wouldn't be able to continue to learn music living this way. The thought of having to give up music almost brought tears to my eyes. I had loved music more than anyone and had worked at it harder than anyone. I felt drained all of a sudden at the thought of how this might be the farthest I could get. I was not a young man dreaming to be a vocalist, but a mere laborer who was barely making ends meet, working more than ten hours a day.

Come to me, all you who are weary and burdened,
and I will give you rest.
Take my yoke upon you and learn from me,
for I am gentle and humble in heart,
and you will find rest for your souls.
For my yoke is easy and my burden is light. (Matthew 11:28–30)

I depended on this Bible verse and went to church every week. But even on Sundays, I only had time for a short worship and had to head to work to struggle with heavy loads. When would I be able to rest peacefully? When would my soul be able to find rest?

When my mind, afflicted with futility, was reminded of how vocal music was an extravagance, I began to think that the reason why the teacher was not giving me lessons was to awaken me to the fact that an insignificant body like me shouldn't be doing vocal music.

Around the time when my inner struggle was steadily building up and increasing proportionately to my physical fatigue, the cotton factory where I worked in the evenings began to have more night shifts. There was so much work that I would work there all night, and when I went to the other factory where I worked during the day, I would always doze off, totally flat out.

"What are you doing? Sleeping while working? What in the world did you do during the night that you end up sleeping while working?"

Despite being heavily berated, I couldn't say that I was working in another factory at night. I simply apologized. "No, nothing; I'm sorry."

Worried that I might be injured again if I continued to work that way, I tried my best to stay wide awake while at work. The thought of having to first quickly pay off my debt made my heart sink. I could only clench my teeth with grim determination and carry on. Having become a wreck after the exhausting labor at the factories, I mulled over whether I should continue with my musical pursuits. I had no answer. All I wanted then was to sleep to my heart's content.

I gradually became distant from music.
It felt as though the hardscrabble life was
whipping me nastily to make me give up singing.
That life itself was a continuation of meaninglessness.
I was simply holding on to the will power to pay back my debt—
there was not a single support left for me.

It was around then that I received a notification for a physical examination from the Military Manpower Administration. I'd thought that an orphan like me didn't have to go to the army. When I went to take the physical examination, however, I was assigned to Class 2 active duty. I was astonished that I had been assigned to duty despite my physical condition. When I made an inquiry at the MMA, they told me that people whose parents were listed as unknown in the Family Relations Register, or whose parents had died before they were thirteen years of age and had no family to support them, were exempt from duty. That would have applied to me since I had lived on the streets since five years of age, but of course, I was surprised to find out that I had parents, according to the documents. It seemed unfair that I had to go to the army even though my parents had not taken full responsibility in supporting me.

I didn't think that I would get enlisted into the army, and so I didn't bring any medical certificates or documents about my physical condition when I went for the physical examination. The cruciate ligament that had ruptured when I was in high school had considerable aftereffects; it had affected my physical labor such that I would limp when I was working. More than anything, however, I doubted whether I would be able to have a successful army life with my deep illness of mind. Not many people would welcome army duty anyway, but the fact that it came to me at a time when I had become distant from music and was feeling aimless in my life felt very burdensome to me.

I lived that way working in Daegu for about one year. In the end, I only got to meet the teacher who had told me that he would take responsibility for my life once or twice. I never managed to figure out why he had rejected me. Had it been in the past, I would have gnashed my teeth and sought revenge. But having become exhausted with reality, I had completely given up my musical pursuits by this time, and I didn't have the will or the energy to take revenge. Once again, I felt only emptiness inside me.

An Utterly Foggy Future

WHEN THE DAYS of mental anguish became more frequent, I wanted to get away. I had been holding on to music precisely because I had wanted to get away, but music did not prove to be a way out. I just wanted to disappear. It felt like things would be okay if only I could get away from here. Whether it would be to die suddenly in some place where no one knew me or by starting over again, I thought about leaving this place somehow. That was all I could think of.

My country was a land where I had been abandoned; a land that only gave me despair; a land that did not give me opportunities no matter how much I tried. I wanted to leave this land. I had no idea, however, about how to get together the airfare. I decided to make one last request to Mr. Park.

"Sungbong, where have you been all this time?"

Mr. Park greeted me with a welcome. I told him about the things that had happened in Daegu, and carefully made my request to him: "Mr. Park, please lend me some travel money to go to the US."

"What kind of offbeat request is that? Why the US?"

"Just, I'll migrate there and…"

"No, Sungbong, what do you think will change by going to the US? Besides, do you think they take any random person for immigration? Just return to Daejeon. Come to our office and practice singing here again."

He tried to persuade me for a long time. I was disappointed that he did not lend me even that amount of airfare, but as I listened to him, I realized that he was right. It did not make sense to go to the United States and find a way to study music there when I didn't even speak English. Even if I were to go and, say, die there, my life's problems weren't just going to be solved. The reason I wasn't able to realize my dream in music and was wandering aimlessly wasn't because I was in Korea. And I was tired of lamenting my misfortune. I decided to listen to Mr. Park and moved out from my room in Daegu and got myself a small studio apartment again in Daejeon.

I was too discouraged to get back my hold on music after having let go of it once. Mr. Park's academy had moved and grown into an entertainment company that used up all four floors of a building. He told me I could sing at his office anytime, but my affection for music had already grown cold.

I spent the days barely surviving—by not starving. Losing your motivation in life really puts you in a state of torpor. Anyway, I had to finish paying my debt, so I spent the days of my twenty-two-year-old life doing motorcycle quick service, delivering food, waiting in bars, and working as a day laborer at construction sites.

Since graduation it had been almost two years of not being able to sing. The mental pain that rushed upon me in flashes of chill had increased to a fearful degree. It seemed that now I shouldn't simply leave myself alone. I'd heard the advice many times since high school to try psychiatric treatment. At that time, however, I'd been worried that people might take me for a crazy person, and because I feared such gaze from people, I'd endured patiently alone. Now it seemed that I had to do something about it.

At the first hospital I visited after having made such a firm resolve, I ended up making trouble, unfortunately. The moment the doctor saw my face, he showed a clear sign that he was tired, and he wasn't interested in patients. Thinking that I might be mistaken, I carefully told him my story.

"I've been this way since I was little...I easily think suicidal thoughts."

"Yeah. It's supposed to be that way."

He cut off my story midway and replied with awful insincerity. How could he judge me with such a brief comment? I felt my blood boil.

"What do you mean 'supposed to be that way'? What do you know?"

My hand flew out before I knew it. I slapped the doctor's face hard—once, twice.

"What in the world! What do you think you are doing?"

He dodged my attack by pulling back his chair and stood up, then called the people outside. Soon, male nurses stormed into the office. They grabbed my arms and legs and bound me up. Then they pulled me out by force and locked me up. I was in solitary confinement. Alone, I screamed at the top of my voice and struggled frantically, but there was nothing I could do with my arms and legs tied up.

Despite being injected with a sedative, it took four hours for my fury to subside and for my arms and legs to relax. After the great fury, a commensurate lethargy followed. I was lying there limp when nurses came in. They must have judged that I was fine again, as they freed my arms and legs. I said to a nurse, "I got no money to pay for the bill."

"Pardon?"

"So I'm going to leave. You need money to be hospitalized, and I'm saying I got no money."

When I jumped out of bed and went out, the nurses tried to hold me back. I avoided them and yelled, "You really wanna die?"

When I threatened them, they stepped back. When I came out of the hospital, the words "you wanna die" that I had spat out at them revolved inside my head. Those words were words that I was speaking to myself.

I was walking, but could not see the way ahead.
I just couldn't make out the road in front of me.
It was simply murky and dark, just like inside a thick fog.

Part 4: Will I Be Happy Now?
One Step into the World

Am I Really a Psychopath? Two Weeks in an Isolation Ward

———— ❧ ————

A SENSE OF oppression weighed down on my shoulders, but it was different from what it used to be when I had been a little abandoned child. I was now an adult. Nothing had really changed other than my physique, yet I was an adult. I was still wandering aimlessly, having lost the will to work and the aspiration to sing again. Immersed in dejection, I wanted to know what exactly the illness in my mind was: why I was suddenly getting depressed every so often, why I was feeling anxious and suicidal, and why the pain in my heart was visiting me every night without respite.

I wanted to be assured that I wasn't crazy but just sick. I went to another psychiatric clinic and pleaded with them about my condition. I went from one hospital to another and received diagnoses. The emotional deprivation, the risky environment, and the severe level of trauma that had continued since childhood; the chronic depression due to that trauma; the anger, antagonism, and problems with emotional control; and the suicidal impulses—all these continued and were getting worse. There were variations in the doctors' diagnoses, but antisocial personality disorder, repetitive depressive disorder, borderline personality disorder, and major depressive disorder were mentioned in common by almost all of them.

One hospital even diagnosed me as a psychopath. Having heard that 8 percent of serial killers were psychopaths, I fell into a shock and felt a sense of crisis about my own condition. Through an Internet search, however, I discovered that the meaning of psychopath was different from my vague knowledge. The probability that a psychopath patient would become a serial killer was five hundred to one, taking into account all crimes. Moreover, I wasn't someone who couldn't feel other people's emotions. On the contrary, it was almost a problem that I could grasp the things that were going on with people's emotions and minds so well through my wits and tact.

When I found out that I did not remotely resemble a psychopath, I felt relieved that I wasn't a monster. Clearly, though, there was a mental problem that I had to deal with. I made a resolution and started going to the hospital but was always short on money because I didn't want to work and also because the wages went unpaid. In addition, there were months when my welfare recipient payments didn't come in due to employee mistakes at the dong office, and I began to struggle with poverty again.

The days that followed were a continuation of aggression, fights, and drinking, because I could not cope with my anger. The doctor advised me four times to be hospitalized. I didn't want to see people, and I wanted to end the pain of insomnia. Counting on the possibility that I might get better by being hospitalized, I went back to the hospital. At the first hospital I went to, I'd gotten tied up by force and placed in a ward, but this time I'd gone in of my own accord. They told me that I needed a guardian, so I contacted the social work manager at the dong office. He found out that I was in a poor condition and got something called a Work Capacity Assessment Certificate, and with that I was reinstated as a welfare recipient. He's another person I'm grateful to.

There was no television in the ward, which was shared by six people. We had to turn in our cell phones, and visitations were banned. I'd heard that even a normal person becomes batty when he enters a mental hospital. When I entered one, I could see that those words weren't a lie. As the days passed, one day after another, I felt like I was going crazy because of boredom. Besides, staying with people with strange eyes and unnatural behavior all day, I feared I would also appear that way to other people.

The control was severe too. Even when you tried to go outside the ward, a nurse would come after you and ask where you were going. All behaviors were observed and kept under control. Anyway, I wasn't in a condition to roam around freely. Taking the medicine that the nurse brought, I would become drowsy and sleep for hours. When I wasn't sleeping, I would lie on the bed and have all sorts of delusions. At other times I would brood over my bottomless and endless anxiety and anger toward the world.

When I told these things to the doctors during consultation time, they would reply, "Oh, right; oh, right," as though they were recording machines. It was as if they believed that simply by repeating those words, I would deceive myself into thinking that they were supporting me. It was the regular doses of medicine more than the consultations that calmed my heart.

One of the basic rules in closed wards was being respectful of others. Nevertheless, when I heard voices outside the ward, I felt anxious about whether they were bad-mouthing me. When the anxiety grew severe, I felt the impulse to go outside and hit the person who was—or to be more precise, who I *thought* was—speaking ill of me.

"I feel anxious. Would you give me some medicine please?"

When I took the medicine the nurse brought, the uncontrollable impulse would gradually subside. As the anxiety symptoms worsened, however, there were days when taking medicine wouldn't change the way I felt. When I continued to be anxious, the doctor came to me.

"Please give me more medicine."

"There is a limit to how much we can regulate with medicine. Let's consider the root causes thoroughly, then slowly try to alleviate them."

When I continued to be restless, a nurse told me, "We're trying to help you. This is an environment where you can get the help you need."

I closed my eyes and tried to sleep, but I couldn't sleep. Neither could I calm myself down, so I escaped from the ward. I went to the lounge and ran into trouble again. A patient had put his hand on my shoulder as he was passing by, and the way he looked at me and the way his hand felt made me feel really rotten. I glared at that person and shouted obscenities at the top of my voice. Soon, the nurses and the doctor came running.

"Sungbong, you shouldn't do this; you must follow the ward regulations."

After a prolonged commotion, I was placed in isolation—in solitary confinement. Although they didn't tie me up, it felt similar to the way I had felt when I had been locked up in solitary confinement at the psychiatric clinic. I'm alone, I thought to myself, as always, and yet again. Things were going to be the same even when I left solitary confinement. Since my heart itself was a solitary confinement in a closed ward, no matter where I was, I wouldn't be able to shake off the thought that I was alone.

And surely I am with you always, to the very end of the age. (Matthew 28:20)

As I lay sideways looking at the wall, the above verse came to my mind. Would Jesus be with me in solitary confinement like this? I closed my eyes and tried to feel the invisible being. I didn't feel as though someone was with me—only the scenes of church on Sundays came to my mind. I remembered how I had forgotten loneliness when I was among people—people who held my hands and prayed with me, people who smiled when our eyes met, people who sang with me in one voice.

I continued to sit silently for quite a long while, and then a doctor entered.

"Do you promise to follow the ward regulations?"

"Yes…" I answered submissively. Rather than being by myself, I wanted to return to the ward where there were other people. Although my body had been removed from isolation, it didn't seem that my heart was going to be removed from its isolation.

My hospital fees continued to balloon during those two weeks of inpatient treatment. The aid I had received as a welfare recipient wasn't enough, and the amount I had to pay went to over four hundred thousand won.

"How much longer will the treatment take?"

"It looks like it's going to be difficult to complete within a short period. It'll take a long time."

"But how long?"

"The things from childhood are very potent, so you'll have to continue with constant treatment for the next several years. There is also going to be a considerable amount of residual symptoms."

"Pardon?"

I couldn't understand exactly what he meant, but it sounded like he was saying that there was no way to fix my condition. I felt uncomfortable about having to pay more hospital fees, so I decided to leave that place. I was also worried about military service. I had submitted a report about my physical condition and had gotten a review, but was still assigned to army duty, this time to Class 3.

Would I be able to go to the army? Would I be able to do a decent job there? If they were right about the psychopath diagnosis, how could a person like me be able to hold a gun? How could I, an antisocial and a depressive, guard the country, when guarding my mind alone was so overwhelming?

I left the mental institution, but nothing had changed since before the hospitalization.

When I had been in the hospital for my leg injury, I was treated until I could walk again.

But mental problems seemed to be more serious than a fractured bone or a ruptured ligament.

My mind was still creaking unsteadily.

I'd Like to Meet Her Once before I Die: The Person Called Mother

WINTER CAME. WINTER was a difficult season to deal with even for a person like me who used to sleep in the streets. Coldness seemed to be something that was felt in more than just the body. Every winter, I would feel a deep chill inside my heart. It was with the same feeling that I had gone to meet Mom that winter. I was back to thinking only suicidal thoughts again. When I stepped out onto a street with the resolve to throw myself in front of a running car, I felt an uncomfortable and unpleasant cord clinging to my heart. And I knew that the other end of that cord was connected to those beings called parents.

Most people had parents who would give them guidance and encouraging pats during difficult moments. But for me, the person called Father had avoided the meeting altogether, and I still had that being called Mother, whom I had not yet made any attempt to meet. She may not be very different from Dad, but perhaps I should at least give it a try. In order to cut off the uncomfortable and unpleasant cord and to be able to die with ease, I wanted to meet Mom.

"Let's meet the person called Mom once before I die."

When I obtained a Family Census Register, an unfamiliar address came up. I received help from a public office, and after much difficulty, found the contact information.

The place where Mom lived was a small city in Choongcheong-do. I couldn't be certain whether she lived at that address, but I arrived in front of the house and started to look for her. I'd gone there with a pompous attitude, but I hadn't the courage to knock on the door and enter. I paced up and down for half a day. I would have liked to totally smash the house into bits, but couldn't do that. In the end, when my legs started to ache, I settled myself down and made a call.

All kinds of thoughts came to my mind until Mom showed up: If she starts to cry and hug me as soon as she sees me, how should I react? Would I be crying also and hugging her? If she says that she is sorry for all that had happened and asks for forgiveness, and asks me to live together with her, what should I say? Or what if I can't hold myself back and get violent the moment we meet? What if I start burning with murderous intent as soon as I see her, thinking, "How could I kill this woman?"

Mom appeared at the place where we'd agreed to meet. No words passed between us. As soon as I saw her, I knew she was my mother. I have her eyes. She pointed with her chin—it seemed like she was telling me to get in the car. I looked at the luxurious car that Mom had arrived in. Was she a community leader in this region? How could she be driving such an expensive car—I found out later that it was a Benz—unless she was? I thought to myself as I got in the car.

I was silent throughout the entire journey. Neither did Mom try to speak to me. Although it was a short drive, the unbearable silence in the car felt as if an hour had passed. As I quietly observed Mother through a sideward glance, I saw a very tough woman, not so much someone who was fierce, but someone who was just plain tough. When we arrived at a coffee house and sat across from each other, she finally spoke.

"Why did you come?"

Her question caught me off guard; I was at a loss for words.

"You look just like that person who's supposed to be your father." There was irritation in Mom's eyes as she said those words. I hadn't expected her to be warm, but irritated eyes? I stared at her, poker-faced. Like Mom, I made an effort to speak in an impassive voice.

"What does Dad look like?"

Mom took out a photo and showed it to me. I saw a handsome young man with a smile. I hardly looked like that person. I was puzzled as to why she had that photo with her.

"I don't think we look alike."

"That manner of speech and disposition are exactly the same as your so-called father's."

I'd never even met that "so-called father." How could I possibly resemble someone whom I'd never even met? First, it was her question, asking why I had come to see her. Then it was her callous remarks about how I took after my "so-called father." All of this came from someone who had abandoned me twenty years ago. What wrong had I done? It wasn't my fault that I'd come to look for Mom and that I looked like Dad. I instantly sprang up from my seat. Before I left the coffee house, I took one last look at Mom. But she remained seated where she was and made no effort to call me or come after me. My meeting with my mother lasted only about twenty minutes.

After I left the coffee house, I realized I had three hundred thousand won in my pocket. It was the money I'd received as welfare aid.

"I'll kill myself after using all this money."

It seemed that I was finally able to kill myself this time. I walked senselessly to wherever my feet took me. The sea appeared along the way. There wasn't anywhere to spend the money. Trudging toward downtown, I thought, "What's the purpose of spending all the money if I am going to die anyway?"

I went up to a building. I was standing on a rooftop looking down from the railing when guards came after me and seized me by the scruff of my neck.

"Who are you? What the deuce are you doing here?"

The guards dragged me down by the arms. Not caring a damn about what would happen next, I dashed across the road, but the cars either avoided me or screeched to a halt. All kinds of curses flew at me. Then I checked into an inn. It must have been because I'd heard swearwords, because the coldness I felt on the streets and each blasted human being who did vicious things to me returned to my mind. As I pulled out a pocket knife, all kinds of ideas popped out along with it. I'd heard in the past that at the moment when you are about to die, your mind would go empty. Not for me. Why did I have so many thoughts? Was I hesitant to die because of the medicine from the hospital drugs? Would their effects ever subside?

Death seemed so far away from me as I stayed inside that room in a strange city. What felt closer to me than death was a feeble hunch about the life ahead. That hunch was neither bright nor hopeful.

It was on one of those days when I was obsessing about death in an unfamiliar city that I received a call from Mr. Park.

"Sungbong, would you like to go sing on the television? I got a casting proposal from a program called *Korea's Got Talent*, and I think you'll be the perfect candidate."

"Why don't you go there yourself, Mr. Park?"

I hung up. What does he mean television? I, huddled here with nothing but the thought of killing myself, would go out and sing in front of people on the television?

Mr. Park called again.

"Hey, young chap, why did you hang up the phone like that? It may be a good opportunity, so give it a shot."

"I said I don't want to. I'm not in the mood for that."

"Don't be sassy. Can't you trust my words and just go try once?"

"Stop telling me this nonsense. I haven't sung for almost two years. I'm busy enough trying to make ends meet. What do you mean 'sing on television'?"

"Well, you've got nothing to lose. It's not like there is an application fee. Besides, if you win, the prize is three hundred million won. It wouldn't hurt giving it a try."

"I'm not going to. I'm not even going to win, so it'll be a waste of time."

After I hung up the phone, I thought about my attitude toward Mr. Park. Somehow I felt bad about how I had talked to him. I've always had a soft spot for him. I'd been abandoned by my parents, but Mr. Park had kept me under his wing, taught me how to sing, and introduced me to the church.

"Okay. I'll do it."

I got on a bus to Daejeon. I had never liked television at all. People love and forgive and comfort each other on TV. Such scenes looked like some faraway world, completely beyond my reach. Yet here I was, trying to get onto a TV show…But I reasoned with myself on the bus that even if there wasn't a way, and even if *this*—getting on a TV show—wasn't the way, I could at least give it a shot.

In contrast to me, who'd returned to Daejeon with a grim resolve, Mr. Park was up to the elbows with another project. It was a project called "Praise Concert."

"What are you going to be doing there?" I asked Mr. Park.

"Sungbong, we drink water, but some children in Africa have to live without water. We need to help such disadvantaged people. How about raising a fund through a performance and buying some water for the African children?"

For someone like me with major depressive disorder and borderline personality disorder, Mr. Park's idea sounded like a whole lot of twaddle. I didn't know of anyone with greater difficulties in life than me. Just because they were children who couldn't drink water didn't mean they had nights of the soul as dark and desolate as I had. I wasn't in a position to look after anyone. Besides, I didn't have a generous enough heart to take care of others' misfortunes. Taking care of myself was already overwhelming enough.

Nonetheless, I joined the project because it was Mr. Park's idea.

"Sungbong, you take care of the lights."

I was in charge of putting the spotlight on people when they stood on stage. I thought about how the role behind the stage, rather than in front of the stage, was more suitable for me. It had been a long time since I last sang, and I wasn't confident enough to sing. Even Mr. Park had no plans to tell me to sing.

The concert was held in a small church. Young musicians who shared Mr. Park's vision gathered to give touching performances throughout the concert. As I shined lights onto the stage, I realized how these people weren't expecting to receive anything in return, how they had simply wished to donate their talents and skills to society. When I felt how my position stacked against their skills—skills that allowed them to give freely to society—I faltered a little. I felt that my circumstances did not allow me to do anything for other people. Yet if only I could stand on stage like them! If only what I did for myself could become something that could be done for others!

As the performance was reaching its finale, Mr. Park walked up onto the stage, took the mike, and began to say something unexpectedly: "Ladies and gentlemen, there's a friend who is in charge of lighting over there behind you. He's a kid who's had a hard life since he was little, living on the streets without a home. When I see that kid, I think we just might be living too comfortably within our families. Aren't we being selfish when there are marginalized people who are living such neglected lives?"

I couldn't understand why Mr. Park was telling everyone my story. I didn't want my past to be known to people, and he knew more about it than anyone in the world. After hearing my story from Mr. Park, the audience quieted down, and there was only silence inside the concert hall. I was flustered after hearing what Mr. Park had to say next.

"Sungbong, come down and sing a piece."

I hadn't any song prepared. The first song that came to my mind was "God's Grace," which I'd often sung at church. I felt preoccupied and out of touch, but the people applauded my singing more than when skilled teachers and vocalists had sung. I stared blankly at the audience in front of the stage amid their applause and cheers. My heart choked with emotions, and it seemed like the illness of my heart was sinking down quietly and was slowly being buried somewhere deep below. It was the first time I had ever experienced such a mysterious feeling.

Wasn't this a better kind of medicine than the drugs I was taking?
People's concern and interest; the hope that I'll be able to continue to sing in the future.
If I pursued my dream again and shared it with others, wouldn't I be healed of my illness, which even the mental hospitals had failed to treat?

It threw me into a state of confusion when the hopeless "I" who'd been receiving treatment locked up in a closed ward intersected with the "I" who was finding hope among people. That confusion, however, was entirely different from the confusion I'd felt when I fell into despair.

"Nella Fantasia": Entering My Fantasy

WHEN I RETURNED home after the Praise Concert awash with that fuzzy sense of hope, I realized that the dates for *Korea's Got Talent* were approaching. Selecting the pieces was only the beginning of my worries. There were so many guys out there who majored in vocal music, and if it wasn't even a vocal competition but a program featuring a competition of various talents, what was the use of going there to sing vocal music? Besides, I'd had such a long break from singing. I felt disinclined to do it, thinking how I might just end up embarrassing myself.

It didn't look like the emotions that had moved me during the Praise Concert were going to continue on into the television program. The Praise Concert hall was small scale, where people were gathered with ready hearts to applaud the people on the stage. I might not know anything about the world of television auditions, but it was probably going to be rigorous and brutal.

"Nella Fantasia": that was the piece that Mr. Park, who'd been rummaging assiduously through songs, recommended.

"This'll be a good one. The masses will be able to appreciate it since it's from the popera genre, and it's sung with vocalizing technique."

I didn't know that the song had become popular as a chorus piece through an entertainment program. I'd only just listened to it being sung by Il Divo, the four-person popera group that I liked.

"What does the title mean?"

"I guess 'in a fantasy'?"

In a fantasy. I mouthed the phrase Mr. Park had interpreted for me over and over again. Despite all the longing to die during childhood, I'd had something that held on to me like a thread. That thread wasn't something like a dream or hope, which to me only seemed unfamiliar and distant. Neither was it a groundless presentiment that someday I was going to live a life different from the one I was living then. Perhaps that thread, which had caught my ankle each time I'd wanted to die, was a world that went on existing only inside my head—a world that was totally different from the reality, yet another world known only to me.

Though it was faint and indistinct, that world did indeed exist for me. People might call that world a "fantasy." When I looked up the song's lyrics, I discovered that what they described was similar to that world inside my head, which couldn't be expressed through words.

In my fantasy I see a just world,
Where everyone lives in peace and honesty.
I dream of souls that are always free
Like the clouds that float
Full of humanity in the depths of the soul.
In my fantasy I see a bright world
Where each night there is less darkness.
I dream of souls that are always free,
Like the clouds that float
In my fantasy exists a warm wind,
That breathes into the city, like a friend.
I dream of souls that are always free,
Like the clouds that float
Full of humanity in the depths of the soul.

I warmed up my voice right away. There was only a month or two left to prepare. I liked the song, but rehearsing it proved to be a formidable process. Because of the long break, I couldn't produce high notes like I wanted, and my heart's despair kept on clashing with the dream portrayed in the lyrics. A lot of things had changed since the time when I'd pursued the dream called music. I even began to doubt whether I might be wasting time on hopeless things when I couldn't even heal the illness in my heart.

It wasn't like I could practice a lot either. I had to pay monthly rent and earn my daily living. The only job that paid instantly was day labor at construction sites. My body had become debilitated from ceaseless hard labor, and I'd also become exhausted with fighting the illness in my heart. Yet there I was, singing again. But this would be the last time that I did this sort of thing. And because it was going to be the last time, I didn't want to leave behind regrets or lingering feelings.

Thinking that I'd regressed to the starting point, I rehearsed over and over again at Mr. Park's academy. When I proceeded step by step as I'd learned from school and from my lesson teachers, the senses that I had trained to become second nature during the days of intense practice regenerated: the music that my head had forgotten had remained intact in my body.

On my way to a downtown gymnasium for the regional preliminary, I questioned what I was doing. Was this the right approach to vocal music? What if I merely ended up playing the part of some pointless extra? The gymnasium was teeming with numerous people. People wearing funny costumes, people dancing endlessly, people playing strange instruments, people standing on their heads, were already in the waiting room. I was a vocalist, so why was I sandwiched there among them? Was there a place here where I'd be able to stand?

"Glad to meet you. You must be Mr. Sungbong Choi?"

Program directors and the producers came up to greet me. I wasn't sure whether it was because they remembered the video I'd sent them when I applied to participate in the program, but it sure felt curious to be recognized.

My turn came, and I sang "Nella Fantasia" as I had rehearsed it. The first preliminary-round screening by program directors and the producers didn't get broadcast. My voice didn't sound the way I'd wanted it to, but I passed. A few days after I passed the first preliminary round, the main stage performance of the Daejeon preliminary took place at the same gymnasium. The judging panel—movie director Jin Jang, actress Yoonah Song, and music director Kolleen Park—was there, and participants were told that unless edited out, the audition was going to be broadcast.

I was in horrible condition. It must have been due to having carried brick loads without taking breaks at a construction site the day before; I felt chilly and utterly worn out. I worried that the encephalomeningitis had returned. Although they'd already screened the contestants once during the first round, there were still many of them. Little youngsters dressed all alike were chatting noisily, and people gathered in their own little groups laughed out loud and shouted, "Fighting!"*

Sitting alone in an unsettled atmosphere with a body that ached piqued my nerves. I sat silently in a corner and waited for my turn, but my name wasn't called even after a long time. Already four hours had passed since I'd arrived.

The contestants around me were with their parents or friends: parents patting the back of their nervous daughter, friends passing snacks and drinks in encouragement. Looking at the other contestants, I considered perhaps returning home. My body was feeling more and more chilly. Was it fatigue? I pulled up my collar yet again. Wouldn't it be better to go home and to lie down and rest under the covers?

A guy who looked like a dancer left all the plentiful space behind him and came to practice by me. Why out of all places did he have to come next to me to behave so flippantly? Discontent poured out from within me.

* "Let's go!"

Wary that I might get into a fight, I sang "Nella Fantasia" silently inside and suffered patiently, forcing down the emotions.

A camera was moving up and down to make a sketch of the waiting area, looking for interview opportunities. I tried to avoid the camera but was eventually caught by a cameraman and was led into a small space.

"Why do you single me out to shoot?"

"Sungbong, dear sir, it'd be good if you could tell us a little about your childhood."

The camera was staring squarely at me. Telling the story wasn't going to make people understand. Besides, I didn't want to pull up the pain-saturated details of my life again.

"Why should I tell it?"

"Just so we can make a sketch video. You can tell any story you'd like. Anything."

The waiting room sketch video only took up around five seconds of the actual broadcast. They took a total of forty minutes, however, to sketch me. It took a long time because they kept drawing out stories by delving into details about how I'd lived my life. Those questions were too heavy for me. I was again gripped by the wish to return home, and barely managed to make it through.

Just as I was getting worn out by the wait, I was given something called a cue sheet. There I read the questions that the judging panel was going to ask me when I went up on the stage. They were questions about what I do, and how I'd been living my life. I asked a producer, "Can't I just skip this one?"

"It'll be fine. It'd be better to answer it. You'll feel better after you speak."

"I really don't want to talk about this kind of thing..."

"It's because you might not make it through if you don't say it. Just tell things exactly as they are."

I felt beat after the interview. What's more, I disliked having to bring up memories about my past. And I was feeling sick as well! I climbed the stage with a reluctant heart. I had a short conversation with the judging panel, then sang. I didn't think of anything other than singing. But then—what a surprise! The audience and judges were moved to tears as they listened to me sing.

Why were they crying? Was it because they pitied me?
Were they acting according to script since this was being broadcast out?
Or…could it be that they were actually being sincere?
I descended the stage feeling doubtful and puzzled.
I wanted to quickly return home and rest.

When I got back after having finished the preliminary audition, Mr. Park asked, "Did it go well?"

"I don't know. When I sang, the people there just began to cry."

"Huh? You sang, and why would people cry?"

I didn't understand it either. Anyway, I passed the regional preliminary through unanimous decision, so Mr. Park and I began to rehearse the song that I was to sing next. Mr. Park chose a song titled "Cinema Paradiso." I was actually feeling pretty much composed during the rehearsal until they aired that day's recording. I'd been expecting my part to be edited out since the atmosphere had been all drab with people crying. Neither Mr. Park nor I had anticipated what was in store for me next.

My Story and Song That Became a Worldwide Sensation

—————— ⚬⟋⟍ ——————

I'D NEVER EXPECTED that the saying "to achieve fame overnight" would ever happen to me.

"When's your show getting broadcast?"

"Today."

Even as Mr. Park and I talked indifferently about the broadcast, we were clueless. After the broadcast was released around midnight, however, surprising things poured down into my life like a waterfall.

Watching the broadcast at home, I just thought, "Well, that feels quite strange to see myself on television." After the program finished, I turned on the computer as usual and found that the name Sungbong Choi was the number-one ranking real-time search word. All of a sudden, I was afraid. I thought that I'd be able to calm down after a while, but my episode was spreading through social networks. There was someone who said he was touched by my story and song; another said she cried like a child... Comments about me continued to be posted endlessly.

The broadcast had ended at half past twelve, but I couldn't recover my wits until five thirty in the morning. I didn't know how to comprehend the situation that had befallen me. It was a good thing that people had been touched, but the fact that I suddenly became famous overnight flooded me with anxiety. It was especially incomprehensible to me that the world, which had been hostile to me until then, had suddenly transformed itself. For a moment, I fell into a daze. When Mr. Park called me, I could tell that he too was bewildered.

"Sungbong, what in the world is going on?"

"I don't know."

"First let's meet up. I can't calm myself."

We met at dusk. He was extremely excited, and his eyes were bloodshot as though he had cried all night. He suggested that we go to the church and ask the pastor to pray for us.

Mr. Park seemed to have settled down a little after the pastor's prayer. I, on the other hand, felt the events sink in and was thrilled because I began to think that if this was really the way that God had prepared for me, then God must exist indeed!

I hadn't slept a wink that whole morning, but I didn't feel sleepy at all. The video of me at the regional preliminary was all over the Internet. The next day and the day after, my name continued to be the number-one search word on portal sites. Words about me circulated instantly through Twitter and Facebook, and my preliminary performance was uploaded on the worldwide video-sharing community, YouTube, and shared all over the world. I'd only said a very tiny bit about how I'd fared in life thus far and had thought that people wouldn't bat an eye about such a story as mine, so it was amazing and yet confusing to have so many people who were interested in me and were touched.

At around the same time, the production crew contacted me.

"Sungbong, it looks like you'll have to come up to Seoul. We'll take care of you throughout the broadcasting period."

It would have been reassuring to be with Mr. Park in this unexpected and hectic situation, but considering the upcoming performances, it seemed that it would be better to be in Seoul. When I went to Seoul, the production crew gave me a one-room studio located two minutes from the broadcasting station. It was a fully furnished, neat and tidy little room.

"Um...How about meals?"

"You can just ask us whenever you feel like eating."

"Really? Can I eat even meat dishes?"

"Of course."

Goodness gracious, meat! As soon as I was in Seoul, I could have meat almost every day!

Not only the national media, but the global media too began to take an interest in me. The production crew seemed to be flustered as well by this unanticipated situation. However, the information delivered by our national media was a bit different from what was delivered by the foreign media. In Korea, there was a controversy over how I'd lied about not having trained in vocal music even though I'd attended an arts high school. The foreign media, on the other hand, put the focus on how a kid who used to sell gum had appeared in an audition for an entertainment program featuring a competition of various talents, and touched people.

I'd told the production crew that I'd majored in vocal music at an arts high school, and all the audience and judges at the audition knew about it too. That part, however, was cut out during the editing process, which then all of a sudden turned me into a liar. When the production crew explained that they were going to use that part in the show's subsequent installments, that settled the controversy about my training. But having such a controversy dumped on top of an already disorienting situation made me afraid to get onto the Internet. Because of this incident, the production crew was asked by the Korea Communications Standards Commission to apologize to the viewers. The production crew also received a warning from the commission. When I began to think of myself at the center of the controversy, anxiety and depression kicked in. The production crew introduced me to a renowned hospital where I received treatment.

Being inundated by interview requests, and having attention poured upon me that I'd never experienced before, I was grateful for everything even amid the chaos. I cooped myself up in a practice room and went on to wrestle with singing. The song was "Cinema Paradiso," which Mr. Park had selected. The production crew also provided me with a lesson teacher, after seeing how determined and zealous I was and how I went all out to rehearse, hardly stepping out of the practice room.

What I could do for the people I was so grateful to
wasn't to spread my tragic story further,
but to sing.
I felt that the way to repay them was by singing great songs to them.

What took place while I was rehearsing was even greater in scope than the shock that I'd already received. First of all, a tremendous number of interview requests came in from both the national and foreign media. When channels among them like ABC, CNN, and CBS introduced me as the second Paul Potts and as Korea's Susan Boyle, my video began to be played all over the world. Even the number of views on YouTube exceeded tens of millions. I was amused at how people held up the video as a record breaker in reaching the highest number of views within the shortest period of time. The number of views had hit fifty million and was still climbing. I also checked the number of views by country and saw that apart from Africa and some parts of South America, it was distributed quite evenly all over the world. What on earth! I couldn't believe that the entire planet was watching my video. It seemed like some pipe dream or a pure fabrication.

CNN and ABC presented my interview and video, and the progress of the audition program three times. They also went to Daejeon with me and did some coverage about the streets of Yongjeon-dong, and interviewed the people who'd taken care of me. My video, which appeared on the main page of CNN's website, became the most frequently viewed video.

Articles about me also appeared in the *New York Times* and *Time* magazine. *Time* compared me to the protagonist of the novel *Oliver Twist* and praised how my voice had touched people's heartstrings. My picture and story were placed next to those of actresses Emma Watson and Blake Lively among others on MSNBC's main website, where I was presented as "a Korean singer with skills that rivaled Susan Boyle's." Mainstream media in sixty-five countries put me under their spotlight and published my story. Articles about me were published by the *Mainichi Shimbun* of Japan, the Reuters news agency, and the weekly news magazine *Der Spiegel* of Germany. American pop star Justin Bieber saw my video, which he'd found through his manager's Twitter account, and encouraged me with the following message: "This is awesome. NEVER SAY NEVER and good luck to this kid."

A Korean movie actor also wrote on Twitter, "Sungbong Choi of *Korea's Got Talent*! Cheers to you! During the hard and lonely moments—the endless tears that flowed when I heard the bright kindling of the lonely hope that he'd nurtured in his heart." Reading his words, I felt a tug at my heart.

That was when I understood the meaning of what they called a "sensation." Soon, a fan website was created under my name, and when I began to receive messages from people all over the world who told me about how they had shed tears, were touched, and wished me God's blessings, I realized that this wasn't simply an ordinary happening. Yet despite the international attention I was receiving, the only thing I could do was to sing. My life was changing incredibly, yet the more it did, the more I cooped myself up inside a rehearsal room. It wasn't over yet: I still had performances left to do.

It was the day of the semifinals. I'd had trouble sleeping for several days before the contest. What if I mess up on the live show? What if I totally botch the song while people's attention is concentrated on me? For several days before the live broadcast, I imagined every possible case of bad luck that I could think of.

On the actual day of the live show, my voice was in a disastrous condition. It must have been due to having rehearsed too hard and not being able to sleep properly. I continued to check my voice as I rehearsed, but the way my voice gave out was enough to tell me that I was in major trouble. I pulled together every last bit of the fighting spirit that had been ingrained in me during my life on the streets. It wasn't so much because of the tenacity to win; it was because I didn't want to disappoint the people who'd told me about how they'd been touched by me.

The live broadcast began. When my turn came and the accompaniment began, I started to sing. I was just barely producing the voice, however poised I might have appeared. I was in the worst possible condition, but I sang "Cinema Paradiso" as best as I could. When I came down from the stage, I felt damp with cold sweat that had run down the length of my spine.

The result wasn't bad. Had the people noticed my fighting spirit? I received a 56 percent vote on that stage to advance into the finals. Fifty thousand votes—three times that of the other contestants—had concentrated on me. Again, foreign mainstream media took up the semifinals update as main news. I began to feel even greater pressure about the finals.

Up until the finals, I spent my days going back and forth between the hospital and the rehearsal room. I was gradually being healed of the pains of my past around then, through the messages of encouragement I received from people. I also frequently met in person all the challengers who had made it to the top ten, and got to know them well enough to be on congenial terms with them. They all had outstanding talents, but I deemed Minji Kim to be my strongest rival.

Minji was born visually impaired. But she had a clear, ringing voice and a warm heart. Though I envied her beautiful voice, I marveled more at how she, who possessed less things in life than others, was more cheerful and free of bitterness than anyone. To me, who resented the world and suffered from depression, she was someone I had a lot to learn from. We went around holding each other's hand tightly when we were together, such that people even mistook us for a couple.

I chose "Nella Fantasia" again for the finals, because no other lyrics carried better the message that I wanted to tell the world. There was the risk of being criticized for singing the same song, but I wanted to communicate the message in these lyrics—my dream fantasy—to people once more.

I rehearsed with orchestral accompaniment for the finals. Dear heavens, I was really rehearsing with an orchestra! It was as though I'd realized my longtime dream and become a real vocalist. At the same time, I felt a heavy responsibility being placed on me. I was worried that I had to go on stage after only one rehearsal, because the orchestra had arrived late.

A great crowd of people came to the live show, which took place at Kyung-Hee University's Grand Peace Palace. National and foreign media flocked en masse to cover the show, which was also being broadcast live on YouTube. My legs trembled, and I worried whether I'd be able to walk up onto the stage. Just then, I saw Mr. Park sitting in the very front row. Looking at his face helped me to control my nerves, though just barely. By the time I was to go onstage, I found myself surprisingly calm and collected.

There I was on the finals stage, with the spotlight shining on me. It was brighter than any light I'd seen up till then.

The winner was decided through text voting in the final round as well. I got into the top three, and soon after that, we were narrowed down to the top two: the poppin' dancer Minjeong Joo, and me. I stood composed and serene like a stone Buddha as the show host announced the results. There was a commercial break before the final result was announced. I thought of what I should do during those sixty seconds; I went up to Minjeong and squeezed her hand.

"It's okay. Everything will go well," I said.

Minjeong also squeezed my hand.

"Good work. You've gone through so much."

Watching her dance reminded me of the time when I used to be obsessed with dancing. The two things that I'd been passionate about in life were both there, side by side on the finals stage.

I, who had burst out crying every single day living out on the streets,
cried no longer when I began to dance.
And then: music.
For someone like me, who'd never been able to hold out a hand to someone first,
or strike up a conversation, singing was the first sound I'd articulated to the world.
At last I could speak to people through lyrics that reflected exactly what was
in my heart.

The TV commercial ended. I was calm. Even though the show hosts racked up the suspense before announcing the final winner, I remained calm. It felt as though I was in a separate space by myself.

"The winner is…Minjeong Joo!"

The winner was Minjeong, and I was the first runner-up. Although they said that it was decided by a meager difference of some two hundred votes, I didn't feel sorry or sad. To be honest, I was sorry for perhaps… three seconds? That was all. In fact, I had to comfort Mr. Park, who had come to cheer for my performance, that it was okay, because he was sitting with his head bowed so low.

Foreign press put out the news that although I ended up in second place, my story and voice had touched people all over the world, beyond Korea. I was grateful that they, who had passed on my story to the whole world, had defended me thus against the controversy surrounding my training background:

It was revealed later that Paul Potts had taken a master class with the legend
Pavarotti, and Susan Boyle had also trained and recorded for a charity CD
before her appearance on Britain's Got Talent…
Despite the hullabaloo, it's apparent that this Korean singer has pipes.*

---

* Clara Kim, "The New Susan Boyle? *Korea's Got Talent* Singer Puts Judges In Tears," *Time*, June 7, 2011.

After the three dream-like months, I wrapped up my things in Seoul and returned home to Daejeon. A water disconnection notice was posted on the front door. I also had to pay the delayed rent. I remembered how I'd answered the question about the prize money: I'd said that if I won, I would buy a house with the three hundred million won. I'd wanted to have a pretty cat as a pet as well. Instead, I was greeted by the familiar musty smell upon entering the house. But I had nothing to be bitter or sorry about. That was simply the reality for me.

Sungbong Choi sings "Cinema Paradiso" during the semifinals of *Korea's Got Talent. Photo courtesy of Total Variety Network, South Korea.*

Life after *Korea's Got Talent*: Into the World, into Society

WHEN *KOREA'S GOT Talent* ended, I thought to myself: if I'd won the first prize, wouldn't I have experienced great confusion? It was true that greater emphasis had been placed on my life's drama than on my singing. Had I won the first prize in that kind of situation, I might have suffered a different sense of shame.

"Oh dear, what a pity! You almost made it!"

I had developed the composure to smile at people around me who felt sorry for me.

"Not at all. It's already more than I could ever have dreamed."

Saying thus, I realized how greatly my perception of life had shifted. My life had also changed dramatically. When I walked the streets or went out to eat, people recognized me and encouraged me.

"Oh, it's Mr. Sungbong Choi. Way to go! Cheers!"

There were also a lot of people who asked me for my autograph. Good gracious, who would have thought that I'd be greeted like that on the streets?

Some people offered to become my sponsors, and some people wanted to have sustained communications with me through their fan pages. Still others delivered to me donation money that they had collected voluntarily. I was simply thankful that the world recognized me and was extending helping hands. Foreign media also showed steady interest in me; CNN in particular ran major coverage of me after *Korea's Got Talent* was over. Then again, since I'd never received that kind of love in the past twenty years of my life, I was somewhat afraid. Was it because I wasn't used to being loved? There were moments when I just wanted to run away and hide.

There was no time to run away and hide, however. I had to run toward wherever I was invited to sing. Singing was what I had to do, and I didn't want to stop the healing through singing. Now I finally had the hope that I would be able to connect with people through singing, and I could not betray that hope myself. In the last three months, what I had never been able to dream even the slightest bit, what I had never been able to imagine, and what I had believed to be impossible inside the little hole in which I had been trapped had happened to me. Even the wall that had stood between people and me had begun to fade away like magic.

One Japanese businessman invited me to a Saipan resort he owned; airfare was included. He said that he was greatly touched by my song, and that I should just come and have a rest because he wanted to reward me. There, I slept for as long as I wanted, then walked along the beach. I swam, then lay down still again. I spent a few days that way. It was the first vacation in my life.

After having rested, I was again occupied with several events. I also had to meet a lot of famous people in politics, business and economy, and media. I was already aware that the world wasn't just full of nice people, but there were quite a number of stuffy people among them. Countless people among those who invited me to events and who said that they would give me support merely finished by taking photos with me. There were people who tried to make money off me as well, and people who used me to increase their personal connections and affiliation. It was probably because I had had the experience of living out on the streets, but I had eyes that could discern people.

Mr. Park said, "Sungbong, you have the eyes of a hawk, so you can discriminate gems from pebbles when you meet people, right?"

It was really so. I could immediately tell the difference between those who approached me with pure motives and those who didn't. Once, a sniffy lady said to me, "I've seen a lot of kids like you; I've helped a lot of young orphans and all, so I understand kids like you well."

A person next to her said that she was someone who did many honorable deeds. I lost my temper and shouted, "What do you mean you understand me well?"

Finally, after a noisy commotion, I extracted an apology from her.

"I'm sorry. I didn't know you well, yet I pretended to know."

She was a secretary of some politician, and somehow, her apology didn't seem sincere. I still behaved roughly toward people who weren't true to me. Money wasn't the issue: it was the heart.

On the other hand, those who genuinely tried to help me didn't say much. All they told me was to keep up the spirit. To them, I showed my utmost sincerity. It came about naturally, without the need for pretense.

I, who'd been on the outer fringes of life,
Had finally entered into the world, into society.
Gradually learning how to interact socially
among both the good and the bad people
was also something I had to do upon entering the world.

I was actually wearied by having to repeat the story of my past countless times during the interviews I had with the various media. Nevertheless, if the I in the past hadn't existed, the I in the present would also never have been.

The Praise Concert had reached its third show around then, and Mr. Park was going around finding and presenting concerts in rural schools, nursing homes, and others. My dear, dear Mr. Park—approaching neighbors and continuing to give free performances for those in need!

At the first Praise Concert, I'd been the one receiving help and encouragement, but now I wanted to be the one giving help. Although this was a bit embarrassing, we named the title of the fourth show "A Praise Concert with Sungbong Choi." The seats were packed with people who had come to see me. Some had to stand for over two hours to watch the performance. There were also people from other countries who had come because they had heard about me.

I continued to receive speech requests. Most of them were special speeches on hope, with a main topic that ran something like, "There are actually people like me living in this world, and they should also have a dream in life." They were held at universities, businesses, military camps, probation offices, and education offices. Some people cried when they heard about the story of my life on the streets, while others found hope. For one of the events jointly organized by the Gyeonggi Welfare Foundation and the Gyeonggi Provincial Office of Education, I was pleasantly surprised to hear that the event scored a 95 percent speech-satisfaction evaluation rate.

Whenever people who had been to my concerts or speeches confess to me how listening to my story and songs made them realize again how precious dreams are, I am reminded that I have yet to achieve my dream, and that I have only just begun. I also heard that a foreign coach of a national pro soccer team had shown my video to his players to boost the team morale.

"No matter how hard the situation may be, if you don't stop trying, you will be able to succeed like Sungbong Choi. You are professional players. If you strive on like Sungbong Choi, there will be no opponent you will be unable to defeat."

After listening to the coach, the team put up a strong fighting spirit in their next game and won. Whenever I hear such news, I become determined yet again to stay faithful and carry out my promises.

I remember singing Frank Sinatra's "My Way" on the Praise Concert stage. That song, which I sung in harmony with Mr. Park and five performance staff, made me look back on my life and resolve to decide on the way I must go. I found especially charming the part that goes, "The record shows I took the blows / And did it my way!" That was when I decided that "my way" was going to be one that brings hope to others, and may I never lose that way. I made a promise to myself as I finished singing the song. My heart must have reached the audience, because they sent ardent applause.

I also gave a number of charity concerts and performed at other places that invited me to sing. At the unpaid performances, which I went running to despite not being paid, I found that I actually received more than at places that paid me for my performances. I was once invited to a discharge ceremony at an orphanage. The people there were in similar situations as I was: they had grown up in the orphanage and were just then stepping into society as adults. I received a huge welcome when I arrived there.

When the abandoned children greeted me heartily,
I could feel the exact same loneliness and troubles
that had affected me.
When I held their hands, something connected us,
without having to say a single word.
And my tears, which had dried up over time,
flowed again as I looked into the eyes of these love-starved friends.

I remember that one of the items in my "post television broadcast" schedule was a request from a radio station for a campaign recording. It was the campaign that had become well known for its popular tag line, "Let's try it once now. Let's share love." It was a message that I could identify with, and I found recording it both fun and meaningful. Here is part of what I said:

Hello. This is Sungbong Choi, who finished second as a vocalist in a cable TV audition show. You know, I think the saying "Where there is a will, there is a way" isn't just something that exists as a proverb.

It took all but a flash of a moment for me to be captivated by vocal music. Isn't having a dream like being carried away for just that short moment of time, and then having that memory live on?

In a society that only remembers the winner, I found out that there are things that actually turned out even better because I'd won second place. First of all, there was less pressure to deal with, so I could stay relaxed and have the opportunity to grow, and then, I would also have this courage pulsing in me, to try even harder than I'd done so far. Winners probably don't understand this kind of feeling!

A few versions like this were broadcast over the radio for a week. I felt both excited and responsible about the fact that I'd become someone who could deliver what he wanted to say to people in this way. I was even featured as a cover model for a Christian magazine. I was smiling brightly on that magazine cover but I was shocked to see that I'd put on such an incredible amount of weight! I couldn't believe it, and it didn't look like me. So I decided to lose weight. It was true that I'd eaten too much meat while doing the broadcast shows.

There were many opportunities other than those radio appearances that allowed me to communicate my thoughts to people. One of them was an invitation from the Blue House.* The presidential chief of staff had sent me an invitation to give a speech at the end-of-year Blue House event. I accepted the invitation as it would allow me to help unfortunate children receive attention at the national level and obtain support.

---

* South Korea's presidential residence.

It was an event called "A Performing and Speaking Party." Also present at that event were singer Youngshim Noh, the Buddhist monk Bup-Ryun, and also Jisun Lee. Ms. Lee had suffered burns all over her body from a sudden accident and was operated on over forty times. Despite that, she did not lose her courage and lives to spread hope to people.

It was an event held for the employees of the Blue House and their families. Many ministers were also present, together with their children. I spoke to the best of my ability in order to communicate my thoughts to them. I hadn't even prepared a script in advance. As I told the story of my life, the words just flowed out on their own. I spoke about how I'd begged at an age when I was supposed to have received love, why I'd become captivated by vocal music, and how I'd come to be able to communicate with people. I also told them that there were several terminally ill people among my fans, and that some thanked me after watching my video, saying that they were sorry, and that they loved me before going to heaven with peace in their hearts. When I returned home after the speech, I was overcome by the satisfaction that a mere high school graduate like me had made a speech at the Blue House.

There was another thing that brought me great satisfaction: I received an invitation from the United States, the country that I'd always wanted to visit. I got on a plane and went all the way to the United States "on the wings of song." A fan who was suffering from a severe illness wished to see me once before he died, and had invited me. The place was San Francisco, once the center of the hippie culture—a city of romance, freedom, and love.

When I arrived at the airport, surprisingly many people there recognized me. Since I couldn't speak English well, I couldn't understand what they were saying, and hoping that my true feelings would be understood by them, I just said, "I love you!" Some Americans I met at the airport café approached me and called my name, as they pointed at my video on their mobile phones to confirm whether I was indeed the person on the screen.

Some people said something in English and then began shedding tears. When I asked the people accompanying me what they were saying, they told me that they were talking about how they had received great consolation from listening to me sing. I'd never really received any special reactions on the streets in Korea. When I was greeted by people in a distant foreign country and witnessed how I'd yet again been a source of strength to the people there, it was an even greater source of consolation to me.

When I met the fan who had invited me to the United States, he said that he would be sorry to meet and listen to me sing all by himself. He asked whether he could organize a concert for me and invite people to the concert. When I nodded yes, he reserved for me a four-hundred-seat concert hall. While preparing for the concert, I met people from the Korean community associations, as well as the consul. It was a short mini-concert for charity. The tickets were sold out, and the hall was packed full of guests. Whether through the social network sites or through acquaintances, the news that I'd arrived in the country had gotten around. Some people had flown in just to see me. That concert was also broadcast on the local TV station.

Was I more famous abroad than in Korea? I was bewildered by this situation. At the concert, I sang the two songs that I'd prepared. Many people had come, and I wanted to tell them my story in addition to singing, but I couldn't do anything about that since I couldn't speak English. Anyway, communicating through songs rather than words suited me better. The performance itself was just under thirty minutes, but I still found it incredible to see myself sing in the United States.

I also held a talent donation event at a concert hall in Palo Alto, near San Francisco. The song that I sang there, "Amazing Grace," was a song that truly captured the feelings I had then.

Amazing grace! How sweet the sound
That saved a wretch like me.
I once was lost, but now am found,
Was blind, but now I see.

I'm now living in Seoul. I decided to just move here to save up on transportation costs and time since I get called frequently. The monthly rent and living expenses in Seoul are incomparably more expensive than in Daejeon. Since many events and speeches I got invited for were for charity and I don't have any fixed income, I'm managing by a narrow margin economically. Lately, I was back handing out flyers for a while, and I also did a few days of hard labor.

Just because I received worldwide attention
didn't mean that I suddenly turned rich or became a star.
That's not even something I hope for.
What I must do now is
to steadily create the being called "I" through music.
I've only just begun.

EPILOGUE

To All of You Who Gave Me the Reason to Live: Thank You, and I Love You

I WAS BORN in 1990, and I appeared on the show *Korea's Got Talent* in 2011. That's twenty-one years between the time I was born and the time I was broadcast on television. To me, *Korea's Got Talent* was a game changer that had completely transformed the twenty-one years of my life. In that sense, I might have to call the event not simply a broadcast show "debut," but a "debut" into another life altogether.

As I've already described over many pages, before the "debut," in both senses of the word, my life was like a stretch of time in which I drifted alone along a dark, cold, and boundless ocean. Those were the years when I felt as though my ankles were caught in the perpetual clasp of death that tried to pull me down to the bottom of the ocean depths. Before my encounter with music, I think I simply went on floundering in life, capable neither of cleaving through the water to save myself, nor actively calling for rescue.

After appearing on the broadcast show, it might look like I have been rescued from the depths of the dark ocean. However, I think the fact that I met you through *Korea's Got Talent* is nothing more than having discovered the light from a distant, shining beacon. I mentioned earlier how *Korea's Got Talent* had changed my life around completely, yet another part of me thinks that such dramatic happenings that change everything around instantly do not exist in life. There are still problems in my life that have not been resolved, and I expect that it will take a long time to find the solutions to them. I believe, however, that if I keep on discovering the beacons and swim forward stride by stride, I will be able to reach the shore someday.

Thrown into the rough and hostile world and thinking only of my own survival, I committed a lot of bad deeds in the past and have hurt others as much as I have been hurt. Alcohol, cigarettes, violence, drugs...I might have made you feel uncomfortable with the story of my life, which was steeped in crime and disorder. But I wanted to reveal myself just as I was, without embellishing or romanticizing things. I have tried to ruminate over the times that have made me who I am, without self-flattery or self-degradation.

Of course, I, who had lived a dead-end, bottom-stratum life, couldn't suddenly turn up one morning with a new face and say that the world is a great place to live in and that it's full of hope. Just as life does not switch around overnight, people also do not change instantly. Even so, I would like to speak of hope.

Some call me a lucky boy, having gone from a gum-selling orphan to a celebrity discussed by the various media. Others talk about how greatly fortunate I have been in making it through tremendous competition to win the second place on a television talent show. They may be right. Before going on the show, my death wish had reached its peak, and my mind, which I had barely been keeping sane, was gradually breaking down. What I—whose life was far from lucky in contrast to what people have said— wanted to communicate through this book was not luck, that source of fancy that's wispier than a strand of thread and narrower than the eye of a needle, but rather, hope.

When I lived in the semi-basement apartment, I used to sit absent-mindedly in a room with no sunlight. Even inside that narrow and dark semi-basement room, at some point during the day a thin ray of light would seep in, and for a very short moment, the space surrounding me would brighten up. That light, however, soon subsided, and the room was again submerged in darkness and silence. The existence of the light that had visited me without me realizing it seemed only an illusion.

However, it was just me inside that room who remained in the dark, because outside the window, the sunlight would always be shining. If I had closed the window, drawn the curtains, and stayed crouched under a blanket, I wouldn't have been able to see even that brief ray of light. It is because of that ray of light that we witness momentarily in life that we are able to fully open the window, push away the curtains, and finally walk out into the radiant streets.

When someone who had been diagnosed with terminal colorectal cancer looked at me and said, "Even [this kind of boy] made it through, whereas I just whiled away life grieving my misfortune," I felt a little embarrassed. My mind had always been full of the desire to die. I hadn't made it through because I had tried to live; I had made it through because I had not managed to die. During the time that I attended church with Mr. Jeongso Park, I threw only resentful questions at God: Why do I have to live like this? Why do you give me these kinds of trials in life? Why don't you just leave me alone and let me die?

The world that surrounded me felt utterly gloomy, and I turned away from the fact that light was shining elsewhere in the world. Even if I did see light, I didn't think that it would reach me, so I just kept myself trapped in a dark back room of my own accord.

Looking back, however, there had been more to my life than that: Mr. Jeongso Park, who had taken me—as I was then, without family or friends—as his student and taught me music; Ms. Gyeongeun Kim and Ms. Hyeonjung Yoo, my social worker guardians who had raced around trying every possible means to secure me welfare benefits; the many sponsors who had given me resolute support; the tteok-bokki lady who had given me, the gum-selling orphan, a name; the big sister who had embraced me warmly; the gum-selling brother who had saved me lying on the streets and bought me jajangmyeon;

the turtle lady who had given me clothes and food; the night school teachers who had tried to pull me from mere food-chain relationships into real human relationships; the turtle teacher who had let himself be ripped off for noodle money; Big Brother Yehjong who had taken me to church; the Pepero brother who had given me his warm friendship; the church deacons who had brought me household items to my rented studio…I had been the only one oblivious to the enormous amount of irreplaceable love I had been receiving. Perhaps it was because I had not been able to receive the love from family like the others that I was able to receive greater and bigger love from the people I met.

At the time when I went on *Korea's Got Talent*, I was being controlled by a victim mentality and an inferiority complex, thinking that I had been neglected and had been deprived of love. I was afraid that if a kid like me were to go out and sing in front of people, it would only attract sneers. I'd never told anyone my stories other than to Mr. Park, as I feared that laying bare my dark and depressing past to others would only attract criticisms. When I opened up to others, the complexes and lumps of inferiority that had seemed so massive to me till then actually had no substance behind them. They had been merely taking root inside my heart and branching out disproportionately. Once uprooted and exposed to the whole world, however, they were incapable of tormenting me like they used to.

Since appearing on media shows, I have met people who told me that they found hope and courage because of me; those meetings have, in turn, filled me with hope and courage. I believe that as we find hope and courage through each other in this way, my wounds will gradually be able to heal. When I was living as a street kid, I cried because I was saddened by the fact that no one would be able to remember me even if I died. But now, many people remember me, and that alone gives me a reason to live.

There was a song I remember hearing when I was selling gum as a kid. It's a song that I listen to almost every day even now. It is titled "With

Love," by the group Sunflower. I couldn't identify with pop-song lyrics like "I'm pissed off because my girlfriend doesn't pick up my call," but this song really touched my heart in many places:

> *There's yet another thing I need to do in life*
> *Even when I'm standing on a windy field, I am not lonely...*
> *Ah, we, with our never-changing, constant love*
> *Will reach out to light up the dark places*

Had it not been for these songs that I'd heard amid all the uncertainties, gloom, and faintness in life, I would have remained crouching in darkness to the end, unaware that there was light shining elsewhere in the world. If there is something that I, who had the privilege to cross over the bridge of life through music, need to do, it is to go and sing in places where there is despair. I wouldn't want anything more in life than to be able to "reach out to light up the dark places."

Oftentimes I find that my busy schedule makes me spend time absentmindedly. During those times, I remember the fan with terminal cancer who loved me so much, and I try to awaken myself. She has since passed away. It is through her that I have come to realize how precious each and every day is, and I continue to urge myself to study and practice with greater discipline.

I will devote myself and endeavor to become a crossover tenor like Andrea Bocelli. I would like to ardently return the love that I have received from the countless people who cheer me on.

I don't know what trials await me yet in the days that lie ahead. I will never cease, however, to live on as someone who sings of, and delivers hope to others in each and every situation.

> *To all of you, who have given me the reason to live:*
> *Thank you, and I love you.*

"I chose "Nella Fantasia" again for the finals [of *Korea's Got Talent*] because no other lyrics carried better the message that I wanted to tell the world," says Sungbong Choi. *Photo courtesy of Total Variety Network, South Korea.*

INTERVIEWS

Attesting to Sungbong Choi's Life

COULD IT BE a made-up story?

Might it have been exaggerated?

Sungbong Choi's story really seems too fictional.

In order to ensure the factuality of Sungbong Choi's narrative of his past, we found people who shared the past with him and who could attest to his life.

Here is the version of Sungbong Choi's story seen through the eyes of adults and told in a more objective stance.

Jaeyong Sohn, Night School Teacher

Jeongso Park, Sungbong Choi's teacher, Head of Luce Art Inc.

Gyeongeun Kim, Hyeonjung Yoo, Social Workers, Green Umbrella Child Fund,

Jongyeon Jung, Sooji Kim, *Korea's Got Talent* production crew

"I Hope You Will Be Able to Express Yourself"
Jaeyong Sohn, Night School Teacher

⸎

You met Sungbong Choi at the night school. What was he like when you first met him?

A. It was in April of 2001 that I went to [teach at] the night school. In June, I met Jiseong. We didn't know what his real name was then, so we called him Jiseong. I went to the school around 7:00 p.m. and saw a tiny kid trying to hide in the toilet. I asked him how he had found us. Instead of answering me, he asked what we did there, so I told him that it was where people prepared for their qualification exams. Another teacher said that he remembered how some lady came to drop him off with us.

About Jiseong staying at the night school: he tended to be sneaky that way, and it kind of settled into a pattern. He would sneak in saying, "I'm going to study," but he would be killing time alone somewhere, or he would say, "I came to hang out," then when you went to check back on him, you found that he had actually sneaked in to sleep. Gradually it began to feel natural having Jiseong eat and sleep at the night school. In his own words, he's skilled at doing those kinds of things knowingly or unknowingly—sleeping over being one thing, getting ripped off by him being another [*laughs*].

At first, I couldn't believe Jiseong's story. A kid escaping from an orphanage and living out on the streets—I just thought, how could such things happen? Although I found it hard to believe, neither could I think of it as a mere lie, because he had a starved look. You could sense something like a shadow in the expressions and the impressions he made that

238

he'd lived a hard life. Normally he wouldn't even talk that much, let alone smile at you, but when he became hungry, he would start to grin and say, "Teacher, the poor little lamb couldn't eat his meal, so spare him just one thousand won." It could disgust you, but it also felt poignant to see him like that.

I was a student then, and carried around less than five thousand won in cash. It was a tight sum simply to cover transportation and meals, yet there he was: Jiseong would rip me off one or two thousand won almost every day [*laughs*]. When he used to learn dancing, he often asked me to lend him transportation money, saying that it took an hour for him to walk there. After all, compared to Jiseong, a poor college student like me was considered relatively well off.

Q. The night school is a place that has a special meaning for Mr. Choi. In your perspective, what kind of place was the night school for Mr. Choi?

A. Well, in simple terms, I might say that the night school was, to Jiseong, a place where he asked for food or got his transportation fare when he needed to go somewhere. Of course, it was also where he could sleep. Classes finished around ten o'clock, and he would always come by around then and ask for food. He didn't come to classes. Even when he did, he didn't actually take the classes, but went in and out of the room creating distractions. He would sing loudly in the teachers' room, act cheeky in front of elderly students, say "Yes, yes," to people who would give him food, then swear at them when they didn't treat him well. He was simply reckless.

There were some elderly students who gave food to Jiseong from time to time, but he continued to be rebellious and unruly. Eventually everyone just seemed to want to avoid him. He probably didn't see much of his peers who came to the school, since he went out before classes began and returned after we were done. There were some kids, though, who sometimes asked about Jiseong, saying, "Where does he sleep?" "What does he eat?" But it was more out of curiosity than concern.

In fact, I don't think people at the night school understood Jiseong. I also think that the biggest reason why he left the night school was because he felt ashamed comparing himself with the others. There was a big gap that separated him from others, and he couldn't close it. Yet he also had a hard time accepting it.

Just like how a bird is born by breaking out of its egg, perhaps the time at the night school was to Jiseong a phase when he was trying to break out of his shell. The night school must have been a precious place for him, but at the same time, a place that instilled in him the feeling of shame and bad memories. It was a place that allowed him to form a self-image, but it seemed that the image was going to form in a direction that was going to be hard for him to accept, and that led him to decide to leave the night school.

Q. I heard that the school held several faculty meetings because of Mr. Choi. What were the main discussions about him?

A. Night schools are places where people volunteer to invest their time to help people. Although I felt that I should give focused care to Jiseong, I found it hard to carry it out in action. The teachers were college students or working employees rather than professional educators, and it wasn't an easy task to hold Jiseong down and make him study when he wouldn't even come in for classes. Also, Jiseong didn't like to be held down.

We had several faculty meetings. The first meeting was just exchanging opinions on whether we should keep Jiseong or make him leave. At the second meeting, the latter opinion seemed to prevail, but when we took a vote at the end of the meeting, there were slightly more votes to keep him. When we voted again at the third meeting, there were more votes to have him leave. One teacher, though, stepped forward saying that he would take the responsibility for Jiseong. So the meeting concluded with the plan that this teacher was going to assume full responsibility over Jiseong, but things went back to square one when the teacher quit the night school two weeks later. I was the vice-principal then, and I went quite strong on how we shouldn't discharge a student who had no place to go. Besides, it wasn't really a problem to be decided through majority vote.

At the final meeting, the opinion that the school could not tolerate Jiseong any longer predominated. Even I was going to tell Jiseong to move on to another place. He must have taken the hint. He left before I had a chance to speak a word to him. That was right after he had the fight with Mr. Hong. There were pictures that he'd taken with other people on school picnic, and I saw that he'd cut his face out of them all. In addition to the photos, he'd erased all other traces of himself and thoroughly tidied up the teachers' room before leaving. Jiseong and I communicated a couple of times even after that.

I heard that you helped Mr. Choi to become a basic livelihood security recipient. He said that it wasn't an easy process. Would you please tell us about that?

A. It's illegal and punishable by law to keep runaway minors like Jiseong without notifying the state. We discovered that Jiseong was neither a missing child nor an orphan. Although he said that he'd run away from an orphanage, there wasn't even any missing report about him. When we ran a background check with his fingerprints, we found that he even had a father. We couldn't contact him, though. We somehow managed to contact the uncle, but he said, "I don't know; he'll manage to live on his own; I don't want you to contact us again," then hung up. I didn't have a chance to tell him how Jiseong was doing. His tone showed that he was absolutely against any obligation to support him. What a pity! His parents had really abandoned him! I heard that there was no legal basis to punish child support evasion, but still, morally speaking, that shouldn't happen. When he discovered from the background check that his name was Sungbong Choi, he became very confused. He found out about who he was only at age fourteen, so he must have had a lot of woes about his identity. He also didn't like the name Sungbong Choi.

Making him a welfare recipient was an idea that one teacher had proposed during the faculty meeting. He first had to get a certificate of residence, and we only managed with difficulty because the night school was a municipal estate. The biggest difficulty, though, was that he had parents listed on his family register. He didn't become a welfare recipient right away, but after he left the night school. There was one dong office employee who felt sorry for Jiseong and gave him a lot of help. It was thanks to him that things worked out. So Jiseong received his recipient benefits after things eventually got processed with the conclusion that his parents had relinquished support. He then probably got around three hundred thousand won per month.

Q. Did you watch *Korea's Got Talent*? I'm curious to know what you felt about it.

A. I thought Jiseong would become a dancer. When he was at the night school, he was all into learning dancing at a dance academy. When we got in touch later, he told me that he was receiving support money as a child head of household, and that he'd entered an arts high school, so I thought, "Good; things were working out well for him." What I wanted most from Jiseong was that whatever he decided to do, he would not go down a wrong path.

Then I was surprised when I saw him on *Korea's Got Talent*. When he was at the night school, he was as thin as chopsticks, and there, I almost didn't recognize him because he'd developed a build. At the night school, he would be like, "Teacher, isn't it obvious that you should help out kids like me? So why should I be thankful?" Then after the TV show, he came to me and said, "You know that I like you." It just drove me crazy [*laughs*].

Q. How would you describe Mr. Choi's character?

A. Jiseong doesn't like to be constrained. Regarding his studies, for instance, the teachers didn't officially teach him anything. A few teachers tried to teach him, but he's not the type who follows orders. Since he disliked instruction, we just had to leave him alone. Then he studied by himself with the books at the night school and passed the exam. He calls himself a genius for that, but he actually passed with difficulty, failing several times on the individual subjects. But it is impressive that he passed the exams through self-study. Jiseong understands situations through wits and tact, because that's what he had to do to survive on the streets, and because he's unique like that, he also solves problems that way. He reads a question, gives it a good stare, and sees the hidden solution.

He must have become that way because he had to live alone without having anyone to take care of him, but he's also got sharp wits by nature. He's lived a tumultuous life since he was little, so he's more experienced than most adults, and that makes him more knowledgeable than others in terms of life experiences. But at the same time, he's got that side of being a frog in a well that's never seen the ocean. It must be because he's had to confront situations where he had to rely solely on his own experiences.

Jiseong's a bit abrasive. When we speak, we just have to simply speak what we think, but he tends to reflexively blurt out something abrasive, without conscious thought. And he tends to avoid expressing his ideas. In other words, he has a different mode of expression from others, but he shouldn't allow that to become a reason that drives people away from him. What I want from Jiseong runs along those lines: being careful about what he says to others and being courteous to them, so that he can get along with the people around him. But to Jiseong, that might be the hardest thing in life. I hope he continues to learn how to express himself.

"Receiving Love for the First Time in Twenty-Two Years: A Grace and Blessing"
Jeongso Park, Head of Luce Art Inc.

———— ❧ ————

Q. We know that you are a teacher who gave a lot of help to Sungbong Choi. What was your first impression of Mr. Choi? He said that you had posted a lesson ad on the Internet. How did you feel when Sungbong Choi came to you?

A. That was around the end of my fourth year in the university. It soon turned cold after we started lessons, so it must have been in early winter that we first met. I was around twenty-seven or twenty-eight then.

I was at school when this kid came up to me saying that he wanted to learn how to sing. When I asked him to sing, he sang some pop song. He wasn't informed about anything. Normally, kids would come together with their parents and first consult me about things like which university they want to attend, and what we should decide for the hourly lesson fee, etc., but Sungbong just told me nonchalantly, "I have no money." He didn't act pitiful. In fact, I felt some inexplicable confidence coming from him. A kid who was in a difficult environment to learn about classical music had, by chance, become captivated by it. I found it astounding. But I was just an ordinary college student, and my graduation was coming up very soon. Since I couldn't give him a definite answer right away, I simply told him that was good for now.

On the other hand, I found what Sungbong told me hard to believe. Sungbong has put on some weight now, but back then, he was this willowy boy with a pretty face and milky-white skin. Even now, Sungbong says that as far as his skin is concerned, he considers himself endowed, and it was utterly so back then. Maybe he had preened himself to his best form before he came to see me. But a good-looking boy who said he had neither a home nor parents would have made a doubting Thomas of anyone. So I said, "Let's go to where you live," and I went there with him together with my now-wife.

There were some container offices behind the vacant lot near the inter-city bus terminal, and they looked like ruins to me. It was early winter and freezing cold. I saw there a tattered, ragged blanket that lay on a worn-out, black fake-leather sofa. He told me that he slept there. The lights didn't work properly, and the place had no heating, but he didn't even have a single electric pad to heat up the floor. I was dumbfounded, and I asked, "How do you sleep here?" He simply told me that he put on several layers of jumpers, pulled the ragged blanket over him, and slept with only his nose sticking out. The faucet outside had already frozen over completely.

I just stared blankly at that unbelievable scene. Then as I turned around and said, "Okay, see you tomorrow at school," tears started to flow suddenly. They just burst out and began pouring out uncontrollably. My wife and I came home bawling like that. How was it even possible to have such a kid in this world? How could there be such a little kid getting beaten up, getting hurt, collapsing on the streets...The only thing I could give him was to teach him how to sing. I didn't know about welfare and all that.

Q. How did the lessons take place? We are curious to know Mr. Choi's attitude about taking his lessons.

A. Students normally take lessons once or twice a week. Other kids would come for the lesson and return home after the lesson was over, but Sungbong came every day and stayed from morning till night since he didn't have anyone telling him to go home early or have friends to play with. He would take his lessons, and then for the rest of the day, he would be by himself playing the piano and practicing. His days began effectively to revolve around music, in a musical atmosphere. He had had no hope or anything whatsoever, but once having found something he liked, he seemed to be holding on to it for dear life.

In my opinion, Sungbong's character now isn't all that different from what it used to be then. First of all, he knows his own mind. Back then, I gave him the nickname Dr. Choi, because he'd talk back to me all the time. As soon as I'd say something, he'd go, "Mr. Park, that's not right," "Mr. Park, this is like this, and that's like that." I come from Gyeongsang-do, so when Sungbong talked back, I'd flare up and bark, "Why not?" Eventually I just went, okay, bring it on, you're the doctor, and started calling him Dr. Choi.

But as time passed, I began to think about why it was inevitable that Sungbong had that kind of personality. He didn't have anyone to take care of him. Other kids go looking for their mom, dad, big brother, or big sister when they feel that they've been treated unfairly or get upset, but since Sungbong doesn't have anyone by his side, he must have had to consider his words as definitive. Believing in his own thoughts was the only way that he could survive. It allowed me to understand him and I asked myself, "Would this kid have been able to survive without such a character?"

Q. It appears that Sungbong's life gained stability from the time you let him stay at your music academy. That wouldn't have been an easy decision to make...

A. Initially, I was thinking of studying abroad after graduation. Circumstances didn't work out for a few reasons, and so I put together the funds I'd saved for studying abroad with my wife's money and opened an academy. That was in January of 2004.

We opened it all right, but it was quite a challenging situation. The academy's location wasn't so favorable, we hadn't recruited any students, and we didn't have the kind of money to put out advertisements. To start off, we printed four thousand flyers. But neither my wife nor I had done things like distributing flyers before. The weather was cold, and standing in the streets distributing flyers felt pathetic and embarrassing.

But then Sungbong came. He led my junior colleagues out and began distributing the flyers like a pro! He would run around deftly in that cold weather, distributing the flyers to people, neatly sticking them into apartment postboxes, barking at my junior colleagues who were actually older than him when he saw them hesitating. It must have been because he'd lived a hard life, but he was tough. Sungbong's never said "thank you" to me directly, but I saw that he was expressing himself in this way what he was unable to say in words.

At that time, Sungbong didn't have a proper place to sleep. So I told him that since he was able to get along well with the other kids, and most of all, now that we'd made a musical environment, he could pack up his things and move over if he wanted to. He did so right away. I wouldn't call him a burden or anything. Sungbong is quick-witted, so he didn't do things that would turn off or annoy other people.

The academy settled in by the end of three months, and two years later, we had over one hundred and twenty students. Sungbong was also on pretty good terms with the other students at the academy. Several of them contacted him even after he got broadcast on TV. But now, it'd be really hard to tell you all the details.

Q. We heard that it was through your advice that Mr. Choi sang in a church choir. Were there people at the church who helped Mr. Choi?

A. Yes. I was in charge of conducting the choir. I used to conduct and sing there, and also received a bit of honorarium to use as pocket money. The church deacons did feel sorry for Sungbong, but since he wasn't their child or relative, none readily stepped forward to help.

Although Sungbong was young, he was given to participating in the adult choir. By moving about here and there in the church that way, he was able to begin naturally his walk of faith. Since he was a kid who loved music, he would be consoled by the message he heard in the praise songs. That had a greater impact on him than a hundred spoken phrases. He became influenced by the religious atmosphere by listening to the praise songs.

Q. What is your opinion of Mr. Choi's musical talent?

A. Musically speaking…when Sungbong started to learn vocal music, he learned breathing and vocalizing techniques from me, but I think he spent more time watching me or other teachers teaching other students. That's the way that Sungbong learns something. Perhaps you could call it an acquisitive ability; he has the ability to watch what other people do and absorb it as his own.

It takes perhaps twenty years to be considered a seasoned vocalist, and Sungbong has learned music only for four years. Even when he went on *Korea's Got Talent*, we had a big fuss because he wasn't fully ready for the second and third rounds. The Sungbong that you see today is just someone who's graduated from an arts high school. He didn't go to the university, and he has had only so much time to really delve deeply into the core of what music is.

In spite of that, Sungbong is gifted with a soulful and smooth voice. I have a strong voice, but in Sungbong's case, his sensibility reveals in his tone. It seems that Sungbong's story interlocks with his voice and becomes elevated. You could express it by saying that the twenty-four years of his life have been dissolved into his singing, and that's what makes people sense a lot of things in his voice. There was a fan from abroad who evaluated

Sungbong's voice this way: that his voice contained depth that could not be described in words, strength that originated from within, as well as flexibility.

He hasn't a brilliant technique because he couldn't get that kind of training, but being able to melt his sorrow into the voice that he was gifted with is his forte. You notice that even in the movie *Seopyeonje*, the singer is intentionally made blind in order to implant sorrow in her. The reason why people are moved even when Sungbong sings with an expressionless face must be because of the sorrowful emotion that they hear in his voice. If Sungbong continues to work with consistent effort, I believe that after a few years, he'll become an artist who touches solely through his singing, without all the background stories.

Q. We heard that you recommended Mr. Choi to the program *Korea's Got Talent*.

A. Yes. Since I ran a classical music academy business and a public performance planning enterprise, the people from the program called me and requested recommendations for people who could appear on the show. There must be more than fifty thousand kids all over the country who learn authentic classical music, so I was a bit skeptical about going classical, thinking it probably wouldn't bring any sort of positive outcome. But then suddenly Sungbong shot up in my mind. There were a lot of good-looking and talented people around me, but I could only think of Sungbong. Talking in terms of faith, I think it had been directed by God. At the time, it had been a year since Sungbong had left for Daegu, so we hadn't been contacting each other much, but I called him right away. He held out, saying he wasn't going to go on the show, but I persuaded him and just barely managed to make him go.

Q. We'd like to hear about the story after Mr. Choi appeared on *Korea's Got Talent*.

A. Sungbong came back from the regional round and told me that he had made it to the preliminary round. I was still clueless then about how things would turn out. I'd also been busy. Anyway, he'd made it through the preliminary round, so we had to prepare the next song. Since we didn't have anything prepared, we were hurriedly practicing a few pieces. Then on June 4, when he appeared on the broadcast, that's when it all happened. As soon as the broadcast came on, I thought, here it is, this is what I've been waiting for all along. Even though I knew about Sungbong's story, I cried a lot while watching that show. Then as soon as the show was over, I started getting all these calls from everywhere. I couldn't adjust to all the uproar and couldn't sleep a wink all night. After that, the global media also expressed their interest and even the production crew and people at *Korea's Got Talent* became dazed by the unexpected sensation.

Things must have been more intense for Sungbong than for me, having those sudden changes in his life. After that, Sungbong went to Seoul, and he must have found the broadcast schedule, preparations, and stress hard to cope with. Had he had parents or siblings or someone, they could have given him support. I wanted to go there myself and help him, but I couldn't since I was working.

Then for the final round, I went to Seoul with my "family" from work and my students. I was watching from the very first row, and of course thought it would be great if he won first place.

When they announced the winner as Minjeong Joo, and not Sungbong Choi, all of a sudden my eyes were filled with tears. I think I cried for around ten minutes. In my heart, I was like, "But God, Sungbong's had such an incredibly hard life till now; how could you not give him first prize?" Sungbong was the one who stayed calm about it and comforted me, saying that it was all right. In retrospect, you could say that the first-prize winner has it all right there and then, and has everything end there, whereas the second-prize winner still has a lot of stories to continue on from that point. That must also have been God's wisdom telling us to continue on with the next story. Sungbong received a lot of help through that broadcast show. He was a kid who used to receive not even the slightest attention from people when he was roaming the streets, and who used to be treated worse than a bug or a worm. When I saw how light was being shed on him and how he was receiving support as his life began to be known, I thought God was rewarding him for the ordeals and hardships that had been his lot over the past twenty-two years.

Oh, when support funds started coming in for Sungbong, I told him not to use them but to save up. That must have been why Sungbong didn't spend even ten won on anything, but then one day, the fellow suddenly brought some clothes he'd bought and tossed them to me, saying that they were for me to wear. I'm a single-suit kind of guy. Once I start wearing a set of clothes, I wear it for six, seven years, and I find it comfortable to wear one set of clothes, and I wear it as long as it's not worn out. Sungbong was bothered by that and had bought me clothes, telling me to pull up my fashion sense. Well, I understood what he meant, but they weren't my style. But anyway, I was proud of him.

Then one day, he asked me to go with him to buy a computer, so I went with him to the computer store. Then he asked the salesperson what the most expensive thing in the store was, and splurged on that. Since he likes computers, I assumed that he was going to use it for himself, but I found that he'd put away the old one at my company and had replaced it. I said, "Hey, what's this?" Then he said, "You're the owner of the company, so you should be using at least this." So I said, "It's not like I didn't have money, so why did you buy this kind of thing with your money?" Then he said, "The first computer I had was from you, and it was something that I'd wanted so much then. I wonder whether you knew how thankful I felt then?" At that moment, I felt a little choking in my chest. I think I learned a lot by teaching Sungbong. But I still use the outdated computer. The one Sungbong bought me is too fast; I can't get used to it [*laughs*].

Q. You are like a father to Mr. Choi. What do you think of your relationship with each other?

A. My wife said that the relationship between us was like the one between a crocodile and a crocodile bird* [*laughs*]. He'd gone to Daegu and then had returned to Daejeon after a year or so and found a room, and it turned out to be right next to our house. There have been many times when we didn't see each other for several months, but it seems that even if we don't forcefully try to put distance between us, or particularly try to be together, we'll continue to live close to each other.

Whenever someone thanked me for having given a lot of help to Sungbong, I would tell them that I was the one who had received help from Sungbong. I learn by telling myself, "I have both my parents and I have lived in a harmonious family, so I'm a blessed person, so I should be doing more." In that respect, Sungbong is like a teacher to me too. When I saw how Sungbong lived diligently without resentment, my life appeared too extravagant in comparison. Since meeting Sungbong, my mind-set about life has changed a lot. You could see ours as a mutual win-win relationship.

A teacher-student relationship that resembles friendship seems to be an asset in life. People think that money is the only kind of asset in life, but I hope people will understand that relationships like the one between Sungbong and me are invisible assets.

---

* A relationship in which each has to mutually depend on the other for subsistence or survival.

Q. Right now, Sungbong manages everything on his own instead of belonging to an agency. Do you intend to manage him by taking him under your company?

A. I'm not sure, since I'm not so greatly qualified…I'm merely somebody with passion, whereas Sungbong has become famous all over the world. You may argue that he's my student, but I think it's only right that a more global company manages him. I think my role goes only up to the time before he appeared on the broadcast show. In the same way that parents abstain from reaping financial benefits through their children—though I'm not a parent—I continue to pray that I will not think of making a business out of Sungbong. In case I begin to have such ideas coming to me without being aware, I'm preparing my mind firmly through prayer. We're still teacher and student to each other like the old days, so I try to help him as far as I'm able to, and share life's blessings. Our hearts are still the same as before; only the situation has changed. My opinion is that we should keep up that initial heart-to-heart relationship. I've never given Sungbong special treatment, but at the same time, I wouldn't abandon him, saying, I don't know and I don't care. I just want to continue to stand by him with a constant heart, like a tree.

Q. Do you have anything you would like to tell Mr. Choi's parents?

A. They must have met and married each other and given birth to their child in love. I don't know the exact details, but I find it hard to understand why they threw away their child when they separated. I'm raising a child now too, and I find my child so priceless and precious and beautiful. Sungbong's mom and dad must have also felt that way. I don't know what could have been so hateful and difficult as to have made them abandon their own child, but it appears to me that they had selfish hearts. It was because of that selfishness that Sungbong ran out and ended up living on the streets. There could be situations where you can't exactly treat your child like gold, but there couldn't be any situation that allows you to simply dispose of your child, who is like your own life. That's how I see it. These days, there are a lot of people who break up and give up on their families. I think in this way, our society has become much more selfish, so much so that some people consider their children to be some lumps that need to be removed.

Looking at Sungbong's face, you would think that had he been born in a noble household, he would have been raised like a gilded youth. He's smart, and he's quick and sure when it comes to his wits, reflexes, and whatever else, so I think he would have been raised well. But had Sungbong died on the streets, no one would have known about the disappearance of this precious life! It's an issue that, through Sungbong, needs to be addressed in our society, by sounding the alarm that people should not separate and abandon others so easily. People should also not decide lightly about ending their own lives. I hope everyone understands how precious and sacred life is.

Q. Please tell us what you hope from Mr. Choi in the coming years, and what you want to say to him.

A. First of all, I would say his health. He might appear completely normal on the outside, but when he lived on the streets, he had to sleep crouching in cold places every day and he'd hurt his leg from car accidents, so his knees are in pretty bad condition. One of his ears is also not good. Malnutrition must have played a part too in his health. What's the use of becoming an icon of hope to people? It's important that he neither gets sick nor dies. I hope he eats well, sleeps well, doesn't get stressed out, and becomes healthy.

Another thing is about religion. I hope that he depends on God and finds his stability in him. Whether he becomes a superstar or an artist, or loses his interest again and returns to being an ordinary person, I hope that he doesn't agitate himself or lose his essence.

The last thing is that although Sungbong has come to live a life that's very different from what it used to be, I hope he will always remain humble. The reason why Sungbong touches other people isn't because he has more things than others but because he's had a needier and a harder life. Also, musically I hope that he puts in ever-greater effort and renews himself continually as a true musician, and in that way, carries on this story.

Sungbong's story is actually a difficult story to make up even deliberately. I saw that foreign press described him as "Korea's Paul Potts," or "the second Susan Boyle," but I think compared to the story of Paul Potts, who was a simple, good-natured mobile phone salesman, or of Susan Boyle, who as a country lady received the world's attention at forty-seven years of age, Sungbong's story is much more amazing. I think it's beyond such comparison. I think God himself was the author of this story. In our country, which has the world's number-one suicide rate, God must be telling his message amid people's mental crises through Sungbong. He's giving us hope. I believe that it wasn't a case where Sungbong ended up delivering hope half-bewildered himself, simply by the virtue of having appeared on a broadcast show, but that perhaps God had been preparing him for a long time to become an icon of hope.

"He's a Miracle Case"
Gyeongeun Kim and Hyeonjung Yoo, Social Workers, Green Umbrella Child Fund

Q. Hello. Would you please introduce yourselves?

Gyeongeun Kim: Yes, I'm Gyeongeun Kim, a social worker at the Green Umbrella Child Fund. Our foundation is a welfare service organization that provides support for the survival, protection, and development of children in need.

Hyeonjung Yoo: I work in the same office with our team leader, Ms. Gyeongeun Kim; as a successor to Ms. Kim, I've been in charge of Sungbong since 2008.

Q. When was the first time that you got to know Mr. Choi? Please tell us also how you felt when you met him.

Kim: Mr. Jeongso Park, who is an acquaintance of Sungbong, gave us a call. He said that one of his students was in great financial difficulty and asked whether we could help him. After that, Sungbong wrote a letter to us too. Hearing Sungbong's story was disconcerting to me at first, because it didn't seem plausible in this age. I had to see him in person and confirm the facts, and determine in what areas and what ways we should provide help, so we decided to meet up. We first met at our office, and after that we went to visit him.

It might have been because I met him with a preconception—that here was a child who'd gone through a lot of hardships and who'd had tough adversities in life. When I first met him, I thought he had a surprisingly good bearing. He was fairer than I had expected, and his expression showed that he'd already been through life. In a way, you could describe it as cute, but I got a strong sage-like impression from him. He had a rather weak voice, and you could feel that he was very tired. He had never been in a system where he could get help, so he didn't know what to do.

Yoo: I was also relieved to see that considering his history, Sungbong appeared healthy. His face was all milky and cute [*laughs*]. I thought he possessed tremendous strength. For a short while at first, I thought about whether he'd really lived such a life, and whether he might be distorting the truth or was simply mistaken about himself. But when I got to know him better, I kept thinking about how he's someone who really needs a lot of care, and I was very glad that Sungbong had gotten to know about us.

Q. Could you tell us what specific help you provided to Mr. Choi?

Kim: As the most urgent priority, we wanted to allow him to live properly. We began searching immediately for sponsors. We have a method of developing our own sponsors to provide support. So we found sponsors and little by little connected him up with support funds. It wasn't a lot of money. Even middle-class families have to pay a lot to give their children music education, and he would have been on a tight budget simply to get by with the funds we channeled to him. So I tried to match him with as many sponsors as possible. Even after Sungbong, we seldom gave so much support funds to one child. They went up to a maximum of six hundred thousand won per month for him, and we normally don't give funds out in one lump sum.

The problem with finding a residence for him continued to worry us, but we found out that if he was declared a child head of household, he would be able to receive two hundred thousand won from Samsung, and he would also receive rental fee benefits, and a lot of other benefits too. So we contacted the gu office through our director and helped him to become a child head of household, got his rental covered, and found him a room.

The problem then was that since it was the first time Sungbong had lived in a big house by himself, he didn't take care of it and lived in such a mess that perhaps he needed to get connected to a housecleaning volunteer [*laughs*].

Yoo: He said so himself, that his house was a mess. Maybe he said that because I was busy and he wanted my attention. I was in charge of over three thousand children then. I did always feel sorry that I couldn't give greater attention to Sungbong because my work tends to be busy and arduous.

Q. We would like to know the detailed process of declaring someone as a child head of household.

Kim: The request is actually supposed to pass from the dong office up to the gu office for the declaration, but for Sungbong, our foundation made the request, which got sent from the gu office down to the dong office; they then made the investigation at the dong level, and he became a recipient. In other words, it happened in the reverse order. I remember contacting the city office; I sent a letter of introduction to the executive secretary, told him that there was a boy in such-and-such circumstance, and asked him to help Sungbong become a child head of household. I called the gu office and made a polite request, asking them whether they should at least allow this child to attend school, and the story must have gone down to the dong

259

office. The terms of arrangement for the recipient are specified in a guideline, but there must have been some leeway for the manager to show some flexibility.

The managers who heard about Sungbong's story cooperated favorably. It might actually have been difficult, but in the end the declaration was successfully processed. There were many people who helped behind the scenes. It was difficult to declare him since first of all, he had parents on the family register, and that's probably why the dong office didn't pass him up to the gu office. Parental rights are like sacred ground: as long as there is a line that links him on the family register, he would go on being ensnared there. That was what used to shackle Sungbong's ankles in the past. But there was a clause in the guideline that allowed the child to become a child head of household if the guardians with parental custody rights were said to be completely disconnected with the child. When the declaration finally went through, Sungbong never forgot to mention how thankful he was every time he met me. I hadn't helped him with the intention of hearing such words, and to me, the declaration was something to be thankful about.

Q. You said that you went with Sungbong to visit his father. How did it go?

Kim: [Basic data about his father] appears on the family register document, so we went to the dong office to ask for his contact information. Sungbong's biological parents had divorced, and his father had remarried a foreign woman and even had children. When Sungbong went to his father's address and made a call from there, he told him to go back because he wasn't going to meet him. Sungbong returned without being able to meet his father, but he didn't cry in front of us. He just tried to accept it serenely. That moment made my heart ache the most. He'd been abandoned once, and as if that weren't enough, when he went back to find his father, he was abandoned yet again. I think that must have been a big shock for Sungbong. It didn't seem to me that his father was all that well off.

Q. Are there many parents who give up on supporting their children like in Mr. Choi's case?

Kim: When they come to a situation where they cannot raise their children, they mostly entrust the children to their relatives. It was the first time for me to come across, in Sungbong's case, where everyone was an utter stranger. That's why I felt the need to step into the parents' shoes, and I used to tell him a lot of things he didn't like to hear. There was no obligation between Sungbong and me to continue seeing each other, and he could simply use the support fund for its intended purpose. But to leave it so businesslike was, first of all, a deviation from professional ethics, and I also felt that as an adult person in society, I shouldn't behave that way toward someone who is my junior in the arena of life.

Yoo: I could see that Sungbong needed someone to tell him the painful truth in areas that really mattered to him and also regarding the way he was living his life. I mainly nagged him about his future career and school life. I sincerely hoped that he would realize the value of the life that he'd struggled through so tenaciously, and grow into a healthy member of society.

Q. How did Mr. Choi put up with your mom-like nagging?

Kim: Right. Whenever I nagged him to do something, he would eventually get it done, except that his progress would be slow. And he really knew how to quibble. Sungbong's biggest shortcoming is that he would keep going on about how I didn't understand his feelings because I hadn't had as many experiences in life. I was disappointed every time I heard him say that.

Q. Are people allowed to receive multiple forms of welfare aids?

Kim: Yes. We've had up to three forms of aid: basic livelihood security, child head of household aid, and children's foundation support fund. On top of that, one-time scholarships were also recommended for press interviews. Also, Sungbong's story had been broadcast on the radio, so listeners sent support items. I made a lot of recommendations here and there for Sungbong in order to let his story be known and be published. I wanted him to receive a lot of money through every possible means, because it costs a lot of money to study music. Since the support money wasn't nearly enough, he took on part-time jobs, but even then, he could barely get by with studying music. He did whatever work there was out there. Kids these days don't do that. So isn't Sungbong admirable in that sense? But it really upset me that he was always broke even though he was working so hard.

Q. How was Mr. Choi's high school life?

Yoo: Sungbong was so happy simply for being able to attend school, but that was only until he realized that he couldn't have deep relationships with friends at school and that he wasn't getting along well with his teachers. The part-time work must have been hard on his body, because he couldn't concentrate in class, and he always seemed daunted and low spirited due to the pressure of having to work part-time unlike ordinary students.

So it's probably right to say that was the reason why he was so awkward in relating to his friends and didn't know how to develop friendships or how to adjust to a school life that's geared toward university entrance. I once asked the school teachers and other students to please try to understand Sungbong.

Kim: At the foundation, we thought that we'd removed the big obstacles by providing Sungbong with a certain amount of financial support in order for him to have proper music training, but suddenly during his first year in high school, he told us that he wanted to transfer out of the school. When we looked up the information for him, we found that it was too late during the year to transfer. We also looked up alternative schools, but none were open for him. We'd thought that he'd be able to handle things by himself once we helped him to settle financially, but as might have been expected, we realized that money alone wasn't going to be enough. We were stumped as to how we could help him when these kinds of problems began cropping up. He pulled himself together anyway and made it through the remaining years, but he almost had to repeat a year.

Yoo: That was probably the hardest period. Despite all the difficulties, he'd wanted to enter an arts high school to become a musician, yet things were hard enough to make him consider transferring to a normal high school. I can just imagine how hard it must have been for him.

Q. You seem to have a special affection for Sungbong.

Kim: Yes. Sungbong was a kid who came across to me not as someone to manage, but someone I needed to take care of like his real older sister. There were around two thousand children I was in charge of; and of course, there is the saying that there wouldn't be any finger out of the ten that wouldn't hurt when bitten. Should there indeed be a finger that would hurt more than the others, it would be Sungbong. He's got no blood relations and grew up in a place that was full of adult entertainment venues.

Had he resolved to make his life there, he would have gone in the direction of becoming a mugger or a gangster, but even amid those circumstances, he found what he wanted to do, and in spite of everything, endeavored to actually go as far as entering an arts high school. It was his own abilities that took him there, and that alone showed that he was a sufficiently capable person, and that's why I was more concerned than usual about him.

Had I been in his situation, I wonder whether I would have been able to pass qualification exams, find a teacher and learn how to sing, and enter an arts high school all by myself. I don't think anyone would find it easy to make one's own way through life like Sungbong did. He must have learned how to make easy money in Yongjeon-dong. He could have easily thought that the good-for-nothing wastrels were cool brothers to look up to, and he must have seen how quickly they got their cars and how they splurged their money. I find it really admirable that he did not falter. He was also sociable, and would rather be wronged and suffer than ask others for favors or wrongfully acquire something.

Q. What was it like the time when Mr. Choi got hurt?

Kim: I was very upset. He fell while doing a part-time job somewhere and seriously hurt himself but didn't even tell us about it and just suffered alone. It was only much later that we heard about what had happened. Ms. Yoo and I wanted Sungbong to count on us as the first ones he could speak to when he had difficulties, and we were ready to run to his aid, but he always tried to solve the problems himself. From our perspective, we simply felt that it was too bad, because if he had asked for help, we'd have found a solution for him somehow. It really distressed us to see him not being able to either receive help or earn enough money, but just all the while living off his hard-earned money.

Yoo: Exactly. Since Sungbong worked early mornings, he had a reversed, night-to-day schedule and frequently skipped meals. We feared that he would start having health problems. In fact, that's how he did end up getting hurt. Sungbong has this very unusual financial sense, and he didn't want to work in low-stress, low-paying jobs. He tried to take high-paying jobs even if it meant doing hard physical labor in the early morning.

We visited him while he was in hospital, and to our relief, saw that he was enduring well. He must have been in so much pain due to the injury, and we were proud to see him enduring and overcoming the pain.

Q. Did Mr. Choi often attend the events held by the foundation?

Kim: Yes. Whenever we asked Sungbong to appear on a program we had organized, he would come willingly. That was his forte. There was no one in the office at the time who didn't know Sungbong, because he would act up so much. Even the director asked about Sungbong periodically. When we told him to do things, he would get them done after all, even though he'd be resistant and act all chic. Sungbong appeared on programs periodically, and although he tried to put on a bright expression, he had a lot of worries inside.

The programs run by the foundation were camp-type activities: some were designed only for the children, and others were accompanied by the sponsors, and there would be Christmas parties as well. They were for recreation and play. It must have been because he'd met and lived with a lot of people, because he got along well with the kids who went there with him. They were either his peers or younger kids. Actually high schoolers don't attend camps very often, but Sungbong would come along willingly.

One memorable camp was a two-day camp to a water park hosted by a sponsor company that Sungbong attended during his final year in high school. The children were sitting around chatting with each other after eating dinner; Sungbong suddenly went, "Miss, could you please hug me just once?" Since he was already in the final year of high school and was almost a grown-up, I felt a bit awkward, but it seemed that Sungbong wasn't just playing around asking to be hugged. So I hugged him, and I almost burst into tears because I think I might have really given him the help that he needed. I had the hunch that it was going to be the last camp that Sungbong was going to participate in under sponsorship. It felt like good-bye. I thought he'd go to university right after that. He did end up leaving.

Q. What happened after he graduated from high school?

Yoo: It seemed that he wasn't able to properly deal with realistic concerns about how he was going to go on after graduation. Since in Korea, people are considered adults after graduating from high school, the support money that guaranteed him even the modestly stable life could all be cut off after graduation, so I told him a couple of times to make preparations in advance. I also explained Sungbong's situation to the sponsor and requested a little extension of the sponsorship. I thought that it would be a real human triumph if Sungbong, who has a weak academic background, could continue on even to university.

I felt certain that going to university would give him not only self-development opportunities, but also add an even greater asset for his future, so I urged him to try his best to make it to the university. Although he did eventually make it to the university, the tuition fee for the arts division was too expensive. The university that Sungbong wanted to attend was a top-tier school. I think he had a strong desire to escape from reality and to live the ideal life that he had dreamed of. But we couldn't find a sponsor on such short notice. Even though he'd been accepted, he didn't succeed in actually entering the university. It was regrettable.

Kim: Our foundation is a system that recruits sponsors and delivers funds, without an independent reserve. So we searched in a hurry, but we couldn't manage in just those one or two days. Since there was no money to help, there was no way to find a solution. So we blew the opportunity, and we felt really sorry for Sungbong. We told him to try again the following year, and that we would get together the tuition fee for him by looking for some companies from then on so that he could start university the following year. We also told him that he should just consider it a dud year. Anyway, since he had a weak academic foundation in music, he could go to an academy that specialized in reapplying to universities and get funding support from us to pay his academy tuition fee. Since there was such an academy right by our office, we were going to liaise for him to attend the academy for free, but he just said, "I'm going to Daegu!" And he left.

Going to a different region meant that he would lose all the benefits he could receive in Daejeon, and that we would have to start all over again from scratch, so we were worried. He consulted with Ms. Yoo many times then, but all the convincing didn't work. He fell out of touch, and then later we heard that he'd toiled like a dog for the one year that he was in Daegu. We could only ask for some cooperation from the municipality of Daegu. For them to have a keen grasp of the situation, we needed to explain everything from the beginning, which would take a long time. Anyway they also didn't seem to believe what we were telling them.

The government also makes investigations on the actual condition of welfare recipients, and they used to check whether what Sungbong was saying was really true. I think it's arrogance to think that such a kid couldn't possibly exist. These are society's margins, and they seemed to be denying the blind spots. The social welfare network in Korea is still not complete.

Q. How did you feel when Mr. Choi appeared on *Korea's Got Talent*?

Yoo: At first, I thought, "He's gone and done it; now what?" Then I was relieved, thinking, "So he's been doing well." It's true that I was very worried about him, because after failing to enter university, Sungbong said he was going to move to Daegu, and that he was going to migrate to the United

States, but then he fell out of touch after that. I was proud of him, and I thought, this relentless chap has shown us what he's about once again.

Kim: The first time I watched *Korea's Got Talent*, I thought I was going to faint when I saw that the contestant talking to the emcee while on standby backstage was someone I knew. The only link I had with Sungbong then was through his mini personal web page. After he was broadcast on the show, I thought, how many countless people must now be sending him messages, and if I were to contact him too, wouldn't it be burdensome to him now that he has turned into somebody famous? I posted a comment on his web page only much later. It was an encouragement message. After that, I got a call from Sungbong.

I did feel that something extraordinary was happening after watching the broadcast show. I thought, "I bet he's going to come up as the number-one Internet search term tomorrow morning," but the reaction was more explosive than I'd anticipated, and when the hype spread to other countries as well, things began to stir even in our company. When I went to work after having watched the show, both the director and the manager were going, "Sungbong's created a storm. We hope everything goes well for him." And everyone cheered for him.

Q. Please tell us any other episodes about Mr. Choi that come to your mind.

Kim: As a foundation program, we have a Christmas party for sponsors at the Nuclear Engineering and Technology Institute, and we used to perform there. When Sungbong was in his final year of high school, he attended the party and sang "Silent Night, Holy Night," really quite terribly in fact [*laughs*]. Even then, the sponsors liked it. For these people, who thought that they were always only giving to others, it came as an experience of actually receiving something back, so we got many comments about how it touched them with a warm end-of-year spirit. We always talk about "giving" to others, but I think giving is synonymous with receiving.

Yoo: Oh, I chose the song "Silent Night, Holy Night" for that event. I didn't know what kind of level would be appropriate for the piece, so I just chose one that's familiar to everyone. I had never checked how good a vocalist Sungbong was, and I had high expectations. He was going to sing as a soloist along with a children's choir. The prerecorded music accompaniment that I'd prepared was in a female register, however. It was fine for the children, but the range must have been too high for Sungbong. I remember assuring Sungbong—who was flustered because he couldn't make his voice sing—that everything was okay. He barely managed to wrap up the performance. Actually, that was being very discourteous to Sungbong, since I didn't ask him in advance but just made the preparation according to my wish. I'm only saying this now but, I'm sorry, Sungbong [*laugh*].

Q. Please tell us if you have anything that you would like from Sungbong in the future.

Kim: People took interest in Sungbong's story, but I think in order for him to be truly happy, he needs to sing well, since he communicates through music.

Also, I hope that Sungbong gets a family so that he can eat proper home-cooked meals for a change. That's if he gets married in the near future. I don't serve my family great meals myself, but when I went to Sungbong's house, I only saw things like a pot that he had used to cook noodles with—and he would eat all alone by himself—piled on top of a frying pan, and then cockroaches...He's lived without proper food and cooking. I hope that he'll be able to have a life in the future where he can eat warm, home-cooked meals.

Sungbong had a lot of things that seemed to work out well but didn't turn out to be so in the end. He wanted to sing, so he entered a school, and it appeared that things were going to work out well, because there was even a foundation that was helping him. That must have taken a load off his mind, but then hardships came again. It must have been really hard for him. He's a chap who has a very strong inner energy to take responsibility of his own life, so I trust that he'll do well for himself.

Yoo: Whenever we asked Sungbong what his goals were in life, he would smile bashfully and answer, "To be well off." I think that he's pretty well off now, receiving the love and affection of so many people, but there are also many aspects I worry about. People have different standards and ideas of being "well off," and Sungbong still seems to be giving the same answer that he used to give when he'd had to worry about his meals. I would like Sungbong to become someone who thinks through and studies things in detail for his future. As we can see from the lives of entertainers who have been forgotten by the masses, the interest and love one receives from people might only last for a short while, and then disappear. In order to become someone who succeeds in the long run, he needs to follow up with self-development efforts. Also, I hope that he becomes a person whose life isn't simply controlled this way—by other people's love and affection, but instead is decided through his own effort and will.

Q. Do you have any final comments you would like to make?

Kim: Shouldn't the government at least be providing minimum living expenses to impoverished children like Sungbong? One TV station experimented with making people live one week on minimum living expenses, and they showed scenes with people giving up midway because they couldn't put up with it. They would have had an absolute lack of expenses, and also relative deprivation. There are so many difficulties we come across in doing social welfare work. The children who have been set to receive minimum living expenses and government subsidies have almost no chances of getting private education. If the children in low-income families want to have an average standard of living when they become adults, the only way they can pull themselves up to that level is by studying, but that's become harder to do now than before. It seems that the polarization is becoming more and more severe. It would be wonderful if the children could be given the opportunity at least in their studies to start in equal and identical circumstances, and to have public education fill the gap by providing additional learning opportunities in areas where people with money are able to get ahead through private education. Giving more government subsidy to a family, say, is all good, but the society as a whole needs to come up with a system that can fill the gap [between the rich and the poor].

Sungbong also went to an arts high school, and had there been a voucher system* or a talent donation system or something that could have filled in his needs when he couldn't pay for his lessons, it would have helped him to adjust to his school life. We have many such systems now. Academies with vision are giving their support, for instance, but we'd like to see the systems expand.

Yoo: There are still many people who think that donation or voluntary service is the preserve of particular groups or classes of people. Voluntary service and donation are no other than helping needy people in what they lack. They are simply giving support funds to people who don't have enough money, sharing warm affection with people who are deprived of affection, and giving medical support to sick people so that they can return to being healthy. If we could put aside the fact that we live in a capitalistic society, whose characteristic is to make things work out using money, but rather focus on the fact that we are all people who are capable of helping and comforting others, and donating and offering voluntary service—that's something I'd like to share.

---

* A system where the government gives out cash cards that the recipients use in areas they select to purchase goods or services.

"Rough, but with a Desire to be Good—An Ambitious Kid" Jongyeon Jung, Program Director, and Sooji Kim, Creative, *Korea's Got Talent* Production Crew

Q. How did you come to cast Mr. Choi for the show?

Sooji Kim: I was in charge of the Daejeon region for recruiting the cast for the program. I contacted all the various arts and athletics academies in the region, requesting them to present anyone they thought would be suitable to appear on the show. Mr. Jeongso Park's academy, which was one among them, introduced Sungbong to us. We found the uniqueness of his life story to be promising.

Q. What came to your mind when you heard about Mr. Choi's story?

Jongyeon Jung: At first, I questioned whether Sungbong's story was 100 percent true. I was surprised to hear how his background was entirely different from ordinary people's. That must have been the reason that from the beginning, we considered him more special compared to the other participants. Even when he spoke to me over the phone once during the casting call process, he would keep saying how he wanted to die; so I thought that he was someone I should take special care of. He was in a very unstable condition then, and we worried that there might be accidents. So after he was cast, I told the creatives to accompany him around and to take care of him. Our creative, Sooji Kim, always accompanied him to places. In any case, I thought that Sungbong would be a key person for the program. And I was also concerned about whether I should disclose his story on the broadcast show—whether to have him compete simply with his singing talent or to let him be aided by his story. In any case, the story got exposed to a certain extent in the broadcast show, except that Sungbong shied away from opening up about his parents, since they are still alive. Whether or not their story was true, since we already figured that he didn't want to see them at all, we too decided against disclosing it.

Q. How did you feel when you met Sungbong?

Kim: Prior to the broadcast, we only talked over the phone. Then I saw him for the first time at the regional preliminary. I had an image of him in my mind based on the story I'd heard, but he turned out to be not as gloomy as I'd thought. I remember that Sungbong didn't like crowded places. When he was in the waiting lounge, I made a lot of effort to help him resolve his emotions. I asked him if he wanted to see his parents. Sungbong said that they just had to live their way, and that he had to live his way. I was heartbroken.

Jung: It must have been because Sungbong had lived a rough life till then, because he would treat people quite rudely when he met them. Being the impatient person that I am, I would blurt out things like "Don't talk like that," "You shouldn't do that to your elders," and so on. He only had one meeting with me the day before he came to the regional preliminaries, and I think this chap has two ways of treating people. One is to play the baby as though he were younger than his peers, and the other is to treat them as if he'd basically constructed a wall between himself and them. The two behaviors coexisted in him. We met on the first floor of the preliminaries venue, and I chatted with him about various things because I was worried that he might mess up from being nervous, and it was tough to do because he was so walled up. Fortunately, our creative Ms. Sooji Kim spoke a lot with Sungbong and communicated well with him.

Q. How was Mr. Choi's singing in the beginning?

Kim: We asked him to sing over the phone, and also to make a video and send it to us. There were many opportunities early on to hear him before he went out on the show. I told him to practice more, not because he sounded bad, but because I wanted him to succeed by singing well on the show.

Jung: I tried to be objective about Sungbong's singing. I didn't want him to stand out simply by virtue of his story. Singing was one of the more common talents among the performance cast, so there was also a side of me that wanted him to stand out more not only through his story, but also through his singing.

Q. I heard that you continued to manage Mr. Choi after the first broadcast.

Jung: Yes. For two days after the show's broadcast, he was the most popular search word on the Internet. So I proposed to my company that it would be good to have Sungbong come up to Seoul, and we would take care of him. We couldn't go as far as putting our lives on the line and take care of a complete stranger as though we were his parents, but we thought that he should at least have someone to help him out. We thought that if people who watched the show contacted him, they may affect the ongoing contest. My proposal was accepted, and he got a room near the broadcasting station. The company covered all the costs for food and lodging. Sungbong ate a lot of meat. Probably because he's a kid who's lived doing physical work like hard labor, after taking a break from work and just eating, he quickly gained weight.

Q. Did he have lessons and such after the first broadcast?

Jung: Yes. Around twice per week. We tried to provide Sungbong with every possible support we could give. What Sungbong said he needed, we found for him. You could say that it was special treatment. Other singers would normally practice with their teachers, but Sungbong needed to be connected. Also, since singing is a relatively common talent, we thought that lessons were needed in his case. We found the teachers through many different routes, and due to frictions that happened in communicating with them, we changed the teachers a few times. In my opinion, Sungbong made the lesson teachers very uncomfortable, but they bore with him and treated him well. With them, music probably served as the medium for communication. Once they began to understand each other through music, Sungbong would change his attitude. Sungbong had such an enormous desire to do well, so had he gotten himself ten hours of lessons per day, he would have done the ten hours. He probably wanted to practice a lot.

Q. How did the rehearsals take place?

Kim: He would be alone by himself playing the piano and singing every day in the rehearsal room. Sungbong's solo rehearsal time was around six to seven hours a day. Since practicing too much would damage his voice, he controlled the time and took rests in between. He seldom stepped out of the rehearsal room. For two months, practice took up the majority of his daily routine. Other than that, he would also take lessons when a teacher came, around twice a week. The lessons were for the songs that he was going to sing on the show. He took the lessons in a general vocal practice facility in the neighborhood; he acted all sensitive with the teachers before they were able to communicate with each other. Only when they began to understand each other through music did he start to follow the vocal trainer, going, "Hyeong, hyeong." At times, he would get all excited. So the teacher found him a vocal trainer and came by now and then to watch his progress. That's how things progressed.

They would say things like "This song needs to go this way in this part, but you are going like this. Your vocal cords and tongue need to be rounded but you have them standing sharp. The sound is resonating in such-and-such way." There were two teachers, one for piano and another for singing. I did not stay with them during the lessons. I greeted them and left. Once I saw Sungbong receive a lesson from a professor who seemed to know that the kid needed to feel comfortable through a sing-along style of instruction in order to sing. He stroked Sungbong generously and made a comfortable atmosphere for him. He didn't seem stiff.

Q. Would you please describe his broadcast appearance in detail?

Jung: He appeared a total of three times on the show. The first broadcast went out in early June; in early July there was the semifinals, and August 21 was the finals. Although he had the desire to do well, the circumstances surrounding him at that time didn't allow him to. He practiced all day and tried to control things by himself. He even brought up a sharp observation about problems during the rehearsal. He looked like he was trying his best to do well. He was most sensitive during the semifinals.

Q. Did the judging panelists give him advice?

Jung: No. There was zero contact with the panelists other than when he was on the stage, since it isn't like there is a lesson arrangement with the panelists.

Q. Did he seem determined to win?

Kim: He had said that he wasn't greedy about winning. But he spoke up honestly once, that of course everyone would want to win the competition. It seemed that he was suppressing it inside. He thought that being affected by greed could spoil the singing. Well, I would have been greedy, if I were in his position.

Jung: He would say that he wasn't greedy and that he probably was going to lose, yet he would tell everyone he met, "Please remember me for the text voting." That would make everyone crack up [*laughs*]. Even when he was quarreling sharply with people, he would end with, "Please vote for me in the text voting." He probably did want to win first place.

Q. Mr. Choi received quite a lot of attention after the first broadcast went out. How did he respond?

Jung: He seemed like a child. He checked people's reactions to him in real time, the number of hits on YouTube went up like an explosion, and tens of thousands of comments were posted. Thousands were posted each day, and Sungbong would be reading all the comments that came up on the Internet. He even tried to read the comments on the CNN article with his broken English. He actually had enough time to do that. He had a lot of free time since he just stayed in his room after practice and didn't have friends.

Q. Wasn't he nervous on stage?

Jung: Sungbong said that he was the type who was strong during the actual performance, but his anxiety level shot up and he was very stressed out before the live show. Before the live show, he would turn edgy, repeatedly checking himself on the video alone. During the practice, his intonation

277

seemed insecure, but he managed to do okay during the live show. Then he seemed to be gradually adjusting to the program, because he went through the process pleasantly without getting stressed, and he was in a good mood after the live show. Although he got second place in the final, he was pleased.

Q. It was said that Mr. Choi had been continuously suffering from mental instability; did that side of him show while he was participating in _Korea's Got Talent_?

Kim: He wanted to die every day. He told us that he'd been to hospitals in Daejeon, so we introduced to him to a hospital in Seoul. The doctor was one recommended by a creative I knew. I said, let's allow him to meet the best doctor that we know, and the creative thought that it would help Sungbong a lot to listen to what this doctor had to say. I took him to the hospital every week. Depending on his condition, he would take one hour of counseling, or it would take just five minutes. I felt that Sungbong shouldn't be left alone, and that he really might commit suicide. Probably because of the stress he had from his bipolar disorder, he had trouble sleeping. He said that thoughts would come into his head when he was alone, and that he couldn't figure out himself what those thoughts were. He struggled that way.

Jung: In any case, I could see that he had an illness. Sungbong was hard to deal with because of his severe mood swings. It was probably due to those scars since childhood. He would guard himself against everyone at first, and then carry on his interpersonal relationships street style. He's also the kind of person who gets hurt or nitpicks on one single comment. I once said to him, "You're rather strong minded," as a passing remark, and he still talks about it now. He seemed to be trying to judge, define, and figure out quickly a way to deal with people.

Q. Were there any episodes during the show?

Kim: During his stay at his lodging, he injured his head while riding his bike. He would exercise, bike, or take walks since he was running out of breath when he was singing. I wasn't there with him when he broke his head, but my friend found him bleeding profusely from a split head and called me. I then called the program director who was nearby to take him to the emergency room. When the program director rushed to help him, evidently Sungbong was going, "Please remember me for the text voting" even as he was bleeding from a split head [*laughs*]. They stitched him up at the hospital with four punches, using something like a stapler. If you watch the semifinals video carefully, you'll be able to see the scar. When I asked him why he hadn't contacted me even though he was injured, he told me that it was because he thought he might get scolded for riding a bike at night.

Jung: He had a wild life to begin with, and being a kid who used to go around riding motorcycles, he would obviously have ridden the bike wildly at night too. Oh right, after the program finished, I met Sungbong in Saipan as well. I was there on personal vacation, but our schedules happened to coincide. I only saw him once, but even there, he was riding a motorcycle. He wasn't afraid of night time and liked to just ride around freely. He must have been very bored while he was in Sangam-dong. Imagine how he must have raced on that bike. There he was, out in the park and racing, when he failed to see a net and tripped and got thrown over.

Q. What was the audience's evaluation after the show?

Jung: You know that he attended an arts high school, right? Even at that school, he wasn't an ordinary student. Arts high schools have strict senior-junior relationships, but Sungbong evidently didn't play along with the system. Now, people who knew about his time in high school put up some blog comments, and the stress from that was intense too. Sungbong didn't go on making up stories, but he did have some anxiety over the fact that he wasn't a well-behaved student during his time in the arts high school, that people might have a bad impression of him. He must have had fears that all those details would get exposed to the world, and that made him all the more keen on checking every single reaction that was being posted.

Q. What did the uploaded comments say?

Jung: One or two bad comments would come up now and then, but they weren't such big deals. Just things like, he's got a reputation for being impudent. Those comments weren't from the kids who had attended school with Sungbong; they were like, "I heard from a senior student of his at school that...etc." You can't really deal with those kinds of things. Besides, they weren't even that important.

Anyway, since we also had to confirm whether Sungbong's story was true, we went to Daejeon one or two weeks after the show was broadcast and visited the arts high school there. Sungbong evidently didn't have good feelings toward the teachers. He wouldn't talk politely to them, and would even quarrel with them a bit. So we asked the teachers for their cooperation. In any case, much of his story about his days in Daejeon Arts High School got opened to the public via the Internet. Anyway, he wasn't a well-behaved student at Daejeon Arts High School. Frankly speaking, how much must they have looked down on Sungbong for being an orphan among themselves? Sungbong must have now become, well, a celebrity of the school.

We also met the people he's connected to in Daejeon, and the social workers who had been in charge of him, collecting testimonies, so to speak. They weren't intended for broadcasting purposes, but to have minimum confirmation of facts. We didn't find anything to be majorly problematic, except that he'd frequented the police station so much as to have become a notorious kid in Daejeon. There wasn't any criminal record.

Q. How was it during the finals?

Jung: Two hours before the live show, we got the permission to do an all-recorded* show with the orchestra. It gets done that way in some cases and not in others, but after the tryout, it seemed safest to put on prerecorded music. It didn't seem like a good idea to have the orchestra go in and out while the stage keeps switching around. In fact, all-recorded music is supposed to be better in terms of sound. The conductor had good manners too. He led the performance to sync† assuredly, and having come to provide live accompaniment, he still took into consideration the many opinions that Sungbong expressed to him.

Sungbong tried not to be intimidated on the stage and instead to appear like a veteran vocalist. Knowing that many eyes were watching him and that there were high expectations of him, he seemed to be very conscious of the need to not disappoint, and that was perhaps greater than his desire to win. That was probably why he didn't feel sorry for being the first runner-up.

Q. We are curious about what happened next after the show ended.

Jung: He met a lot of public figures, and there were lots of sponsor-related contacts. He also went to church events and fan-meeting invitations. So he met his fans and performed, with Mr. Jeongso Park by his side.

---

* In an all-recorded (AR) show, both the voice and the accompaniment are prerecorded for the performance.

† Making a prerecorded performance seem as though it were a live performance.

He also received many offers to participate in events. We also received them, but there was a separate company that managed the *Korea's Got Talent* performance cast for a given period of time after the program ended, so we used to pass those offers over to them.

Kim: He stayed at the lodging we provided him for a month or two after the show ended in August. Apparently Sungbong had grown affectionate toward us, the creatives, and thought fondly of us. He probably felt very lonely thinking that everyone had become distant, because we were all busy after the *KoGotTal* season. The work that we had going later on for business didn't work out, so we had to return the lodging, and it was good-bye to Sungbong.

Q. Please tell us any comments you would like to conclude with.

Jung: We've never contacted his parents. Sungbong told us that he'd gone to meet his mom. I think Sungbong needs people like foster parents. Korea's living standards are now decent enough that his story is a rare one, but I think there are many blind spots in our social welfare. He'd basically leaped out of the welfare system at a tender age, at a time when there used to be many news stories about how people kidnapped children and made them into panhandlers.

He's a chap who's risen through adversities, so I trust that he'll continue to do well in life. If there is anything I might want from him, it would be just that he would take good care of his wounded heart, meet good people, and continue to have wholesome communication with them.

Glossary

ajumma: Middle-aged woman.

all recorded (AR): Meaning both the voice and the accompaniment are prerecorded for the performance.

annyonghaseyo: "Hello" in Korean.

Bacchus drinks: A noncarbonated South Korean energy drink, manufactured since 1963.

Blue House: South Korea's presidential residence.

bung-eo-bbang: A fish-shaped waffle stuffed with red-bean paste.

crocodile and a crocodile bird: Refers to a relationship in which each has to mutually depend on the other for subsistence or survival.

"cut open my stomach": A Korean expression that means "Sue me. I have nothing left."

dong: The smallest urban submunicipal administrative region that has its own government office and staff.

fighting: Let's go.

gopchang: Fried intestines of cow or pig.

gosiwon: Special accommodations for exam candidates.

Go-Stop: Korean card game.

gu office: Borough office.

Gyeongsang-do: Gyeongsang Province.

hyeong: The word that boys and men use to address older brothers.

jajangmyeon: Noodles with black-bean sauce.

Jeollabuk-do: North Jeolla Province (*buk* means "north" in Korean; *do* means "province").

kimbab: Dried seaweed rolls that look like sushi rolls.

Korean won: One hundred Korean won is approximately 10 US cents. Although the exchange rate has fluctuated over the past decades, it is usually between 900 won per dollar at the least to 1,300 won at the most. In 1995, when Sungbong was five years old, 775 Korean won was equivalent to about one US dollar.

lodging venues: Hotels and inns.

noona: The word that boys and men use to address older sisters.

old young and a sharp spoon: According to the Naver dictionary, "old young" refers to a child who looks or behaves like an old person. It is not used to criticize someone but more as a tease or mockery. Also according to the Naver dictionary, "sharp spoon" is defined as a person who seems to be knowledgeable (usually because of his or her high academic background or knowledge-related career) but does not know what he or she is supposed to know or fails to make the right choices in real life.

oppa: The word that girls and women use to address older brothers.

Pepero: A cookie stick dipped in chocolate, manufactured in South Korea since 1983.

seolleongtang: Stock soup of bone and stew meat.

soju: Korean distilled liquor.

soondae: Korean sausage.

sync: Making a prerecorded performance seem as though it were a live performance.

telephone room managers: Phone-sex parlor owners.

touter brothers: Young, well-dressed promoters who distribute advertising flyers to potential customers.

tteok-bokki: Stir-fried rice cake.

Ursa capsules: Pills that some South Korean people believe will improve liver function.

voucher system: A system where the government gives out cash cards that the recipients use in areas they select to purchase goods or services.

Sungbong Choi's English autobiography was published
with the support of

Julius Bär
FOUNDATION

39373309R00188

Made in the USA
San Bernardino, CA
24 September 2016